W9-BVD-745

T. S. ELIOT

Literary Lives
General Editor: Richard Dutton, Reader in English,
University of Lancaster

This series offers stimulating accounts of the literary careers of
the most widely read British and Irish authors. Volumes follow
the outline of writers' working lives, not in the spirit of traditional biography, but aiming to trace the professional, publishing and social contexts which shaped their writing. The role
and status of the "author" as the creator of literary texts is a
vexed issue in current critical theory, where a variety of social,
linguistic and psychological approaches have challenged the
old concentration on writers as specially-gifted individuals.
Yet reports of "the death of the author" in literary studies are
(as Mark Twain said of a premature obituary) an exaggeration.
This series aims to demonstrate how an understanding of
writers' careers can promote, for students and general readers
alike, a more informed historical reading of their works.

Published titles

WILLIAM SHAKESPEARE   *Richard Dutton*
JANE AUSTEN   *Jan Fergus*
JOHN DRYDEN   *Paul Hammond*
JOHN DONNE   *Joseph McMinn*
GEORGE ELIOT (MARIAN EVANS)   *Kerry McSweeney*
VIRGINIA WOOLF   *John Mepham*
PERCY BYSSHE SHELLEY   *Michael O'Neill*
JOHN DONNE   *George Parfitt*
T. S. ELIOT   *Tony Sharpe*
JOSEPH CONRAD   *Cedric Watts*
CHARLOTTE AND EMILY BRONTË   *Tom Winnifrith and Edward Chitham*
D. H. LAWRENCE   *John Worthen*

Forthcoming

JAMES JOYCE   *Morris Beja*
JOHN MILTON   *Cedric Brown*
GEORGE ORWELL   *Peter Davison*
THOMAS HARDY   *James Gibson*
HENRY JAMES   *Kenneth Graham*
BEN JONSON   *David Kay*
W. B. YEATS   *Alasdair MacRae*
ALFRED, LORD TENNYSON   *Leonee Ormond*
JOHN KEATS   *David B. Pirie*
EDMUND SPENSER   *Gary Waller*
GEOFFREY CHAUCER   *Barry Windeatt*

T. S. Eliot

A Literary Life

Tony Sharpe
Lecturer in English
University of Lancaster

St. Martin's Press   New York

First published in the United States of America in 1991

Printed in Hong Kong

ISBN 0–312–06203–6

Library of Congress Cataloging-in-Publication Data
Sharpe, Tony, 1952–
T. S. Eliot : a literary life / Tony Sharpe.
p.   cm.—(Literary Lives)
Includes index.
ISBN 0–312–06203–6
1. Eliot, T. S. (Thomas Stearns), 1888–1965—Biography.   2. Poets,
American—20th century—Biography.   I. Title.   II. Series: Literary
Lives (New York, N.Y.)
PS3509.L43Z86485   1991
821'.912—dc20
[B]   91–9079
                                                                        CIP

For Peter Newman (1948–1990)
O quam te memorem

Contents

Preface   vi

Acknowledgements   viii

Annotation and Abbreviation   ix

1   The Paradoxes of Eliot   1

2   Before the Beginning   12

3   1914–1920   37

4   1921–1925   69

5   1926–1934   103

6   1935–1945   133

7   After the End   167

Further reading   181

Index   182

Preface

In H.M. Bateman's series of cartoons for *Punch*, 'The Man Who . . .', an individual who has innocently committed some minor infringement of custom or etiquette is shown, surrounded by onlookers manifesting the most extravagant outrage and disgust at his *faux pas*. As 'The Man Who Has Written Yet Another Book On T.S. Eliot', I may well provoke indignant dismay in those who know how many there already are; and I have not even the excuse of innocence.

My justification, in the first place, must be enthusiasm: the interest in Eliot's poetry excited when, as a schoolboy, I borrowed my elder sister's set-text *Selected Poems*, and read it in a parked car in Portsmouth. This enthusiasm has survived the intervening years, and made some sort of book seem necessary. This sort of book, in the second place, because now that a quarter-century has elapsed since Eliot's death, and with the increasing availability of biographical information in recent years, we are better able to set his work in the context of his life, and to make an assessment of what has almost certainly been this century's most notable and influential literary career in English. In examining how a Missouri-born American became the most prominent English man of letters of his time, we encounter the first of many apparent contradictions in the phenomenon of Eliot, who was – in his own words about Tennyson – 'the most instinctive rebel against the society in which he was the most perfect conformist'. The contrary impulses of rebellion and conformity, desire and control, secrecy and openness; balancing the demands of the private life and the public world; these are some of the tensions observed in Eliot's career. In exploring them, I hope not to have arrived at any simplistic resolution.

I hope, also, to have borne in mind the requirements of the general reader as well as the specialist. Whilst I was completing this, news came of the death of my brother-in-law in a car-crash; this was an event which helped me appreciate a passage in *The Dry Salvages* whose truth I had disputed (11. 108–14). A scientist by training, a teacher and then systems analyst by profession, Peter had talked to me about the *Four Quartets* some months before his death; and I dedicate the book to him because for me he represents the non-specialist reader whom Eliot, for all his difficulty, is able to attract. Peter deserves a better memorial; but this is the book that I have written.

Acknowledgements

Thanks to: The Humanities Research Center at the University of Texas at Austin, where I spent happy weeks amidst the Eliot material; to Virginia Taylor, who was a very thorough research assistant for me, in the Eliot material at the New York Public Library; to the General Editor, Richard Dutton, who advised on the manuscript at an important juncture; and to Jane Atkinson, who commented on the nearly-finished work. To Lyndall Gordon, for a detailed reply to a textual enquiry; and, of course, to all the other Eliot scholars from whose labours I have profited in writing this.

Extracts from T.S. Eliot's verse are reprinted by permission of Faber and Faber Ltd, from *Complete Poems and Plays of T.S. Eliot* by T.S. Eliot.

Extracts from *The Letters of T.S. Eliot*, Volume I and previously uncollected letters and articles are reprinted by permission of Mrs Valerie Eliot and Faber and Faber Ltd, and Harcourt Brace Jovanovich, Inc., © Valerie Eliot 1991.

Excerpts from *Collected Poems 1909–1962* by T.S. Eliot, copyright 1936 by Harcourt Brace Jovanovich, Inc., copyright © 1964, 1963 by T.S. Eliot, reprinted by permission of the publisher.

Excerpts from *Four Quartets,* copyright 1943 by T.S. Eliot, copyright 1943 by T.S. Eliot and renewed 1971 by Esme Valerie Eliot, reprinted by permission of Harcourt Brace Jovanovich, Inc.

Excerpts from *After Strange Gods: A Primer of Modern Heresy* by T.S Eliot, copyright 1934 and renewed 1962 by T.S. Eliot, reprinted by permission of Faber and Faber Ltd and Harcourt Brace Jovanovich, Inc.

Excerpts from *Selected Essays* by T.S. Eliot, copyright 1950 by Harcourt Brace Jovanovich, and renewed 1978 by Esme Valerie Eliot, reprinted by permission of Harcourt Brace Jovanovich, Inc., and Faber and Faber Ltd.

Excerpt from *On Poetry and Poets* by T.S. Eliot. Copyright © 1943, 1945, 1951, 1954, 1956, 1957 by T.S. Eliot. Renewal copyright © 1985 by Valerie Eliot. Reprinted by permission of Faber and Faber Ltd and Farrar, Straus and Giroux, Inc.

Excerpts from *To Criticize the Critic* by T.S. Eliot. Copyright © 1965 and renewal copyright 1983 by Valerie Eliot. Reprinted by permission of Faber and Faber Ltd and Farrar, Straus and Giroux Inc.

I am grateful to Mrs Eliot for allowing me to quote from Charlotte Eliot's letters, and also from Vivien Eliot's contributions to the *Criterion*.

Annotation and
Abbreviation

I believe that endnotes are disruptive, and because this book does not masquerade as weighty scholarship, I have tried to keep annotation to a minimum, without (I hope) denying the reader essential information. I incorporate most reference-sources for Eliot's own writing in the running text, according to the following system of abbreviation:

CPP:	*Complete Poems and Plays of T.S. Eliot* (1969)
SW:	*The Sacred Wood*
FLA:	*For Lancelot Andrewes*
SE:	*Selected Essays* (1951)
UPUC:	*The Use of Poetry and the Use of Criticism*
ASG:	*After Strange Gods*
OPP:	*On Poetry and Poets*
TCC:	*To Criticize the Critic*
Ts:	*The Waste Land: A facsimile and transcript* (ed. Valerie Eliot)

Where an essay has been gathered in *Selected Essays*, which had previously been part of another volume (for instance, SW or FLA), I have given the SE reference as likely to be the more accessible.

I hope that my other sources are identifiable from context, where not exactly referenced; I have not, for example, annotated my allusions to Conrad Aiken's letters, on the assumption that the reader can easily trace these in *Selected Letters of Conrad Aiken*, ed. Killorin (New Haven, 1978).

1

The Paradoxes of Eliot

On 21 August 1914 an American graduate student arrived in London from Rotterdam. He was twenty-six years old, and came from a distinguished family which was spiritually and temperamentally rooted in New England, although geographically located in St Louis, Missouri. He was reading for his doctorate at Harvard University, and was in Europe on one of its Sheldon Travelling Fellowships, under the terms of which he would spend one year (and possibly a second) advancing his studies in philosophy at Merton College, Oxford. It all looked like the beginning of a creditable academic career of the sort that his family had envisaged for him; a career whose culmination would be (his mother in particular hoped) an eminent professorship in the United States.

He had not intended to be in England at that precise moment: his plan had been to spend the summer at the University of Marburg before coming to Oxford, but the rumblings of what was to be the Great War had hurried his departure from Germany. His plans were to undergo much more radical adjustments than this, however. Although he did complete and submit his dissertation on the philosophy of F. H. Bradley, his doctorate was not awarded because he did not undergo the necessary oral examination. He was not destined to become a professor, although his career would indeed have its academic aspects. More significantly still, although he could not know it he had left America for good, and his 'home' would never again be found on that side of the Atlantic. He had already visited London briefly in 1911, from Paris; but in spite of the fact that on this more sustained inspection he was not at first inclined greatly to like England (the food disgusted him), and although he was not particularly stimulated by Oxford – which in wartime was empty and subdued – he was nevertheless to make the country in which he landed his own.

This was not done painlessly. His parents were opposed to his life in England, and his father died before the son could achieve much to justify it to him. Themselves imbued with the family

1

ideals of service, duty and high achievement, his parents saw their
youngest child estrange himself from their expectations for him, by
living abroad, contracting a furtive and unsuitable marriage (in
1915), and thereafter by scraping a living as a schoolmaster and
subsequently in a bank. They knew of his aspirations to become a
poet, but these were hardly to be considered as providing solid
prospects.

He kept at it, however; both at the poetry and at his adoption of
the country in which he undesignedly found himself in August
1914. Through one disastrously unhappy marriage to an Englishwoman, through baptism and confirmation into the Church of
England and the assumption of British nationality, through rising
prominence as a man of English letters, he did his best to assimilate himself to what he considered England to be. And when, a
little over fifty years later, he died in London on 4 January 1965 (the
Fates having relented somewhat, and granted him, late in life, a
very happy second marriage), T. S. Eliot was almost a British
national institution.

His name, that is to say, signalled something – even if only
'high-brow poet' – to many more people than those who read his
work: and yet, considering that he was hardly a populist writer,
there were more who *did* read his work than might be supposed.
His prestige was great and what might be called his cultural
authority enormous: his fame was international, and he had accumulated enough honorary doctorates to make up for the one he
hadn't taken at Harvard. His mother, who died in 1929, had lived
long enough to see something of her son's growing reputation, but
even she might not have foreseen the pre-eminence he was finally
to attain. Considered as a literary career, Eliot's was the most
successful seen so far this century: the uncertain American graduate was to become the most influential man of English letters of his
time.

I want in the following pages to examine how this came about. In
doing so, I shall not be principally concerned either with literary
criticism of the writing, nor with biographical analysis and psychological speculation concerning the writer – although neither of
these elements can be entirely absent from an adequate account of
the career, which is connected both with the nature of the poetry
and of the poet. A 'career' obviously enough follows and to an
extent dictates the contours of a 'life' – especially when there is a

strong element of vocation. But as with a life, the question remains of how far the final shape is actively produced, or passively received. This is particularly relevant to the case of Eliot: whose prose writing tended to advance the claims of the consciously critical faculty, with its need to choose, to discriminate and to decide; but whose poetry seems to spring from a level below that of conscious intellection – or to be most characteristic and powerful when it does. The speaker in 'The Love Song of J. Alfred Prufrock' exclaims 'It is impossible to say just what I mean!'; and however much the theoretical Eliot might espouse 'classicist' virtues of self-regulation and lucidity, his poetry can powerfully evoke the *disparity* between the psychic 'material' in which the poem originates, and the shaping procedures involved in putting it into words. His repeated imagery of the sea communicates a sense of hidden submarine life, occasionally glimpsed on the surface; and some critics have implied that when Eliot finds it possible to say just what he means his poetry becomes nerveless, because it is no longer the site of an important struggle.

It is tempting to draw an unbroken line ascending from the young man disembarking in 1914 (with 'The Love Song of J. Alfred Prufrock' in his baggage) to the eminent Eliot with the literary world at his feet; but a comparison with that other great figure of Modernism, James Joyce, is instructive. When Joyce left Ireland on the ferry from Dublin, his was a conscious expatriation; whereas Eliot's, in 1914, was not: he was apparently taking the first steps on the road toward an academic career, and return to the United States. Nevertheless, Eliot was in Europe at least as much because of his poetry as his philosophy, no matter what his family thought: because Europe – and especially France, whose poets were so crucial to his development – offered him the most stimulating literary climate. Indeed, if in 1914 there had been no war and Eliot had been obliged to choose a European country to live in for the rest of his life, it is almost certain that he would have chosen France. But the choice did not arise then, and when in 1927 he took British citizenship, this was more the formalisation of his status quo than a radically decisive step. It seems to have been necessary for Eliot to cross his Rubicons without quite realising that was what they were, although in retrospect their finality became clear; looked at another way, he had an uncanny knack of turning his accidents into his purposes, of giving direction to surprise, or of bringing ages of prudence to bear upon his moments of surrender.

The opening of *East Coker* has it that one's end is implicit in one's beginning; but thirty years earlier the interlocutress in 'Portrait of a Lady' had observed that human beginnings never know their ends. The relation between subconscious impulse and conscious shaping, between experience in its moment and in retrospect, is everywhere relevant in Eliot, suggesting the poet as opposed to the critic, the private as opposed to the public man. In the very act of becoming so consciously and electively 'English' as he did, Eliot remained profoundly something else: when, as Richard Aldington reported, he doffed his hat to the sentry outside a royal residence, he was making a gesture of assent to England and its institutions that by its nature was most un-English. But the theatricality of such a gesture is not proof that it was insincere; in Rome three years later (1926), Eliot surprised – and probably embarrassed – the relatives he was with, by falling to his knees before Michelangelo's *Pietà*. Such incidents may strike us as stagey and self-dramatising; but they can just as easily be seen as unmediated impulses, the spontaneous reaching out to something larger than the self, the sudden need to make a public testimony.

Eliot was not compelled to spend a long, obscure apprenticeship before winning recognition of his talent, nor did he have to establish his reputation in the teeth of widespread or persistent opposition; those few who continued to write against him simply looked out-of-date. But in spite of what might from our perspective seem like a continuous and quite speedy ascent of Parnassus, his own sense of his career was beset by crisis, and by fears of exhaustion: he repeatedly imagined that he had written himself out, that silence beckoned. He was kept on his way partly by external factors, partly by something within him. In the mid 1930s, having at length extricated himself from his miserable marriage, but feeling that his career was at an end, his involvement in the Christian pageant *The Rock* required him to write some serviceable verse; this led to the commission to write *Murder in the Cathedral*, and rejected lines from this play were the starting point of *Burnt Norton*; a poem which turned out to be the inauguration of the series *Four Quartets*. As well as Eliot's poetic frugality, his reluctance to waste words and images, such a sequence again demonstrates how accidents became purposes: when he wrote *Burnt Norton*, he had no notion of composing further Quartets; he did not, in fact, know that this poem *was* a 'quartet'.

No amount of external stimulus would have been sufficient, however, without that 'something within'. Eliot was highly motivated, as well as highly gifted; and I use this American term to identify a sustained directedness that perhaps distinguished him most sharply from any British tradition of literary amateurism. The form in which it was present in him distinguished Eliot, as well, from the more blatant and embattled energies of his compatriot Ezra Pound, which found themselves better suited to the Italy of Mussolini than to London literary decorum. Even so, there were those of Eliot's contemporaries who suspected him of being a manipulator, a manoeuverer; and as we shall see, there *were* aspects in which he mounted a strategic campaign to get on and get noticed in the literary world. To have had Eliot's high motivation without his high gifts could, of course, lead to strategies of the market-place like those pilloried by Pound, in the figure of 'Mr Nixon' in *Hugh Selwyn Mauberley*; but Eliot was remarkable in not compromising with any audience: he was, as Pound denoted by his approving word, '*echt*', the real thing.

As I have implied, there were those who considered Eliot to be in some ways the unreal thing: deceptive if not actually deceitful, at any rate somehow untrustworthy, not quite what he appeared to be. Since Eliot's writing, early and late, is permeated by an almost corrosive distrust of the world of appearances, this may not be surprising; it remains the case, however, that most major steps affecting his life (his first marriage, his religious 'conversion', his separation from his first wife in 1933, and his second marriage in 1957) were undertaken either in conditions of absolute secrecy, or were brought about in ways that avoided the possibility of open conflict. Taken together with Eliot's wish that no biography of him should be written, it was half natural to assume that something was being suppressed: there were, after all, a suppressed poem ('Ode' from *Ara Vos Prec*, 1920), a suppressed book (*After Strange Gods*, 1934), and even, it was to appear, a suppressed wife (Vivien Eliot died in 1947, in a private mental hospital to which she had been committed in 1938). After Eliot's death, his friend Herbert Read wrote of his feeling that Eliot was like 'one who had some secret sorrow or guilt'.

There is, however, more smoke than fire. Eliot's decision against a biography was apparently taken as early as 1925, rather than at the end of a life of hidden remorse; and any 'guilt' might be the natural reaction of a sensitive man to a life which had for the most part been unhappy. Other reminiscences than Read's present a more genial figure, with a memorable laugh; but there was certainly darkness in Eliot's life: his first wife was physically unwell and became mentally so; her condition was hardly helped by the fact that they seem to have been incompatible personalities. In consequence of all this theirs was on the whole a spectacularly unhappy marriage, prolonged by what appear to have been bursts of desperate devotion and loyalty on either side. It was natural enough to wish to keep such misery from being generally known. 'We knew fantastically little about him', I.A. Richards was to recall of the early Eliot whose poetry he so admired; Wyndham Lewis similarly was led to remember that at first he had had 'no idea where Mr Eliot lived' even after meeting him; and there were many whom Eliot struck as aloof, beyond a certain quantity of friendliness.[1] Others, however, such as Virginia Woolf and Ottoline Morrell, were to complain between themselves about the extent to which he inflicted on them details of his private life, almost garrulously concerning them in his matrimonial affairs.

It is true that there was a secretive side to Eliot, which seemed also connected with a taste for play-acting; we might think, for example, of the fact that in 1923 he took a small flat by himself in an arcade off the Charing Cross Road, where visitors were instructed to ask for 'Captain Eliot'; a personage whom they also observed to be wearing coloured powder on his face, and painting his lips, at times. Yet all this is less furtive than it might appear; if it was a secret, it was a fairly open one, known to quite a few of Eliot's literary friends, who visited him there and have left various references to it in their papers. One supposes that the principal object of the conspiracy was his wife; but given Eliot's very real need of a haven in which to get on with his work, this does not seem to be a serious breach of marital fidelity, whatever it suggests about a secret life.

As Peter Ackroyd demonstrated in his biography of Eliot (1984), so far from there being a paucity of information about the poet, there is in fact a very considerable body of material to sift through. Although the primary material is for the most part located in various research libraries, substantial insights and reminiscences of his life and character have been published in the autobiographies, journals and letters of those who knew him, such as Conrad Aiken, Bertrand Russell, Virginia Woolf and others. To anyone conditioned by the notion that Eliot really is an 'invisible' poet, it is surprising to discover how much is in print and available, albeit disparately. Since Ackroyd wrote, the long-awaited edition of Eliot's letters has started to appear; but for the time being his biography is likely to remain standard.[2] Its existence enables us for the first time to review both the life and the work side by side; and what I would define as the 'literary career' is a compound both of the life and the work. My study, therefore, proceeds with Ackroyd's researches in the background, and I presume that the reader who wants the detail and the approach of a straight biography will read his book.

The linkage between the writer's private life and his published work, between 'the man who suffers and the mind which creates', was one which Eliot in his early criticism sought to minimise, for reasons attributable as much to professional ideology as to personal reserve. Yet, as I have suggested, he was aware of the inadequacy or the untrustworthiness of public appearances, of the purely external record:

> By this, and this only, we have existed
> Which is not to be found in our obituaries
> Or in memories draped by the beneficent spider
> Or under seals broken by the lean solicitor
> In our empty rooms.
>
>   (*The Waste Land*)

However much he attempted to diminish the significance of a writer's 'personality' as a factor in the value of his work, it has become ever clearer that his own writing is most animated when its concerns or its sources are most deeply personal. Thus, what we might call the internal record needs attention. The man of letters is of course entitled to preserve his privacy; but as Wyndham Lewis put it in his reminiscence of Eliot, written from the viewpoint of a fellow-writer: 'We are all public figures. A man becomes that of his own free-will – in fact the becoming it entails quite a lot of work, frequently requiring many years of pretty close attention and solid labour'.[3]

Although elements of indecisiveness and self-uncertainty can be discerned in Eliot's character, there was also something which may as well be called ambition. It is probably true to say that in many respects he achieved what he desired; indeed, whatever dream of influence and success the younger Eliot may have indulged, it could hardly have been more extravagant than what actually happened. No doubt the young man would have accepted eagerly enough, had the future of his career been unfolded to him, in his early days of close attention and solid labour. Only the old writer could be in a position to report how high the price, and how radically different the experience of being 'famous', from the prospect. As Ackroyd points out, through his influential critical essays Eliot was able to put into currency the terms most favourable to a discussion of his own poetry. To a large degree, he thereby created a readership in his own image; but his readership also created a poet Eliot in its own image, and some of those who believed him to be articulating the disillusion of their generation could not happily adjust to the Christian affirmations of his later poetry.

Some who found this later work more congenial were anxious, on the other hand, to detect redemptive intimations in the early poetry as well. In both cases the writing was being used to confirm what the reader wished to believe; this is to take Eliot seriously, but at the cost of making him safe, by conscripting him as role-model for a desired spiritual attitude. I would like to recover the sense of Eliot as a more continuously surprising writer. Although he was from the beginning a master of 'deliberate disguises', keen to blend in with social and institutional background, and although latterly he seemed to develop what has been described as a carapace of respectability, both early and late he was as much the poet of discomfort and homelessness as of reconciliation. We should retain a sense of the challenge of his work, that it disconcerts as much as it reassures; just as we should remember that the same man could strike some observers as humble, self-doubting and generous, who yet could seem to others, or at other times, to be disdainful, conceited and frigid.

To consider Eliot at any depth is to confront such challenging disparities, at various levels. There is the contrast between the achieved edifice of the public career and the sometimes tormented circumstances of his private life; there is the fact that this institution of English Literature was born an American, and in certain aspects remained one. There is the difference between his early poetry and his later; and there is the contrast between his critical theory and his poetic practice. It would be a mistake to consider one side of these contrasts 'truer' than the other – that, for example, he was an American who pretended to be English, or that his poetry of 'glowing despair' is more genuine than his poetry of 'melancholy faith' (the terms are George Orwell's). Rather, it seems to me that we must see Eliot's career as composing itself out of the tensions between these opposing aspects of his life and art.

I am not proposing to offer an exhaustive account of that career, which enfolds diverse activities: as poet, as literary critic, as dramatist, as writer on religious topics, and as social theorist. There are quite clearly relations between all these areas, so that all will be touched upon; but my primary focus will be upon the first two – Eliot as poet and as critic. I make this choice because this seems to me to reflect the probable interest of the general reader; and more significantly because it was as a poet and a critic that Eliot established his reputation, and it is, I believe, in these functions that it is likely to survive. His contributions to social and religious debate tell us something about Eliot and the times he lived in, but are not inherently interesting as religious or social thought, since it is difficult now to read them and feel that he asked quite the right questions or found quite the right answers. His plays cannot so easily be set aside, because they are more closely interconnected with the poetry; yet only the most indulgent and uncritical reader will pretend that in them he matched his achievements in the poems, and they don't seem wholly satisfactory as literature, nor yet as drama. They have not established themselves as part of the theatrical canon, and are likely to be subject to spasmodic revival.

In considering the poetry and the criticism, I try to account for some of the 'disparities' mentioned above. How is it that the spiritual bleakness of the earlier verse gives way to the religious affirmation of the later writing? How can one who is so much a Modernist in practice, be so much a traditionalist in theory? These correspond to a debate about Eliot which took place as his career was unfolding, and which continues, albeit that the vocabulary may be more sophisticated. I have already said that there were those who felt betrayed or deserted by Eliot's religious conversion; they simply could not believe it possible that the poet of, say, 'Gerontion' or 'The Hollow Men' could write *Ash-Wednesday* or the verse that followed without breaking faith with his earlier vision (and themselves). I hope to suggest the ways in which Eliot's religion can be seen to be of a piece, both with the poetry and the literary criticism which preceded his announced conversion; but I do not want to underestimate our sense of the difference. The 'shock' of Eliot's Christianity to his readers is part of a now

historical reaction; but it is a very current question in criticism of
his poetry whether *Four Quartets*, rather than *The Waste Land*, is his
crowning achievement.

Towards the end of his life, Eliot and his second wife held a small
dinner-party in their London flat; their guests were Groucho Marx
and his new wife. The conjunction of so serious a poet with so
zany a comedian is not what we might have anticipated, but it also
reminds us of these surprising facets of Eliot's character. It was
their first and only meeting, the result of a correspondence between these two celebrities initiated by Groucho several years
earlier. Because they were virtual strangers, conversation was a
little strained, with each man addressing himself to the public
achievements of the other: but Groucho was no more interested in
discussing scenes from Marx Brothers films than Eliot was in
responding to Groucho's quotations from *The Waste Land*. When
told that Groucho's daughter was studying his poetry in college,
Eliot's reply was that he was sad, because he had no wish to
become required reading.

This was not, I believe, false modesty: Eliot knew that to achieve
the status of 'set text' for courses of literature conferred doubtful
honours; for although it ensured a steady conscripted readership,
it also tended to embalm a writer, making him, as a 'modern
classic', a visibly impressive corpse enshrined in the mausoleum of
his reputation. He also knew the importance of a reader's response; and much of his writing is concerned with the present
relevance of past literature, the living-ness rather than the dead-
ness of the great writers. His major effort was to affirm that the
classics have to be read in the context of a vital present rather than
in a museum hush of the august past; and that the reader's modern
consciousness is part of that vital present, inescapably forming
those aspects of the classic texts which seem contemporary to the
age. The problem implied by this is whether there can be objective
criteria of merit, by which the major writers can be distinguished
from the minor (which for Eliot was an essential part of the critical
process), yet which also accommodate the equally necessary subjective component of the individual reader's personal evaluation.

These are the issues which can be observed to operate at various
stages in Eliot's career. Both a spiritual and a professional journey
are implied: the interior development of the poet, and the external
shape of the life, in its connections with the worlds of the univer-

sities and of publishing. It may be a mistake to think that there are two Eliots, one full of doubt, one full of assurance; one who wrote the early verse, and one the later; for as he put it in a lecture given in Dublin in 1936, the ideal poet is 'submissive, reactionary or revolutionary', depending on his perception of what the times require.[4] There may seem to us an enormous contrast between the man who wrote 'On Margate Sands./I can connect/Nothing with nothing', and the one who later wrote 'History is now and England'; yet it was the same man. One question that arises out of this, is how 'Margate' and 'England' came to be items in the poetry of an American-born poet; and it is to Eliot's American origins that we turn first of all.

NOTES

1. Herbert Read's and I.A. Richards's reminiscences are amongst those collected in *T.S. Eliot: the Man and His Work*, ed. Allen Tate (London, 1967); hereafter cited as Tate. Wyndham Lewis, untitled reminiscence in *T.S. Eliot: A Symposium*, eds March and Tambimuttu (London, 1948); hereafter cited as March.
2. *The Letters of T.S. Eliot*, ed. Valerie Eliot, Vol I (London, 1988); this volume goes up to 1922, others are expected in due course; hereafter page references for this will be given in the text, thus: (L 3). Peter Ackroyd, *T.S. Eliot: A Life* (London & New York, 1984); hereafter cited as Ackroyd.
3. March, p. 28.
4. T.S. Eliot, 'Tradition and the Practice of Poetry', *Southern Review*, 21, no. 4 (October 1985), pp. 873–88. This is the first publication of this 1936 lecture; the title is not Eliot's.

2

Before the Beginning

Thomas Stearns Eliot was born in St Louis, Missouri, on 26 September 1888, the sixth and youngest surviving child of Henry Ware Eliot (b. 1843) and Charlotte Champe Eliot (*née* Stearns), who had married in 1869. There was an appreciable gap in ages between young Tom and his siblings, with the nearest of them, his only brother (Henry Ware Eliot, Jr) nine years older. It can be seen, then, that the future poet was born into an established marriage and an established family, the child of middle-aged parents, with no obvious playmate for him amongst their other children. In the immediate circle, one of those of whom Eliot seems to have had fond recollections was his Irish nurse, Annie Dunne; on one occasion at least she took her young charge with her to her Catholic church, whose atmosphere impressed him as distinctly different from the Unitarian establishments in which the Eliots worshipped.

What did it mean to be a member of such a family? It was something to live up to: perhaps it is not surprising that one of T.S. Eliot's early and abiding concerns was how a new individual could find an appropriate relation to the illustrious and formulated past. For the Eliots were prominent citizens of St Louis: at the time of Tom's birth, his father was President of the Hydraulic-Press Brick Company, an influential and successful man of business; and his mother, who had once been a school teacher, was involving herself in social concerns, after the pattern of high-minded and well-off American matrons. Although situated in Missouri, they had lost none of the ideals of dedication and duty fostered by New England roots – and Charlotte herself came from an old Massachusetts family, which she memorialised in her youngest child's middle name.

It was because of the family sense of duty and dedication that they found themselves in St Louis, where Eliot's grandfather, William Greenleaf Eliot, had gone in 1834 to create and practise a Unitarian ministry on what was at that stage the American frontier. He had left Harvard Divinity School to become, in essence, a missionary; and in spite of a frail constitution he was extraordinarily successful in all branches of this calling, both as a spiritual leader and as an effective fund-raiser and social organiser. He vigorously espoused a variety of worthy and enlightened causes, and founded what was to become Washington University (insisting it should not be named after himself) and more than one school, in St Louis. He was widely respected; Ralph Waldo Emerson admired his preaching, and many who met him felt themselves to be in the presence of a saintly man.

This, as the saying goes, was a hard act to follow. The expectation was, however, that his children would emulate his example; but although two of his four surviving sons did become ministers, his second son – the poet's father – declined to do so, offering in later life only the laconic explanation, 'too much pudding choked the dog'. If this was a gesture of rebellion on Henry Ware Eliot's part against an overshadowing father or the subtle tyranny of family expectations, it seems to have been his only protest; for in all respects other than pursuing the ministry he conformed to the mould, and subsequently became an amateur historian of his American forebears. It was doubtless researches such as these that would enable his wife to declare in a letter she wrote in 1916, 'I am glad all our ancestors are English with a French ancestry far back on one line' (L 139).

W.G. Eliot died before this grandson was born, and it may seem odd that we should concern ourselves with a relative the poet never met. There are, however, many ghostly presences in Eliot's poetry, and in the family from which he came the past was definitely not dead. This can be seen in Charlotte Eliot's letter already quoted (to Bertrand Russell, whom she hoped would dissuade her son from his poetic ambitions), where she goes on to write: 'I am sending Tom a copy of a letter written by his Great-great-grandfather in 1811, giving an account of his grandfather (*one* of them) who was born about 1676 – in the county of Devon, England'. His mother's attachment to the family history would be echoed by Eliot himself, when he quoted from his namesake and ancestor Sir Thomas Elyot, in *East Coker*; a poem whose title alludes to the Somerset village from which Andrew Eliot set out for Massachusetts in the seventeenth century.

More significantly, Charlotte Eliot was engaged in compiling a biography of this eminent grandfather; an uncommon enough tribute for a daughter-in-law to pay, one supposes. This she eventually published in 1904, dedicating it to her children, 'lest they forget' (she later sent Russell a copy). Her younger son, when he was himself a famous and respected figure, would make it clear how much the atmosphere of his childhood home was permeated by the memory of William Greenleaf Eliot; not simply as an object of retrospective piety, but as an embodiment of living principles of conduct:

> I never knew my grandfather: he died a year before my birth. But I was brought up to be very much aware of him: so much so, that as a child I thought of him as still the head of the family – a ruler for whom *in absentia* my grandmother stood as viceregent.
>
> (TCC 44)

His, then, was a 'dignified, invisible' presence in the lives of following generations of Eliots.

The Unitarianism of which he was so respected an exponent was not to prove an adequate faith for his celebrated grandson, who would eventually find it necessary to be re-baptised into the Church of England. In a simplified account, Unitarianism is the terminal evolution of that fierce and uncompromising Puritanism which led many early settlers to hazard the Atlantic crossing, and the colonial deprivations of New England. Retaining a Puritan focus on the necessity for hard work, and on material success as one of the indications of God's favour, Unitarians had lost that sense of the awesomeness of the afterlife and the fearsomeness of God, which for Puritans had been enshrined in the superb capriciousness of the doctrine of predestination. As a rational and enlightened creed, Unitarianism was well enough adapted to the phase of America's optimistic expansion; but it was more or less devoid of religious mystery, and of the terror that can accompany such mystery. Unitarianism does not acknowledge the divinity of Christ, and hence rejects the doctrine of Incarnation; Eliot underwent baptism, later, because he did not consider the faith in which he had grown up to be truly Christian.

So young Tom was raised in this household, presided over by the spirit of the grandfather he had never met, but whose example was recommended to his attention from very early on. Given the ages of his parents, and of his sisters and brother, it could hardly have been otherwise than that he should have had a somewhat solitary childhood; which, it is probable, answered to his natural inclinations: a clever child spends much time in the company of its own imagination. By contrast to his grandfather's quantifiable presence in the life of the family, his father Henry seems somewhat shadowy. Eliot paid him the tribute, shortly after his death, of dedicating his volume of criticism *The Sacred Wood* (1920) to 'H.W.E.', putting the Eliot family motto into the past tense to describe his father's achievements: *tacuit et fecit*.

Keeping his mouth shut and getting on with the job, Henry Ware Eliot has left glimpses of a less unrelenting character (he used to paint faces on his children's boiled eggs); but his son's commemoration highlights attributes of personal remoteness and absorption in affairs. He was apparently becoming deaf when Tom was growing up, a circumstance which cannot have aided communication and the easy flow of affection between them. His younger son's expatriation and sudden, unannounced marriage were to place barriers between them; and the absolute nature of his paternal care is perhaps suggested by the fact that his will ensured that this son's inheritance would, in the event of Tom's premature death, revert to the Eliot estate rather than pass to his widow. When in 1916 he saw a copy of *Blast* (in which his son's poetry was first published in England), he commented that he had not known there were enough lunatics in the world to support such a venture (L 131). It was to be a source of permanent regret to the poet, that his father had died believing him to have made a failure of his life.

Henry Ware Eliot's own side-step from the predicted family path did not, it appears, render him entirely sympathetic when confronted by his son's more radical departure from what had been expected – although he continued to pay him an allowance, despite his disapproval. But the more significant influence upon T.S. Eliot was his mother's, and in her case there were reasons which might have incited her to sympathise with what he proposed to do with his life. She herself suffered from a sense of having been denied the full flowering of her gifts, by the limited opportunities then available to an intelligent young woman. She, too, had leanings toward poetry, and had written a long poem, 'Savonarola' (which in 1926 her son would publish privately in London). Although she is reported not to have been much interested in him as a baby, once into childhood and showing signs of promise, she seems to have seen his life as a vicarious version of her own.

As the youngest of her children, gifted, and apparently the most

like her, it is not surprising that Tom became an important focus
for his mother, and was in his turn devoted to her; although his
devotion was one which could envisage, and perhaps required,
that they should inhabit different continents. The family circumstances were such as to make his childhood solitary, but it is clear
that he was in no sense neglected; rather the reverse. He was the
object of fond attentions on the part of his elder sisters, as well as
of the mother who would direct his early reading and encourage
his writing – until the day when, shown a poem written as a school
exercise ('A Lyric', CPP 590), she acknowledged it to be better than
anything she had herself produced. He was not a robust child
(although later he appeared slightly to resent suggestions to this
effect) and suffered from a congenital double hernia, which de-
barred him from the more boisterous physical activities of school
life. His mother watched over him anxiously, and when he was at
college away from home was worried lest those *in loco parentis* took
less good care of his health than she did.

By the time of his enrolment at Harvard University his sisters
and his mother felt sure that he was destined to high achievement;
but his mother was not easily to relinquish her belief that this
would be in the field of academic philosophy. What can be seen is
that, added to the burden of expectation that would naturally
attach to an Eliot – and especially to a gifted Eliot – there was also
his mother's special and self-implicated solicitude for the course of
her son's life. She wrote to him at Harvard: 'I hope in your literary
work you will receive early the recognition I strove for and failed'
(L 13); but later on, at a time when the family was trying to
persuade the erring son to return to more conventional paths, it
would be clear that her vision of his future evoked the professor
rather than the poet: 'I have absolute faith in his Philosophy', she
wrote to Russell, 'but not in the vers libre' (L 139). Herself feeling,
as she put it in her letter to her son, that she had 'made a dead
failure', it was presumably a matter of anguish with her when this
favourite child showed signs of doing the same. There would
certainly be occasions when it appeared to Eliot, in spite of literary
success, that this was precisely what he had done.

There were, then, many claims and many pressures to bear
down upon the youngest member of the family at 2635 Locust
Street, St Louis:

The heavy burden of the growing soul
Perplexes and offends more, day by day;

Week by week, offends and perplexes more
With the imperatives of 'is and seems'
And may and may not, desire and control.

But whether or not memories of his own childhood inform these lines from 'Animula', we should not paint too gloomy a picture. Eliot was a serious child, without being joyless and repressed; he had a sense of humour, which was usually expressed verbally, and later in life he was to acquire a reputation as a practical joker (which can, of course, have its darker side). Although there are images of childhood thwarted in his verse, there are also images of childhood as an alert and self-communing secrecy: 'the leaves were full of children, / Hidden excitedly, containing laughter' (*Burnt Norton*). This sense, hardly unique to Eliot, that childhood is essentially a private condition which cannot be comprehended by adult outsiders, should remind us how much we cannot know about his own boyhood.

We do know that the house in which he spent his boyhood and youth was situated in an area of the expanding city of St Louis which was becoming less and less fashionable, and even bordered upon slums. The family stayed on because of the association with William Greenleaf Eliot: the house adjoined one of the schools he had helped found (the Mary Institute for girls, in whose yard his grandson would sometimes play after school hours); his widow lived nearby. The urban squalor nearby was probably noticed by the impressionable young Eliot, who in many of his poems would evince a sort of negative zest for such scenes and their inhabitants. During his time in St Louis, he travelled regularly to the North; for the family kept up its associations with New England by annual visits there during the hot Missouri summers. In 1896 Eliot's father had a large seaside house built at Eastern Point, Gloucester, Massachusetts, commanding a fine view out to the harbour and beyond across slabs of rock and overgrowth. In this setting, Eliot grew familiar with the atmosphere of the fishing town of Gloucester, and himself became a keen and proficient yachtsman, with his own small boat.

So we can discern a certain doubleness in his experience: the comfortable, respectable home with its protective women, tenanted also by austere figures from the past; contrasted with the ambient slovenliness of the industrial city, its smokes, smells, scenes of low-life and decay, and other insignia of disorganisation and entropy. This 'doubleness' can also be observed in Eliot's divided heritage, as the scion of a New England family, but born and raised in the South: heir, therefore, to different types of society and familiar with contrasting geographies. If St Louis gave him its city fogs, its big, slow river and its rank vegetation, New England endowed him with its sea and its fishermen, its rock and golden-rod and sea-mists, and its Boston. The result, according to Eliot himself, was a sense of displacement; in a letter to Herbert Read in 1928 he contemplated writing 'an essay about the point of view of an American who wasn't an American, because he was born in the South and went to school in New England as a small boy with a nigger drawl, but who wasn't a southerner in the South because his people were northerners in a border state and looked down on all southerners and Virginians, and who so was never anything anywhere'.[1] This should probably not be taken too directly as a statement of fact; but it communicates a mood which may well have been real enough, and suggests something of what lay behind Eliot's droll but not entirely flippant thumbnail sketch of a chameleon personality, in his poem in French, 'Mélange Adultère de Tout'.

The Eliot family was sure that Tom would become somebody, somewhere, and no less confident that Harvard would be an important part of this. He had been educated in St Louis until the autumn of 1905, when he was sent for a year to Milton, a select private college near Boston, before proceeding as destined to Harvard; his mother described him to Milton's headmaster as 'quiet and very dignified' (L 6). He arrived at university in October 1906 as a privileged young man from a distinguished family, by which he was distantly related to the then President of Harvard, and which also furnished him with an *entrée* into Boston society – to be the object of satirical probing in some of his poems. He came from having spent his preparatory year in the company of other rich and intelligent young gentlemen, to take up lodgings in a select student neighbourhood; he became a member of the right clubs. The conventional undergraduate career of a gilded youth, with much social show and little intellectual exertion, seemed in prospect: for by December Eliot had been placed on probation for his poor grades (this was lifted the following February). Much later he told his second wife that he had 'loafed' through his first two years; but there was soon evidence of his capacity for work: in his own choice of courses for his first degree Eliot was eclectic and rigorous – opting to do seven of his eighteen courses in classical studies, for example, which was far from being the usual pattern.

He wanted to earn his laurels, not to rest on them. His chosen courses, it has been observed, show a characteristically American concern with breadth of coverage rather than with depth of study; but he was to prove himself capable of depth, as well as of knowing how to deploy his breadth to best effect in his writing. His commitment to his own education is seen in his decision to complete his undergraduate studies in three years rather than the customary four; using the fourth year to study for his master's degree. The grades with which, in June 1909, he obtained his bachelor's degree were good, without being outstanding; but during the following year he completed the work for his master's degree in English literature with all-round distinction – although he was to fall ill in May of that year, and was unable to sit his final examinations. The illness was not so serious as to prevent him from attending the graduation ceremonies at the end of June.

It has been suggested that this illness may have had its connection with a small crisis in Eliot's relations with his parents: for in the spring of 1910 he had formed the project of spending the following year in Paris. This was not a scheme his mother could contemplate with any equanimity; 'I can not bear to think of your being alone in Paris, the very words give me a chill', she wrote to her son, adding for good measure, 'English-speaking countries seem so different from foreign. I do not admire the French nation . . .' (L 13). In her letter to Bertrand Russell – written during the Great War, it should be remembered – Charlotte Eliot berated the Germans ('a synonym for all that is most frightful'): it is difficult not to detect a fierce parochialism generating these sentiments. But such was probably the common attitude of her class and type, good education notwithstanding; and this suggests something of the mental climate in which Eliot grew up: which both formed him, and also made it urgent that he should make an escape – as well as from the mother who perhaps presumed too much on her interiority with him.

The doubleness of experience already referred to must have been apparent to Eliot, as he became aware of the difference between the gentilities of the University environment and the slum or waste areas of Cambridge and Boston, which he explored and evoked in early poems: the 'Second Caprice in North Cambridge' of November 1909, for example, considers the charm of vacant lots.

The vision of life suggested by such places seems to have carried more authority with the young man than the prevailing ethos of Harvard, which was at that time attuned to practical and affirmative notions of American destiny. Although there were eminent thinkers at the University, it is reputed to have been an unexciting period to be a student there, and Eliot does not seem to have been unduly stimulated. By the time he arrived, he had completely lost interest in the Unitarianism in which he had been raised; he was hardly likely, therefore, to be much moved by an institution whose tepid optimism seemed like a philosophical counterpart.

Although Eliot joined clubs, became in his third year an editor of the University's literary magazine (the *Harvard Advocate*), occasionally got drunk, and in certain externals resembled other undergraduates, there was also a slightly reclusive aspect to him: he was marked off by a seriousness. It is probably no exaggeration to suggest that the most important relationships which were established during these three years were not with fellow students (apart perhaps from Conrad Aiken), but with poets: in particular Dante, Baudelaire and Laforgue. He was introduced to the first on a course, and may also have been directed to Baudelaire by his studies in French Literature; his acquaintance with Laforgue he owed to Arthur Symons's book *The Symbolist Movement in Literature*, which he came across in the library of the Harvard Union in December 1908.

A studious child, such as Eliot was, is liable to have been open to a variety of literary influences as he forms his taste. Those which he himself identified as having had sway over his imagination in childhood and adolescence were Edgar Allan Poe, and Edward Fitzgerald's translation of *The Rubáiyát of Omar Khayyám*. Shakespeare he reports having read without genuine enjoyment, to gain the approbation of his elders. Dante, Baudelaire and Laforgue were important to Eliot, not because they excited a transient youthful fervour – as was the case with his earlier enthusiasms – but because they answered to a more mature requirement. His acquaintance with Dante preceded his knowledge of Italian, and he read the poetry in parallel text, with the translation facing the original; he memorised passages and repeated them to himself – for example, on train journeys.

The precise nature of the need these writers met in Eliot is a matter for conjecture, although he would himself write about it. The scope and authority of Dante's achievement, the beauty, technical mastery and moral rigour of *The Divine Comedy*, would be likely to impress one engaged as Eliot was in his preliminary wrestle with words and meanings, and afflicted by a sense of the fortuity of experience. The diversity of Dante's material and its judicious disposition within his structure, each sin assigned appropriate punishment and each virtue its reward, offer a sweeping spectacle of imaginative vigour and of disorder ordered. Eliot would later claim that the *Comedy* exhibited 'a complete scale of the *depths* and *heights* of human emotion' (SE 268): such comprehensiveness, and the enlargement of human actions by the perspective of the eternity to which they led, in Dante's scheme, were potent features of his achievement. Eliot would never outwear his admiration for this writer.

Dante, however, was too elevated and too distant a master to be directly useful to an aspiring poet as any kind of model. Eliot was most typically to be a struggler with fragments rather than the architect of a massive whole; and indeed, his relation to Dante's work is characterised by a retention of vivid images and isolated episodes from the poetry, as much as by any appreciation of Dante's cosmology. Although Baudelaire's poetry, as well, was connected with a system of belief unlikely to be digestible by Eliot, the French poet's example was more immediately fruitful. The technical interest and verbal accomplishment of his verse were surely important, but his significance as the first great poet of the modern consciousness is what is likely to have struck a highly intelligent young man like Eliot, who was aware of the inadequacy of the orthodox thought and belief which were his own inheritance. In Baudelaire the 'I' becomes theatrical, its sexual encounters are reveries of a fetishistic imagination, its discontents are projected onto the backdrop of the contemporary unreal city. Prey to unformulated longings, the disconsolate ego presides amidst the débris of its worn-out enthusiasms.

Baudelaire was a subverter of the bourgeois sensibility, an investigator of the spirit damned rather than the spirit saved. He enlarged the scope of poetry with his quasi-diabolical depiction of the modern mind, its rootlessness and its dissatisfactions; but insofar as these are representative of modern reality, such a vision offers an escape from the arbitrariness of personal experience, by showing how the unfixedness of the self, its sense of alienation and its imperative fantasies, are a revelation of the human condition. To a mind like Eliot's, more open to the sordid than the conventionally beautiful, Baudelaire showed a way of making poetry that was not a surrender to the trivial. Both Baudelaire and Dante, with their respective atmospheres of hell-fire, offered a perception of life with a sense of ultimate seriousness as well as the dimension of a spiritual trial.

Baudelaire's seriousness, his somewhat egotistical defiance, were appealingly masked within the pose of a dandy; this was a pose even more marked in the poetry of Jules Laforgue, whose influence on Eliot was to be more obviously identifiable, if shorter-lived, than that of the other two. After his introduction to Laforgue in Symons's book, Eliot went out and ordered the complete works from a bookseller; he quite plausibly supposes himself to have been the only Harvard undergraduate to possess these volumes at that time. Within a little while the poetry he was writing shows the influence, with Laforguian props such as marionettes making their appearance, together with a dandiacal posturing, evidenced in a disdain for bourgeois pieties and a quizzically disaffected view of manoeuvering between the sexes.

Eliot would not draw the profoundest sustenance from Laforgue, however much he acknowledged a debt. There are elements of Laforgue in poems such as 'The Love Song of J. Alfred Prufrock' and 'Portrait of a Lady', with their mocking self-consciousness, and especially the movement of their verse, which owes much to Laforgue's *vers libre*; but there are other elements besides. The best of his most undilutedly Laforguian poems is probably 'La Figlia Che Piange': 'I should have lost a gesture and a pose' distils the essence of a self-protective dandy. But however much this poem seems to offer its speaker as stage-manager of emotions, it also implies a critique of his separation from these scenes of passion he spectates; and the glacial understatement of its final lines (which in fact contain an echo from Baudelaire's poem '*Les Bijoux*') betrays an impassivity that has been deeply, unaccountably ruffled:

Sometimes these cogitations still amaze
The troubled midnight and the noon's repose.

It is important not to be simplistic in assessing the 'influence' of these three writers, first read by Eliot during his undergraduate years; his appreciation of Dante would develop and grow. But it is probably fair to say that one common trait between the three, which may be relevant, is that in each the poet is a being apart, and by implication superior: elevated, if you like, by his more comprehending response. Dante's is the most clearly privileged vision, passing untouched through infernal and celestial regions; but Baudelaire, too, is an explorer of the inferno of the modern city and its night-lit streets, a charter of individual damnations. With Laforgue, the poet throws a *cordon sanitaire* between self and experience, fastidiously unmoved or quizzically amused, a model of elegant detachment. The inference to be drawn is that life is not simply what it seems or what it declares itself to be, but is more truly recognised from a subversive angle: by which, for example, the passionate lover is perceived as a gesticulating puppet, or hordes of city clerks going to work are seen to be the souls of the damned. 'The thing is', he would write to Conrad Aiken in September 1914, 'to be able to look at one's life as if it were somebody's else [sic]' (L 58).

On the whole, then, these literary discoveries are what seem to have counted most for Eliot as an undergraduate, rather than anything Harvard accomplished for him. But in his fourth and final year, studying intensively for his master's degree, he came into contact with a teacher who was to have a significant effect: in the autumn of 1909 he took Irving Babbitt's course in French literary criticism. As with the poets, it would be difficult to ascertain how far Babbitt was responsible for implanting thoughts in his pupil's mind, as opposed to strengthening and focusing tendencies already there; what is certain, is that the concerns of this course were remarkably close to some of the fundamental positions of Eliot's thinking, as it was later to reveal itself.

Babbitt was apparently an academic who had set himself against Harvard's prevailing liberal and scientific notions of a sufficient education; the consequence of this on the students was to repel the many but attract the few, and Eliot was one of those few. The course ranged beyond its defined subject (it was Babbitt who pointed Eliot toward a study of Eastern philosophy and religion); but essentially its concern was to analyse the weaknesses of the traditions of thought, writing and behaviour which derived from Rousseau, with their emphasis on the individual as the measure, and their presumption that the greater the individual's freedom, the better the life. Opposed to this was the 'classicism' that insisted on the past as a component of the present, asserted the validity of established standards of wisdom, and argued the need for the naturally anarchic impulses of the unchecked self to be shaped by social and cultural contexts. Along with this went a distrust of art whose emphasis was on the expression of emotion, and which put a premium on the 'sincerity' or 'originality' of the artist. What was preferred, was the art which derived a strength and maturity from its continuity with the achievements of the past.

Ideas such as these were to become essential to Eliot's critical thought; but however congenial he found the majority of the premises on which this view was based, there were aspects of Babbitt's thinking (specifically his humanism) with which he was to disagree, and against which he would argue with some vigour. It is hardly to be doubted, however, that Babbitt's course gave an added impetus to his desire to go and study in Paris, even if the primary reason related to his poetry rather than his studies. The period of his master's year up to his departure for Europe was one in which Eliot wrote a considerable amount of new poetry, and this shows (Ackroyd suggests) that his interests and energies were predominantly focused in that area. Certainly, in 1944 Eliot would give the following account: *'Mais ce n'est pas un accident qui m'avait conduit à Paris. Depuis plusieurs années, la France représentait surtout, à mes yeux, la poésie'* ['But it was no accident that led me to Paris. For several years, France had above all represented poetry to my eyes'].[2]

To find himself in France in October 1910 was a significant step; not only was it his first crossing of the Atlantic, he had also carried his design in the face of family opposition – although in the event his father subsidised the trip: as far as he was concerned, his son was continuing his studies in French and philosophy at the Sorbonne. In an interview he gave in 1959 Eliot would look back on it as 'a romantic year', but it seems that this applies as much to the conception as to the reality: there is some reason to suppose that he was quite solitary for much of his time there (he would later recommend this as the best way to get to know a city).[3] Nevertheless he made acquaintances: with a fellow-lodger at his pension, Jean Verdenal, to whom he would dedicate his first volume of poetry (1917); he practised French conversation with the young writer Alain-Fournier, who like Verdenal was to lose his life in the Great War, and he also met Jacques Rivière, editor of the *Nouvelle Revue Française*, to which Eliot subscribed. He read *Bubu de Montparnasse*, a popular novel about the Paris underworld, which influenced the imagery of some of the poems he would write; and he walked in the Luxembourg Gardens. There was in the city at that time (Eliot would recall in 1934) a pervasive sense of intellectual and artistic excitement and discovery: the young American became aware of the researches of several figures previously unknown to him; but probably his two most decisive encounters during this visit were with the thought of Henri Bergson and of Charles Maurras.

Bergson was a philosopher then very much in vogue: Eliot was later to evoke his 'spider-like' figure as in some ways the presiding intelligence. He attended a course of seven lectures by Bergson in January and February 1911; these were held on Fridays at the Collège de France, where it was necessary to arrive well in advance in order to secure a seat: the atmosphere of intellectual fervour this suggests must have offered a contrast to what Eliot had been accustomed to at Harvard. Bergson was more of a prose stylist than many philosophers; indeed, subsequent criticisms of his thought demonstrated its reliance, at crucial points, on metaphors which would not submit to logical analysis. It is possible that his significance for Eliot lies less in any influence his philosophy exerted ('Rhapsody on a Windy Night' is often cited as a poem that suggests Bergson), than in the reaction it provoked. Although Eliot admitted a period of attachment to Bergson's ideas, this was short-lived: within two or three years he would be mounting serious objections to them, as a graduate student in philosophy.

Bergson became popular, it has been argued, by offering a subversion of the scientific determinism which had been a dominant intellectual legacy of the nineteenth century. For those dissatisfied by such an account of reality, Bergson elevated the fact of flux into a quasi-mystical category. This was indeed, he argued, the basis of reality; but the consequence was that the only true perception could be the perception of flux, and since all science depended upon the artificial segmentation of the continuous flow of existence into stable units for investigation, science never addressed itself to the actuality of flux, and was therefore untrue. Bergson proposed an absolute level of reality, '*la durée*', a kind of pure time, the ongoingness of being which is, so to speak, the essence of flux. The more we structure our experience analytically or rationally, by dissecting its textural continuity into units, the further we are from apprehending this fundamental reality. '*La durée*' seems to be both immanence and transcendence; and we can only come into alignment with it by 'intuition': which involves the suspension of ordinary consciousness. It is almost as if intuition discloses the secret of time.

Bergson also advanced the notion of an *'élan vital'*, a cosmic dynamism which has resemblances to a fundamental spiritual principle; although Santayana suggested it amounted to no more than a 'tendency to life' on the part of everything. In diminishing the authority of the physical sciences as explications of reality, and in demoting the operations of the consciousness with its categorical procedures of labelling and identification, Bergson by implication elevates the significance of the unconscious, the unformulated; and the experience of 'intuition' seems akin to an unwilled epiphany. There is, then, a certain mystical absolutism here; about which Eliot's mother, commenting to Russell on her son's declining enthusiasm, made the following dry observation: 'In Bergson's emphasis on *life*, its power and indestructibility, I think some persons found an intimation of immortality, which excited their interest' (L 130).

The moment of intuition, when things come unbidden and unsought before the mind, was an experience important to Eliot in various ways, as was the feeling that, at some deeper level, the randomness of experience makes (not always pleasant) sense. He would, too, become aware of the varieties of religious experience which can only be communicated through a subversion of positive definitions – where 'what you do not know is the only thing you know'. But his temper and his training attached him to difficulty, to arduous procedures, as well as to the structures of reason; Bergson dissolves the personality, which is a conscious construct, and at best leaves the 'self' that remains in an incommunicable intuitional communion with *'la durée'*. This is a state that precludes apprehension of the past as the past, and also precludes moral responsibility. Whatever the temporary attractions of a philosophy that displaced the certain certainties of reductive materialism, it could not in the long term answer Eliot's questions.

By contrast, his attachment to the thought of Charles Maurras was not to be short-lived, and was to be maintained (like his support for Ezra Pound) in adverse circumstances. Eliot became acquainted with his work in the pages of the *N.R.F.*, and in it he found an intensification of the attitudes and values promulgated by Irving Babbitt, with a more overtly political issue in the organisation *Action Française* (co-founded by Maurras in 1899) which

engaged in right-wing demonstrations and other patriotic viol-
ences. Maurras was opposed to any emphasis on the freedom of
the individual, whether expressed artistically in Romanticism or
politically in democratic egalitarianism. He espoused an active
monarchism, which expressed his sense of the need for a stable
and hierarchical organisation of society; and although he no longer
professed Roman Catholicism, that Church was an institution
whose authoritarian structure and capacity for social control he
applauded. The Pope did not reciprocate Maurras' enthusiasm,
however, and denounced *Action Française* in 1928.

Maurras reacted against what he perceived to be the disintegrative tendencies in contemporary French politics; emotionally, he
hankered after the immobile stratifications of feudalism. In his old
age during the Second World War, when strong government
visited itself upon his country in the shape of Hitler's stormtroopers
and state torturers, Maurras became a member of the Vichy puppet
administration set up by the Nazis. It seems a somewhat com-
promised position for so uncompromising a political theorist; too
subtle indeed for his fellow-countrymen to grasp, and he was tried
and imprisoned when peace returned. He was doubtless being
made a scapegoat, but this episode, together with the virulent
anti-Semitism which was a feature of *Action Française*, make an
unendearing figure of Charles Maurras. His influence on Eliot,
nonetheless, was important, and acknowledged: the latter would
imply that it was through the atheist Maurras that he himself had
been led to Christianity. Eliot was less extreme than Maurras; what
he seems to have imbibed was a social, political and religious
extension of views which were originally formulated in the realm
of literary aesthetics or philosophy. The influence of Maurras lies
behind his idea of a Christian society, for example, with its oddly
anachronistic belief in the Church of England's capacity to generate and sustain a social structure.

Although it is clear that Maurras was more important to Eliot
than Bergson, just as Dante was more important than Laforgue, it
is interesting to consider them together: Eliot encountered both at
the same period in his life, and it can be argued that they pull in
opposite directions, perhaps suggesting contrasting compulsions
within Eliot himself. For Bergson – with his subversion of scientific
categories, his elevation of the realm of the subconscious, and his
implication that ultimate truth lies beyond and within our experience of the phenomenal world – points toward those private,

intuitive areas from which, for Eliot, fragments of poems unaccountably arose, 'the depths of feeling into which we cannot peer' as he was to describe them in 1933 (UPUC 148). Whereas Maurras, emphasising the need for structure and control, preferring regulation of impulse by an external order to inspirational spontaneity, indicates not only a social reality, but also concerns of discrimination and evaluation which manifest themselves in Eliot's critical writing.

It is rash to be schematic about what is a complex matter; but if Eliot was subject to conflicting tendencies of this kind it helps to explain why the upshot of his year abroad was that he went back to Harvard. It has been suggested that a potent factor in his decision to return was his desire for a period of sustained logical application, a rededication to the modes of enquiry Bergson sought to devalue. He went to France because of poetry; and to the extent that he composed a considerable amount of verse during his absence from America, his visit justified itself in that regard. But in spite of this, the ensuing three years were to be notable for his dedication to philosophy. Speaking of his year in France in 1959, he recalled that 'I had at that time the idea of giving up English and trying to settle down and scrape along in Paris and gradually write French'.[4] This may have been his vague plan at the outset; but by the time he was visited by his Harvard friend Conrad Aiken early in the summer of 1911, these ideas had undergone a change: for Eliot told Aiken that he intended to return to America and read for a doctorate in philosophy. In April he had visited London, where he had made a point of visiting several City churches; and in July he travelled in Northern Italy and visited Munich (where he finished, among other poems, 'The Love Song of J. Alfred Prufrock'); but by October 1911 he was enrolled in the Harvard Graduate School.

Family pressure would have played a large part in his decision. His mother wanted him back from Paris, and his father was unlikely to subsidise another year abroad in any case; Eliot's time for scraping along had not yet arrived. But there was probably more to it than this: the deflection from his poetry to philosophy was emphatic. Although he completed 'Portrait of a Lady' that November, between then and the second half of 1914 the evidence suggests that he may have written a mere handful of poems. In a later reminiscence he would declare that in these years his philosophical studies 'were' him. Yet if he acted the philosopher, he looked the poet; Charlotte Eliot's 'quiet and very dignified' son returned to Cambridge somewhat dandified: perceptibly Europeanised, in Aiken's recollection, with a malacca cane and declaratively foreign apparel and hairstyle, causing – as presumably he had intended – 'a sensation'. A reproduction of Gauguin's 'Yellow Christ' found its place on his wall. If such were his visible credentials, less public but more substantial were the drafts of poems copied into his notebook. By this time Eliot had composed all the important poems of his first volume of poetry: 'Preludes', 'Portrait of a Lady', 'Rhapsody on a Windy Night', and 'The Love Song of J. Alfred Prufrock'.

Which may make it all the more surprising that he turned away from such achievements; yet Aiken (who was himself to become an expatriated American writer, and with whom Eliot would maintain a constant – if fluctuating – friendship) read 'Prufrock' admiringly in manuscript, but remembered Eliot as 'heartlessly indifferent' to its fate. In 1920 Eliot told Virginia Woolf that 'a personal upheaval of some kind came after Prufrock' (as she put it in her Journal); this turned him aside from his desire 'to develop in the manner of Henry James'.[5] We cannot know what this upheaval was; but possibly he was referring to the fact that in 1912 he had fallen in love with Emily Hale, whom he had met during amateur theatricals at the Cambridge home of his vivacious cousin Eleanor Hinkley. This followed on from his Parisian year, during which, as he told Aiken in December 1914, he had been prey to 'nervous sexual attacks' (L 75). Emily Hale was to be a woman of great importance in Eliot's life; it is not clear whether she encouraged or hindered his immersion in his academic studies, but it does seem that by contrast to the reclusive studiousness of his MA year, the post-Paris Eliot led a more active social life, which included dancing and skating lessons as well as concert parties and amateur dramatics. By his own account (half a century later), Eliot declared his love to Miss Hale before he left for Europe in 1914, but her response seems to have implied to him this was not what she meant, at all (L xvii).

He embarked on courses in Indic philology and Indian philosophy, which he abandoned after two years and one year respectively, and also (Ackroyd tells us) took a year's course on Buddhism. Then, he turned toward European philosophy, and was taught by Josiah Royce, whose book *The Problem of Christianity* (1913) deals both with the relation of the individual to the community of belief, and with the relation of the past to the present. In

June 1913 Eliot acquired a copy of F.H. Bradley's *Appearance and Reality*, which was to give him the subject of his doctoral dissertation, 'Experience and the Objects of Knowledge in the Philosophy of F.H. Bradley'. He was an assistant in the Philosophy department from 1912 to 1914, teaching undergraduates, and for the second of these years was the President of the University's Philosophy Club. He delivered papers on the significance of ritual in primitive religions, on the nature of belief, and on the value of illusion. In March 1914 he met Bertrand Russell, then a visiting lecturer at Harvard, and made a comment about Heraclitus which caused Russell to think this rather formal young man a cut above his predominantly dull contemporaries. Russell, for his part, struck Eliot as a much more lively person than the Harvard academics.

Eliot, with his malacca cane and other European affectations, was something of a *poseur*; later in his life he would adopt a variety of protective colourations, but within them all was the fact of a formidable intelligence. His dissertation, on which he was working between 1913 and 1916, has been described as showing an acquaintance with the specialist literature 'far in excess of what might reasonably be expected in a graduate student'.[6] This was eventually published in 1964, a year before Eliot's death; by which time its author declared himself unable to understand it. Other readers, their appetite whetted by hopes of what it might reveal about the formative years of a major poet, fared little better: the thesis is obscure and even convoluted in expression, in ways that may suggest a mind seeking refuge within the labyrinthine density of an intellectual system, from the importunities of external circumstances – these by the time of its completion included an already troubled marriage and an uncertain future.

It is hazardous for the non-specialist to ascertain what led Eliot to Bradley. Bradley had criticised the philosophy of Bergson, but there are also some broad continuities between the two: each is concerned with what might be designated an absolute, and with the difficulty of approaching this by means of rational or categorical procedures. In Bradley's case there is something called 'Immediate Experience', or 'Feeling', which is the undifferentiated datum on which all the interpretative superstructures of consciousness are subsequently erected. This, at as it were the lowest, initial point of the scale, is similar in its irreducible unity to the highest, unattainable point, which would be perception of the unity of the Absolute, within which everything is a whole. The loci of perception are 'finite centres', similar to souls, but different from person-alities. It was, at any rate, to tease out such concepts that Eliot left for Oxford (via Marburg) in early July 1914.

The period from the autumn of 1906 to the summer of 1914 can be seen as the inaugural phase of Eliot's career. This phase begins with his admission to Harvard, and ends when he left on his Travelling Fellowship to Europe – left, as it would turn out, for good. These years were those in which he moved away from home, published his first 'serious' poems, first visited Europe, and felt the conflicting attractions of poetry and philosophy. Having already touched upon home and philosophy; it now remains to deal with the poetry from this period, which falls into two categories: published and unpublished. The published poems are those which were either printed in the *Harvard Advocate* (between 1907 and 1910), or those written during the period under consideration but published later, such as 'Prufrock'. The unpublished poems are almost entirely those preserved in the material which Eliot sent to John Quinn in 1922, in gratitude for Quinn's efforts over American publication of *The Waste Land*.[7] In addition to those papers relating to *The Waste Land* (which were published in facsimile in 1971), there is a notebook and a folder containing drafts of other poems in various stages of correction; many of these have been dated by Eliot, or can be dated on the evidence of his handwriting – which underwent a change during his year abroad.

The years 1909, 1910 and 1911 stand out as the most fertile in terms of quantity, with the later two years combining quality with this; only one poem from 1909 ('Conversation Galante') would be admitted by Eliot into his canon, and it is not a strong contender for immortality. Poems from the previous years are included in the appendix, 'Poems Written in Early Youth', in *The Complete Poems and Plays of T.S. Eliot*. Here are most easily to be found the ten poems which make up his *Harvard Advocate* contributions, of which one ('If space and time, as sages say', June 1907) is a revision of the 'Lyric' written as a schoolboy, which had so impressed his mother; and the last, 'Ode' (which appeared in June 1910, and should not be confused with the 'Ode' cancelled from *Ara Vos Prec*), was a poem of tribute to Harvard which Eliot had been elected to write: convention decreed the form it should take, its melting anapaests and poetic diction do not denote any crazed reversion on the part of the poet who had already composed some of 'Portrait of a Lady'.

In the summer of 1910, after graduating, Eliot bought a note-book, which he entitled 'Inventions of the March Hare', and amplified by the description 'Complete Poems of T.S. Eliot'. For the next four years he would copy into this the poems he had written, frugally filling up blank portions of pages wherever poss-ible, but fortunately for us also recording the date in most cases. None of the poems published in the *Advocate* was transcribed: even at this early stage, an editorial eye defined the 'completeness' of the collection, and Eliot would continue to be a poet characterised by a scanty and discriminating output. It is highly likely that this omission signified a rejection of his pre-Laforgue poetry; but it is probable that he didn't include poems like 'Nocturne' or 'Spleen' simply because they existed in print, and saw no need to waste paper; whatever the reason, 'Conversation Galante' is the first poem in the book.

As well as this one, before he left for France in October 1910 Eliot had written 'Preludes' I and II, and 'Portrait of a Lady' II; the following month he wrote part I of 'Portrait of a Lady' (which quite possibly he had already started before leaving). In March 1911 he wrote 'Rhapsody on a Windy Night', and in July he completed the third 'Prelude', and arrived at the final version of 'Prufrock'. Then he returned to America, where he wrote 'Portrait of a Lady' III and the fourth 'Prelude' in Cambridge. Along with these, there was a body of poems which he never published; common to both pub-lished and unpublished poems of this period is a sense of the vulnerable or untrustworthy nature of the world of appearances – especially in its social manifestations. There is a feeling that some-thing darker underlies the civic façades and the posed brittleness. Hugh Kenner has argued that Eliot's 'unvarying dramatic method . . . is to set loose, in a drawing-room full of masks, some Lazarus'.[8] Would it, however, be possible to disturb this universe, to disrupt what Eliot would much later describe as its 'deliberate hebetude'? This is the predicament repeatedly delineated in the early poems, whether in Prufrock's inability to say just what he means, in the failure to communicate anatomised in 'Portrait of a Lady', or when the speaker in the fourth of the 'Preludes' appar-ently finds his confession – 'I am moved' – scoffed at by the companion to whom he makes it.

The unpublished poems which Eliot wrote in the summer of 1910 present life as a charade, and although he would himself become a frequenter of drawing-rooms, on the evidence of his writing he was never wholly to lose his scepticism, nor a kind of pleasure in reflecting on the futility of such display. When, for example, in 'Rhapsody on a Windy Night' he declares 'I could see nothing behind that child's eye', it's difficult not to receive this as a disclosure of a rather satisfying vacancy. It is not uncommon for young poets to expose the artificiality of other people's behaviour; what elevates Eliot's poetry beyond an attitude of smug superiority is the sense of being implicated in the falseness: a poem like 'Portrait of a Lady' is not merely a presentation of her gushing insincerities (if that *is* what they are); it also probes the helpless posturing and self-recriminations of her gentleman caller.

This poem is probably the clearest exposition of the pressing issue in all the early poetry: that of authenticity. When its speaker is disturbed by hearing the street-piano's 'mechanical' evocation of 'things that other people have desired', or when he reflects that he 'must borrow every changing shape / To find expression', there is dismay at the ease with which personal experience becomes second-hand, or is distorted by the only modes available for its communication. The world of the poem (which he fears may be the only world) is one in which men are for the most part quite happy to adjust their individual perceptions to conform to a received pattern – to 'correct our watches by the public clocks'. The lady of the title (who is reported by Conrad Aiken to be based upon a Boston original whom Eliot visited) sets a trap, although she may not mean to, because she creates an atmosphere of expectation which he finds emotionally coercive; she is, to borrow Eliot's later phrase, a 'lady of situations'. In Prufrock, we see a man entangled in a still more complex web of what he thinks he feels and wants, and what he thinks is expected of him. He finds practically the whole of external reality transformed into impediments – 'the sunsets and the dooryards and the sprinkled streets', the novels, the teacups, the skirts that trail along the floor, the downy hair on a lady's arm: all these importunate details refuse to form them-selves into a coherent whole, yet are obstinately there, in a way that his visionary mermaids are not.

Eliot's most pressing sense seems to have been that of a funda-mental emptiness; in 1928 he would explain his Christianity as a response to 'the void that I find in the middle of all human happiness and all human relations'.[9] At this stage of his life he appears to have had a sense of 'the void' without any philosophy or theology that could redeem it; and a problem for the personae presented or implied in these poems is that theirs is not so much an apprehension of truth as a conviction of falsity: the negative vision is much stronger than any positive, and they can feel the artificiality of what passes for 'reality' more readily than they can articulate a truer system. Prufrock knows that he is not Prince Hamlet, but does not know whether he dare disturb the universe, or eat a peach. From these early poems to *The Waste Land* and beyond (we could think of *The Cocktail Party*), Eliot is a notable poet of acedia, of spiritual listlessness or disability. Yet it is not a question of the self being distorted by the world of externals, for what lies inside the self may as easily be madness, as truth (and a cancelled section of 'Prufrock' deals explicitly with madness). The 'I' in these poems is unstable, generating questions rather than answers: as in 'Are these ideas right or wrong?' in 'Portrait of a Lady', or the more radical doubts that begin an unpublished poem (possibly from 1913), whose speaker asks, does he know how he feels, does he know what he thinks?

At this stage Eliot was the poet of doubt rather than assertion. This manifests itself not only in scepticism about what happens in the drawing-room, but also in scepticism about what happens in the mind. If social behaviour is characterised by elaboration and artifice, so is much of our mental life; and a poem like 'Rhapsody on a Windy Night' 'dissolves' the 'clear relations' established by conscious process, to replace these by the random associations of involuntary memory. Its Baudelairean wanderer through city streets encounters the arbitrariness of his experience, and the automatism of what constitutes his 'self'; the 'rhapsody' is not evidence of deep romantic feelings, nor is the wind the wind of inspiration. Read in sequence the 'Preludes', written either side of this poem, seem to chart an ascending graph of the life of the mind. They move from almost pure objectivity (I), to a notion of 'consciousness', initially impersonal, but then located in 'one thinks' (II); the words 'soul' and 'vision' occur in the third 'Prelude', albeit sarcastically undermined by the context; and, finally, we encounter the word 'conscience', along with the surprising declaration 'I am moved', leading into the complex emotions associated with the 'infinitely gentle / Infinitely suffering thing' (Eliot reportedly had his brother Henry in mind here). But this tender evocation is apparently repudiated, as consciousness once again finds itself at odds with context.

These poems deal with the problem of a structured external life which does not seem to be 'real', and an inner life whose profoundest level is of fragmentary glimpses that resist formulation, but which challenge the received ideas and accepted appearances. A 'Romantic' temperament might glory in the isolation or even madness that could ensue, but Eliot's effort would be to bring his single inner life into alignment with a more general conception of reality, without sacrificing its integrity of vision. His poetry was posing questions rather than providing answers; it is then not surprising that philosophy, with its attempt to expound a coherent system, would engross his energies on his return from France, after a period which had intensified his uncertainties. Nor is it surprising that he turned to the philosophy of Bradley, with its sceptical rigour about the simple imposition of intellectual categories, its postulation of a fundamental unitary 'absolute' behind appearances, and its assertion that 'finite centres', whilst remaining finite, can partake of this 'absolute'.

In 1912 and 1913 Eliot appears to have written very little poetry – 'La Figlia' probably dates from 1912, as may an unpublished short poem 'Hidden under the heron's wing', which enacts a lover's transition from rapture to despair. But his immersion in his studies did not diminish his desire to return to Europe, which the award of the Travelling Fellowship early in 1914 made both financially practicable and – in his family's eyes – respectable. Possibly in prospect of this approaching liberation, he began again to write poetry in some quantity (by his own standards), beginning before his departure, and carrying on after his arrival in Germany and England. Little of it has properly been published, although three samples are amongst the *Waste Land* transcripts (pp. 108–14), and some that he sent to correspondents is becoming available with the publication of his letters. This includes samples from the notorious comic pornographic series about 'King Bolo and His Big Black Kween', which Eliot circulated amongst his friends, and would continue to add to over the years; these turn out to be less shocking than some commentators had hinted, although on the whole they suggest the sensibility of Swift behind the mask of Rabelais. In 1915 Wyndham Lewis would reject some 'Bolo' fragments Eliot had submitted for inclusion in *Blast* (Eliot deduced Lewis's 'puritanical principles').

Poems exist from what Eliot intended should become a sequence entitled 'Descent from the Cross'; he wrote about this to Conrad Aiken on 25 July 1914, enclosing specimens (L 43–7). Although the title and some of the subject-matter suggest a religious orientation, there is little Christian vision operating; instead, there is a fascination with the ways in which martyrdom and luxuriant suffering enable the victim to transcend the world that one poem defines as 'appearances'; but there is more dissatisfaction with that world than affirmation of any other. What the sequence suggests is that, if on his return from France Eliot dedicated himself to philosophy, in the hope of finding answers to questions which his poetry could not provide, three years later he seemed again to be seeking answers through poetry: for the poem, as described to Aiken, is structured and to a degree discursive. Eliot had been working at this sequence in Marburg when it became necessary for him to leave for England; it would be some time before he would return to the consideration of the lives and deaths of martyrs. He expressed his dissatisfaction with it to Aiken; and in the event he turned from it, and embarked during the ensuing year on a series of poetic vignettes, in which he contemplated Boston from Oxford.

NOTES

1. '"St George's Day" 1928', Tate, p. 15.
2. E.J.H. Greene, *T.S. Eliot et la France* (Paris, 1951), p. 10.
3. See Ackroyd, p. 43.
4. *Writers at Work: The Paris Review Interviews*, Second Series, ed. Plimpton, (London, 1963), p. 85. Hereafter cited as *Paris Review*.
5. *The Diary of Virginia Woolf*, ed. Bell, 4 vols (London, 1977 onwards); II, 68. Hereafter cited as *VWD*.
6. Richard Wollheim, 'Eliot and F.H. Bradley: an account', in *Eliot in Perspective*, ed. Martin (London, 1970), p. 170.
7. These papers are fully described by Donald Gallup, in his article 'The "Lost" Manuscripts of T.S. Eliot', *TLS* 7 November 1968, pp. 1238–40. A few of the unpublished poems are published in the *Letters*.
8. Hugh Kenner, *The Invisible Poet: T.S. Eliot* (London, 1959), p. 27.
9. Quoted by John D. Margolis, in *T.S. Eliot's Intellectual Development 1922–1939* (Chicago and London, 1972), p. 142. Hereafter cited as Margolis.

3

1914–1920

When Eliot arrived in England in 1914 he had already written the best poems of his first book (*Prufrock and Other Observations*, 1917); but they existed only in manuscript, known to a chosen few. The period 1914–1920 saw the initial establishment of his reputation, by the publication of his writing. This reputation was that of critic as well as poet: the very beginning of 1920 saw his volume of poetry *Ara Vos Prec* published (which contained, in 'Gerontion', what is arguably his first major poem written in England); and in November of that year his volume of critical essays, *The Sacred Wood*, appeared. Both these books collected material which had originally been published separately, in various little magazines and periodicals. Another reason for treating 1920 as a significant stage in Eliot's career is that toward the end of this year Ezra Pound decamped from London for Paris, and subsequently for Italy. In 1914 Pound had been an influential and active figure on the London literary scene, but by 1920 he had antagonised too many people; to some degree 1920 marks the end of the Pound era in London, and ushers in the era of his less abrasive and ultimately more influential compatriot.

The moment of Eliot's arrival was a moment when a period of innovative artistic activity was about to be interrupted, in England as on the continent, by the 1914–18 war; afterwards, things would never be quite the same. This activity contrasted vividly with preceding years. Looking back, in 1954, on the circumstances in which Pound had started to make his way in London, Eliot had this to say: 'The situation of poetry in 1909 or 1910 was stagnant to a degree difficult for any young poet of today to imagine'.[1] By the time he himself appeared, there were two or three camps vying for attention or posing the question of alignment; and this made it all the more fortunate that Eliot was not an unfocused young aspirant to poetry, ready to conform to any attractive mould, but was instead the author of substantial and highly-accomplished poems. As Pound put it, himself looking back in 1932, Eliot 'displayed great tact, or enjoyed good fortune, in arriving in London at a particular date with a formed style of his own'.[2]

Pound's comment cannot really be appreciated, without some idea of the predominant literary groupings in pre-war London. These fall into three main camps, corresponding to traditionalist, centrist and radical positions. The first is represented by poets such as Sir Henry Newbolt and Alfred Noyes, affiliated to the Establishment in poetry and politics, men who sold well but generated almost nothing that was new; the second, by those poets who were published in Edward Marsh's collections of 'Georgian' poetry; and the third, by those poets who declared themselves to be practisers of 'Imagism'. These are not watertight categories: D.H. Lawrence, for example, was published both as a 'Georgian' and an 'Imagist'; and wide as the gulf might seem between a poet like Pound and a poet like Newbolt (who wrote a poem with the fatuous refrain, 'Play up! play up! And play the game!'), it was not so wide as to prevent the two from being acquainted, nor so deep that Newbolt could not include poems by Pound in an anthology of modern verse he edited.

Reviewing his own career in 1961, Eliot asserted that he had at first been 'in reaction' against Georgian poetry and criticism (TCC 16); and this reflects what was for some time the prevalent view taken of this group: that they represented an encumberingly old-fashioned literary taste. It needs to be remembered, however (as C.K. Stead pointed out), that although as successive 'Georgian' anthologies appeared their stagnation became ever more apparent, at the time of the first collection (1912) they set out to be fresh and innovative – and were perceived as rebellious by the literary establishment.[3] The very name 'Georgian', as well as denoting the pastoral element in their verse, affirmed their sense of belonging to a new age, consciously different from its Edwardian predecessor. After the war, however, when 'Georgian' verse was published by J.C. Squire in his new magazine *The London Mercury*, Squire and the poets in question were themselves 'in reaction' against the modern poetry, which was then sprouting from seeds planted by the short-lived 'Imagist' movement; and it is this third grouping which chiefly concerns us here. As Eliot put it in a backward glance from the perspective of 1948: 'The *point de repère* usually and conveniently taken, as the starting-point of modern poetry, is the group denominated "imagists" in London about 1910' (TCC 58).

The roots of the 'Imagist' movement lay in an exchange of views between T.E. Hulme and F.S. Flint. Hulme, after an abortive student career at Cambridge and London University, had spent time in Canada, then returned to Europe, attended Bergson's lectures in Paris, and began to study literary and aesthetic theory. He was a member of a group in London that called itself 'The Poets' Club'. When a publication of this literary coterie, containing two of Hulme's poems, came to the attention of Flint (himself an aspiring poet and extremely well-read in recent French poetry), he mocked their comfortable pretensions, contrasting their opulent meeting-place with the 'obscure cafés' in which, he claimed, French poetry had been 'remade'. This led to a friendship between the two, after initial controversy; it also led to their forming another society, whose meetings took place at the 'Eiffel Tower' restaurant in Soho (which one supposes to have been sufficiently obscure for Flint's taste). The first meeting took place on 25 March 1909, and Ezra Pound was introduced to the fourth meeting, on 22 April 1909. These weekly meetings persisted throughout the spring and summer, but did not survive into winter.

The first formulations of the doctrine that would later be presented as 'Imagism' were made during the brief life of this group. Flint later identified Hulme as the 'ringleader', with his insistence on 'absolutely clear presentation and no verbiage'. 'There was a lot of talk and practice among us', he recollected, 'of what we called the Image. We were very much influenced by Modern French Symbolist poetry'.[4] The next phase began when Pound re-met the American poet Hilda Doolittle, by this time calling herself H.D.; in America they had been for a time engaged. She arrived in London in 1911, and met Richard Aldington, like her a poet and Hellenist; the two of them took rooms together across the road from Pound in Kensington, and they would discuss each other's poems 'to squeeze the water out of them' – as Pound described the process to Robert Frost, who declined to participate. At one such meeting, in the spring of 1912, Pound informed the two of them that they were 'Imagistes' (the pronunciation, initially, was French). They had not, apparently, suspected this; but there was some point in their consenting to be so, because in August 1912 Pound was asked by Harriet Monroe to collaborate with her in the magazine, *Poetry*, which she was starting up in Chicago. As 'foreign correspondent', he hoped to have great influence in recommending work for publication.

So the movement was born; with Pound's entrepreneurial spirit thinking of the product, and then setting about creating an appetite for it. This was done in *Poetry* (March 1913), in which Flint's 'Imagisme', backed up by Pound's 'A Few Don'ts by an Imagiste', set out to explain matters to the magazine's readers (naturally disconcerted to hear about an important school of poetry of which – equally naturally – they knew nothing). Flint's note, written in collaboration with Pound, denied that the movement was 'revolutionary', but insisted on basic principles, enumerated as follows:

1. Direct treatment of the 'thing', whether subjective or objective.
2. To use absolutely no word that did not contribute to the presentation.
3. As regarding rhythm: to compose in sequence of the musical phrase, not in sequence of a metronome.

For his part, Pound defined an 'Image' as 'that which presents an intellectual and emotional complex in an instant of time'; the amplification which he gives of this is interesting:

It is the presentation of such a 'complex' instantaneously which gives that sense of sudden liberation; that sense of freedom from time limits and space limits; that sense of sudden growth, which we experience in the presence of the greatest works of art.

Meanwhile, after these initial exercises in promotion, the time was ripe – in terms of publicity if not of available material – for an anthology to establish the movement. Thus, in March (New York) and April (London) 1914, *Des Imagistes* appeared, edited by Pound: which contained ten poems by Aldington, seven by H.D., and six of his own; the rest of the book's weight being made up by poems from (among others) Flint, William Carlos Williams and Amy Lowell. This last-named was a large, flamboyant, wealthy poetess from Massachusetts, whose first volume of verse, published in 1912, was reviled by the others as a contravention of all they held dear. Pound, however, by dint of squeezing gallons of water out of her poems made them presentable; and his motive in doing so seems to have been less from any conviction of her merit, than a hope that her money could be put to good use, by setting him up as editor of a little magazine.

He had unfortunately miscalculated her wealth (which he overestimated) and her ego (which he underestimated). Stung by the inclusion of so few of her poems in his anthology, she proposed that in future an annual anthology should be organised on entirely democratic lines. Pound would not consent to this abandonment of standards – which would have had the additional consequence of diminishing his control. His defiant position was undermined, however, by H.D., Aldington and Flint, who had increasingly felt that to be sealed of the tribe of Ezra was a constricting discipleship, and who resented this constriction more, the less they were dependent on Pound to place their poems for them. They co-operated with Amy Lowell's scheme, and duly appeared in her anthologies *Some Imagist Poets* (1915, 1916 and 1917) – although with her, too, there would be disagreements. This Pound scornfully designated as the school of 'Amygism'. But he was found in what would become a familiar situation, of becoming separated from those with whom he had been collaborating. This factor of dissent amongst the original members of the group doubtless played its part in diverting his energies toward his next venture, which was 'Vorticism'; although since Pound's spirit of activity rarely operated within one field at a time, to speak in terms of a simple succession of interests is misleading. He would suggest, a good deal later, that the name 'imagisme' had only been a device to get Aldington and H.D. into print, before they had enough poems to fill a volume of their own. Vorticism, which had grander designs (a reorientation of Western civilisation), achieved much less.

A major influence behind Imagism, as we have seen, was T. E. Hulme, who acted as a conduit for ideas from Europe into England, at this time. Having been an enthusiast for Bergson, Hulme began to reject his philosophy as conducing to a romantic liberalism which he deprecated: Bergson's concept of an '*élan vital*' fed into progressivist creeds that everything was getting better, and encouraged a neglect of the past; his notion that one's true 'self' lies interred beneath an encrustation of imposed mental habituations, which need to be sloughed off, led toward a 'Romantic' exaltation of the unfettered personality. Having become acquainted with more congenial theories (notably Wilhelm Worringer's), Hulme was now moving toward a position which he defined as the new 'classicism', for reasons which seem to have been as much political, as aesthetic. This new 'classicism' was to be exemplified in the 'geometric' rather than the 'organic' – form externally defined rather than internally produced, we might say:

this countered the Romantic's exaggerated sense of the importance of the individual and his emotions, by stressing limitation, discipline, and even promulgating a notion of original sin.

Some of these ideas were operating in Vorticism, even though at the time of its inception Hulme had fallen out with the painter and writer Wyndham Lewis, who together with Pound was a prime mover (their quarrel was about a woman, not about art). The overall effect of Vorticism was not great: intended to focus on a 'Rebel Art Centre', an academy of innovative and dissenting creativity, its most tangible result was the pink publication *Blast*, whose first issue appeared in July 1914, by which time the 'Rebel Art Centre' had closed. The tone of the magazine was abusive, provocative, rowdy and high-spirited: praising and anathematising various aspects of the world with its antiphonal injunctions to 'blast' or 'bless'. For Pound, the most obvious consequence of his involvement would be a letter that October from G.W. Prothero, editor of the staid but influential *Quarterly Review*, in which he declined to publish any more of Pound's writing because of his association with the scurrilous magazine.

For literary periodicals could also be classified as traditionalist (or reactionary), centrist and radical. Pound, and Eliot after him, knew the importance of finding an outlet, as well as the difficulty of doing so: the radical little magazines tended to have short lives and small subscriptions. Part of the venom in a publication like *Blast* came from Pound's growing frustration at the impossibility of denting the complacency of the literary establishment, and his conviction this same establishment would ensure that even an initially successful venture in radical publishing could not survive. His example for this was Ford Madox Ford's *English Review*, set up by Ford and run by him from December 1908 to February 1910 to a consistently high standard; but this had not saved it from economic embarrassment, and consequent sale to the financier Sir Alfred Mond (later to make his appearance in Eliot's 'A Cooking Egg'). Since when, although Pound occasionally published poems in it, its columns also found room for the likes of Newbolt and Noyes: reinforcing the literary status quo along with the *Quarterly Review*, the *Athenaeum* (before Middleton Murry became editor, 1919–21), and the *Times Literary Supplement* – which august newspaper Pound addressed, in a vituperative poem in *Blast*, as a 'slut-bellied obstructionist'.

In the middle ground (and struggling to remain there in the face of Pound's efforts at appropriation) were *Poetry Review* and the later *Poetry and Drama*, both founded by Harold Monro, who had also set up and administered the Poetry Bookshop (he would later start the *Chapbook*). Monro, publisher of the Georgians, was not a radical: when Conrad Aiken had shown him a manuscript of 'Prufrock' in 1912, in an effort to interest him in publishing it, he had returned it saying that it was the work of a madman. Also in the middle ground, as far as Pound was concerned, was the American *Poetry* which, although it would usually accept his work and that of his protégés, would cheerfully print rubbish – and Harriet Monroe was not above interfering with the poems she published (nor, for that matter, was Pound; but his taste was better). A. R. Orage's periodical *The New Age* was to provide a vital and consistent source of income for Pound, and one which introduced him to a wide selection of men of letters; but it was described by Eliot in 1917 as 'a literary organ which has always been strongly opposed to metrical innovations'.

There was on the whole an impressive number of serious periodicals; but the sales commanded by the more adventurous amongst them were small (and Pound's volume of Imagistes, initially rumoured as a 'post-Georgian' anthology, in no way matched the sales of the first Georgian collection). Their financial precariousness necessitated the presence of a wealthy backer to underwrite the losses; such a one as Pound was searching for in Amy Lowell and others, and Eliot was apparently to find in Lady Rothermere when she put up the money for the *Criterion*. Since August 1913 Pound had been associated with *The New Freewoman*, run by Harriet Shaw Weaver and Dora Marsden; and when this changed its name to the *Egoist* from the beginning of 1914, he was given a free hand in the literary section. This became an important early outlet for writers like Joyce and Eliot, until December 1919 when Weaver and Marsden decided to shut it down. Journals like *Blast* may have had a therapeutic function but were, as Pound's case shows, as likely to diminish influence as to enhance it.

Before Eliot arrived, Pound had been energetically trying to establish himself as a major influence in contemporary letters; his failure to consolidate his position within London literary circles contrasts with Eliot's success in doing just that. Nevertheless, at the time of Eliot's arrival on his doorstep, Pound was a source of good contacts and sound knowledge concerning the London scene, a figure of some note and notoriety. Eliot arrived, also, at a period when Pound was in his aggressive Vorticist phase, had seen the failure of the 'Rebel Art Centre', and was in the process of losing his sponsorial role with regard to Aldington and H.D.. He could hardly have wished for a brighter talent to declare itself than that of the urbane fellow American who, on Conrad Aiken's recommendation, presented himself at Pound's Kensington flat on 22 September 1914.

In particular, we can see how, arriving as Imagism took centre stage in English poetry and claimed the future, Eliot's own development recapitulated that of the movement. He had read his French Symbolists; he had discovered *vers libre*, and knew more than most about 'composing in the sequence of the musical phrase'. Whether or not he had articulated a theory of the 'image', it was the case that his poetry was and would continue to be composed in a fragmentary luminosity, whose very unpredictability made it seem as if independent of his personality, at the same time that its forces posed the question of control. He had studied his Bergson, and had sceptically moved beyond, in reaction against inner voices and Romantic tendencies and overemphasis on the present tense, toward a position not dissimilar to Hulme's (although the two never met). He was, also, in partial flight from respectability; and he found himself in the room of one of the collaborators in *Blast* (which he had read), who wore trousers made out of green billiard cloth, who was acknowledged to have his finger on London's literary pulse, and who had already published five volumes of poetry.

Both, of course, were Americans who were to some degree evading what they considered to be the dullness or philistinism of the academic life, with which each had been involved. Pound was more obviously a brash product of the United States than Eliot; and his focus was always distantly upon the land of his birth: he never gave up the notion that his countrymen could be educated, and that when that happened America would be the scene of a new renaissance. So he set himself tirelessly to hector his fellow Americans, with results that would eventually prove catastrophic to himself. Since London offered, as he conceived it, the best base from which to operate, and the best chance to found a literary revolution that could in time be exported to America, he pitched his tent there, and encouraged others to do likewise. Eliot's schemes were characteristically less grandiose; but he became sure, with Pound, that London would provide him with the best chance of establishing himself in what he really wanted to do.

There must have been an element of trial involved in exposing himself, virtually unknown and unpublished, to his established compatriot. The meeting passed off well enough, however, with Pound writing that day to Harriet Monroe in Chicago that Eliot had called and seemed to have 'some sense'. He had asked to see some of this quiet young man's poems, and when these arrived his response was electrifying; writing again to Harriet Monroe eight days later (30 September), he declared 'I was jolly well right about Eliot. He has sent in the best poem I have yet had or seen from an American. PRAY GOD IT BE NOT A SINGLE AND UNIQUE SUCCESS' (this was to be Eliot's own fear). Part of Pound's stupefaction lay in the fact that Eliot had 'actually trained himself *and* modernised himself *on his own*'.[5] On the same day Eliot himself was assessing Pound's own poetry, in a letter to Conrad Aiken, as 'well-meaning and touchingly incompetent' (L 59); and this perhaps showed the degree to which he had 'modernised' himself more successfully than Pound had (he amplified his comment in 1959, saying that Pound's early poetry had struck him as 'rather fancy old-fashioned romantic stuff').[6] By October 1914 Miss Monroe had 'Prufrock' in her hands; but in spite of her foreign correspondent's fervent advocacy (the postscript to his accompanying letter was 'Hope you'll get it in *soon*'), her response was to be closer to that of her namesake, Harold Monro: the poem did not appear in *Poetry* until June 1915, inconspicuously placed at the end of the poetry section.

Almost a year after their first meeting, Pound would write to John Quinn in New York that he had 'more or less discovered' Eliot. This bent the truth a little; he had first heard about him from Conrad Aiken (although in Pound's version Aiken only started talking about Eliot when Pound stopped him from trying to praise E. A. Robinson); it was Aiken who admired 'Prufrock' sufficiently to try to place the manuscript, unsuccessfully, with Harold Monro; and it was Aiken who had told Eliot he should get in touch with Pound. However admirable was Pound's instantaneous recognition of the genius of 'Prufrock', we should not forget that Aiken, too, had seen its quality: both stand out from the preponderant responses to this minor masterpiece. The essential difference between Pound and Aiken, was that Pound had a showman's vigour allied to a fanatical but altruistic desire to advance the cause of modern writing. Eliot's advocate was one whom Wyndham Lewis described as 'The Trotsky of literature'; but Eliot could profit from this zeal, without being overwhelmed by it.

Almost immediately, Pound was trying to arrange a meeting with Yeats. Through Pound, Eliot became acquainted with the literary avant-garde in London; he met H.D., Aldington and Lewis (who later recalled Pound's proprietorial air toward his new discovery). Through Pound's untiring efforts on his behalf, Eliot's work was to receive its first serious publication on each side of the Atlantic. It is highly likely that Pound sharpened his appreciation of Dante, as well as introducing him to the work of French writers like Remy de Gourmont and Julien Benda; and like Eliot, Pound was an enthusiast for a notion of the 'European' cultural heritage. As we shall see later, Pound played a vital role in helping Eliot to organise *The Waste Land* (by which time he had himself moved to Paris); but it may be that his most momentous and long-lasting influence was not as an editor or agent, but as the friend who in the crucial period encouraged Eliot in his choice of career, his choice of country, and his choice of wife.

These were obviously interlinked, although it is probable that only in the case of Eliot's marriage was it a question of his acting on a clear-cut decision. Pound was himself married to an Englishwoman, and may have felt that for Eliot to do the same would consolidate his commitment to the country where – Pound divined – his future lay. His prescience about Eliot's career did not, unfortunately, extend to the marriage, which would illustrate in some depth and at some length the truth of the adage, 'marry in haste; repent at leisure'. Eliot had met Vivien (or Vivienne) Haigh Wood at Oxford, probably in the spring of 1915; they were married in Hampstead registry office on 26 June that year, with neither her parents nor his being informed in advance. Looking back on this in the last years of his life, Eliot described himself as 'very immature', 'very timid', and 'very inexperienced'; probably he had wanted, to rectify these aspects, an affair rather than a marriage; probably he was still in love with Emily Hale (L xvii). But she was an American; and Eliot's uncharacteristically impulsive first marriage was part of his movement away from America.

Shortly after his meeting with Pound, Eliot went up to Merton College to begin working on Bradley, under his disciple Harold Joachim. Brand Blanshard, an American contemporary at Oxford with whom he spent part of that Christmas vacation in Swanage, recollects him reading *Principia Mathematica* at the breakfast table, which seems to indicate a continuing attachment to philosophy. But at the end of the following month (25 February 1915) he wrote to Conrad Aiken about the dilemma facing him, as a result of Harvard's offer to renew his fellowship: he disliked Oxford, and did not think he would ever come to like England; he did, however, think it possible he could be happy if allowed to continue his research in London at the British Museum, and thought it certain he would be miserable back at Harvard. Additional evidence of a reaction against the idea of America lies in the group of poems which he wrote in Oxford in 1915, about aspects of Bostonian gentility. 'The Boston Evening Transcript', 'Aunt Helen' and 'Cousin Nancy' are fairly light verse, but they all evoke an atmosphere of decorous enfeeblement and intellectual inertia (Eliot had that year exclaimed to Blanshard, 'What a lazy mind Emerson had!'). More substantial is the poem 'Mr. Apollinax' – provoked by recollections of Bertrand Russell's spell at Harvard – in which the intellectual and animal vigour of this live-wire visitor is set against the drawing-room decor which, apparently, characterises 'the United States'. Mr Apollinax is a kind of laughing Lazarus, evoking 'submarine and profound' experiences in a genteel setting, a Dionysiac Apollonian who cannot be confined within 'the palace of Mrs. Phlaccus' (a name suggestively conflating 'flaccid phallus'). The poem's ending reads rather like its author's farewell to the academic life which threatened him:

Of dowager Mrs. Phlaccus, and Professor and Mrs. Cheetah
I remember a slice of lemon, and a bitten macaroon.

So when Eliot met Vivien, he had realised that he did not want to return to Harvard, and that he did not want to stay in Oxford (which points up for us the paradox of his dislike for the ethos of universities, in spite of their importance in his career). These were awkward enough conclusions to arrive at, in the face of what he knew his parents supposed his future to promise; more awkward still would be his desire to remain in England, attempting to make a career as a writer. The Travelling Fellowship had offered a temporary respite from such pressures; but the question of its renewal put the problem into sharper relief, because he was by then moving away from his enthusiasm for philosophy. Behind him lay a country which he regarded as culturally vacant, the provincial dullness of academic life, and a family background of smothering respectability and intellectual earnestness; before him was a London in which the likes of Pound and Lewis were operating, the challenge of making his mark as a poet, and a lively, unusual, intelligent young woman. As he saw it from his 1960s perspective, he realised that his heart was not in the study of philosophy, and persuaded himself that he was in love with Vivien 'simply because I wanted to burn my boats and commit myself to staying in England' (L xvii). They were together, and he fell.

Except insofar as it provides the unhappy private backdrop to his public career, Eliot's first marriage does not minutely concern us; but although the available evidence suggests that sexual difficulties, and problems of ill-health (predominantly hers, but also his), put an early, continuous, and finally unendurable strain on their relationship, we should not too quickly assume the marriage to have had a purely negative effect. His American sister-in-law has suggested that Vivien 'ruined Tom as a man, but made him as a poet'.[7] Although in the later years she was to be an obstacle to his career, an active social embarrassment at dinner-parties in their own home and on visits to friends, she was passionately committed to his advancement, and apt to strike out at those she believed were hindering it. Writing to his brother in September 1916, Eliot confessed his fears that 'Prufrock' was a 'swan-song', adding that Vivien was 'exceedingly anxious that I shall equal it, and would be bitterly disappointed if I do not' (L 151). If she had faith in his literary ability, he felt that she, too, had talent: later he would print some of her work in the *Criterion* (whose name was her idea), under aliases; she was an essential aid to him in preparing some of its early issues; and her enthusiastic comments on *The Waste Land* are a matter of record. Whatever the difficulties that affected the early months of his marriage, Eliot could write to Aiken in January 1916 that he was having 'a wonderful life nevertheless' (L 126); he acknowledged that it was 'entirely different' from the one he had contemplated two years previously, but this prompted the reflection: 'Cambridge [Mass.] seems to me a dull nightmare now'.

An immediate consequence of the marriage was their removal to London; at first they stayed with Vivien's parents in Hampstead then, after a three-week visit by Eliot alone back to America and a spell in Eastbourne for both, in September 1915 the newly-weds moved in to share Bertrand Russell's small flat in Bury Street. After Pound and Vivien, Russell may well be the third most significant figure in Eliot's life at this time. Having taught Eliot at Harvard, Russell had been surprised to bump into his former graduate student in New Oxford Street, in October 1914; in the short term, this meeting led to an invitation to address the Moral Science Club at Cambridge, where Eliot read a paper on 'The Relativity of Moral Judgment' in Russell's rooms at Trinity; in the longer term, it led to Russell's intimate intervention in Eliot's life, and a disillusionment with Russell that may have played its part in Eliot's move toward Christianity. Russell's autobiography provides some significant interior glimpses of Eliot's troubled marriage in its early stages.

Russell was introduced to his former pupil's bride soon after their wedding; 'I expected her to be terrible, from his mysteriousness', he wrote in July 1915 to Lady Ottoline Morrell, 'but she was not so bad'. Nonetheless, he diagnosed that things were not well between them – Vivien, who did some typing for Russell at this period, seems to have confided to him that she could not 'stimulate' her husband, and he saw that Eliot was 'ashamed of his marriage'. Although he would observe Eliot's 'profound and unselfish devotion' to his wife, and believe that, in spite of her 'impulses of cruelty' toward her husband, she was 'really very fond' of Eliot, the implication of most of Russell's comments is that the two of them had not known each other very well. Indeed, in the matter of his new wife's character Eliot deferred to Russell's expertise; as late as 1925 he would write in desperation asking for advice, congratulating Russell on the accuracy of his predictions, and confessing that he found Vivien still 'baffling and deceptive'.[8]

At the time of that first dinner with Russell, Eliot and his wife had many years of mutual bafflement ahead of them. They had squared the marriage with her parents, but Eliot still had in prospect the confrontation with his own family (he travelled there alone because Vivien refused to make the crossing for fear of German torpedoes). He asked Russell to write to his mother, and enlisted Pound to write in advance to his father, assuring Henry Ware Eliot that his son's literary prospects were good. If he was 'ashamed' of his wife, it was not for the customary reason of having married beneath himself: the Haigh-Woods were a respectable and moderately wealthy family, who were themselves more likely to have objected to their daughter's marrying an impecunious American 'of no occupation'. They were won over by their new son-in-law's impeccable manners, however, and gave their daughter an allowance of £50 a year. Eliot's parents were less accommodating, although they maintained the errant son's allowance; they strongly opposed his continued residence in England (which was, after all, at war). At their request, he agreed to complete his PhD dissertation, and they entertained hopes that he would return to America and an orthodox career, as can be seen from the letter Charlotte Eliot wrote to Russell in May 1916, in which she expressed her confidence that he could influence her son back to philosophy. When it became clear such hopes were unfounded, Henry and Charlotte Eliot seem to have felt some resentment toward the wife they held responsible for blighting his prospects.

Eliot's marriage certainly inaugurated a period of financial insecurity, aggravated by the increasing medical expenses in which his wife's chronic ill-health involved him. On more than one occasion she came close to death, and by 1920 Pound would describe her to Quinn as 'an invalid always cracking up, & needing doctors' (Ts xix). This was clearly a situation of great strain, but I think it can be said that there was also, for Eliot, a gratifying intensity about life lived under such pressure, in spite of its emotional and psychological demands. The issue of authenticity arises again, as when the speaker of 'Portrait of a Lady' wonders at the end whether her gushing emotionalism does not outweigh his incapacity to respond. As Eliot himself put it to Conrad Aiken in 1916, he had '*lived* through material for a score of long poems, in the last six months' (L 126), in spite of having written none of them. Apparently still a virgin at the beginning of 1915, he may well have feared for himself the predicament familiar in the fiction of Hawthorne and Henry James, of becoming an uninvolved and self-enclosed observer of the passions of others. The attractive and unorthodox Vivien, described by Aldous Huxley as 'incarnate provocation', may have offered him a motive and a cue for passion at a critical moment of dissatisfaction with his life; and however different from their hopes, the marriage doubtless provided a life of sensations rather than of thought. Describing to his brother in September 1916 the nightmarish anxiety of that year, Eliot's comment was, 'at least it is not dull, and it has its compensations' (L 151). A good deal later, Russell offered the uncharitable summary that he had 'endeavoured to help them in their troubles until I discovered that their troubles were what they enjoyed'.[9]

Russell took a paternal attitude toward his former pupil, and a less straightforward attitude toward Vivien, with whom he engaged in what was possibly intended to be therapeutic flirtation. In letters to Ottoline Morrell, he indirectly confessed to a fascination with her, and with the relationship between the two; but his 'help' also took extremely practical forms: not only did he provide a roof over their heads until Christmas 1915, he also made over to Eliot $3000 worth of debentures in an engineering firm which was engaged in war-work (Russell was a pacifist; Eliot, who was not, returned the gift in 1927). Meanwhile, Eliot set himself to earn the money they badly needed, and embarked on what would on the whole be an undistinguished career in practical education, as a schoolmaster teaching immature boys, and as an extension lecturer teaching students who were for the most part mature women.

During the time they stayed with Russell, Eliot was teaching at High Wycombe Grammar School. He resigned this post after one term, in favour of a job at Highgate Junior School which paid more and was nearer home: having left Russell's flat at Christmas as arranged, the Eliots stayed for a while with her parents, before moving into their own small flat at 18 Crawford Mansions. Eliot taught at Highgate during 1916, and was known – one of his pupils, John Betjeman, recalled – as 'the American master', quiet and withdrawn. He had neither appetite nor aptitude for school-mastering, which absorbed much more of his energy than he had anticipated; but extension lecturing, for Oxford and London universities, seemed to promise a more appropriate level of intellectual activity as well as the prospect of liberation from the school. In November Eliot wrote to thank his brother for financial assistance, and declared that he hoped in a year's time to be self-supporting, explaining that 'I am basing most of the hope on lectures, of course' (L 157).

Earlier that year he had negotiated with the Oxford University Extension Delegacy, offering six courses on modern French literature; they invited him to mount just one of these, so during the last quarter of 1916 Eliot travelled up to Ilkley, Yorkshire, to deliver his 'Course of Six Lectures on Modern French Literature'. These took place in the afternoon, and were followed by a discussion class, attended by something like a quarter of the lecture audience. The syllabus for these lectures shows Eliot's debt to Babbitt, and his similarity to Hulme: the first lecture, 'What Is Romanticism?', offers an analysis of Rousseau's influence on subsequent thought and literature ('The two great currents of the nineteenth century – vague emotionality and the apotheosis of science (realism) alike spring from Rousseau'); his second, 'The Reaction against Romanticism', suggests a twentieth-century return to 'ideals of classicism' ('These may roughly be characterized as *form* and *restraint* in art, *discipline* and *authority* in religion, *centralization* in government (either as socialism or monarchy). The classicist point of view has been defined as essentially a belief in Original Sin'). Subsequent lectures examined figures such as Maurras ('reaction fundamentally sound, but marked by extreme violence and intolerance') and Bergson (whom Eliot associates with 'Mysticism' and 'Optimism').[10]

At the same time as he was running these lectures, and teaching his final term at Highgate, Eliot inaugurated a three-year Tutorial Class at Southall, under the auspices of the University of London Extension Board; this involved twenty-four two-hour lecture and discussion classes on Monday evenings in autumn and winter (1916/17, 1917/18, 1918/19); unlike the Ilkley lectures, this course required fortnightly essays from students – although then as now students did not always produce the required essays. The first two years' classes were on 'Modern English Literature', and offered a wide survey of Victorian writers; the third year covered 'Elizabethan Literature'. In addition, at the end of September 1917 Eliot commenced 'A Course of Twenty-Five Lectures on Victorian Literature', sponsored by London County Council, and delivered on Friday evenings at the County Secondary School, Sydenham. These covered similar ground to his Southall lectures, and may not have involved him in disproportionate extra preparation for the extra money they brought in; they did, however, consume at least twenty-five of his evenings.

Eliot was not, as he had hoped, to become self-supporting as a lecturer; in February 1918 he was not accepted by London as a supplementary University extension lecturer (his status at the time was 'tutor'), because of an adverse report on his lecturing. In his final year at Southall, his class suffered from inadequate enrolment, so that he felt obliged to offer to teach it for a reduced fee. The war, of course, created difficulties in sustaining ventures of this kind; looking back on these Southall classes in 1959, Eliot recalled how transport was sometimes disrupted by the primitive air-raids. Because of the war, his pupils were mostly women, some of them eccentric: forty years later, he would remember the lady who bombarded him with letters addressing him as 'Dear Tutor Boy', as well as one whose fascination with the occult involved him in a constant struggle to focus the discussion after class on Victorian literature rather than on ghosts. In this genial retrospect Eliot claimed to have enjoyed his teaching; but it may be that the chief benefit (as he also suggested) lay in his having to read many books which he had omitted to read, in order to do the job plausibly.[11]

Although his lectures clearly connect with critical positions he was formulating, his exertions as a teacher had little to do with the advancement of his literary career, but were undertaken out of financial necessity. The hours he devoted to such labours were hours that were not, as a consequence, spent in composing publishable prose or verse; but even if 1916 was a fallow year for poetry, his typewriter was far from idle: his thesis had been completed and despatched in the first few months of the year, and more significant still, that year saw the inauguration of a steady stream of prose that was, in time, to establish Eliot's reputation as a critic. Between January 1916 and the end of 1920 he published approximately ninety prose items – articles and reviews of varying length – in a number of periodicals, ranging from the avant-garde to the worthily established.

Eliot's first British publication came in July 1915, when 'Preludes' and 'Rhapsody on a Windy Night' appeared in the second (and final) issue of *Blast*; by November 1919 he had made the first of his appearances in the *Times Literary Supplement*, with an unsigned review (then standard practice in the *TLS*) which he reprinted as 'Ben Jonson' in *The Sacred Wood*. This progress, from Wyndham Lewis's 'puce monster' to the sanctified atmosphere of the periodical Pound had insulted in its pages, might seem like the transition from outrageousness to respectability; but it did not mark a transition on Eliot's part: he still had *The Waste Land* to come, and he was capable of being simultaneously outrageous and respectable. It does, however, illustrate the variety of his outlets; and this in turn attests to the breadth of his contacts within the literary world, and to the assiduity with which he cultivated them.

Bertrand Russell, we have already seen, helped the Eliots in material ways. He also made introductions which were extremely important, in providing Eliot with an entrée into circles to which Pound had no access. It was he who introduced Eliot to the *New Statesman* – whose literary editor, J.C. Squire, might not have seemed a promising acquaintance for an associate of Lewis and Pound: yet Eliot was a regular contributor between July 1916 and July 1918 (by 1920 Eliot would bemoan Squire's influence and ignorance: '[he] knows nothing about poetry; but he is the cleverest journalist in London', L 358). Russell also introduced him to his then mistress, Lady Ottoline Morrell, who maintained one of the

three important salons of the time (the other two, according to
Leonard Woolf, were in the drawing-rooms of Ladies Colefax and
Cunard). She first met the Eliots with Russell at a Soho restaurant
in March 1916, and invited them the following day to tea at her
house in Bedford Square. Shortly afterward, Eliot and Russell went
down to her other home at Garsington (near Oxford), and in that
most Jamesian of settings, the English country-house week-end,
he met figures like Lytton Strachey, and subsequently Aldous
Huxley, Katherine Mansfield and John Middleton Murry. Ottoline
Morrell was to become a friend, but this first visit of Eliot's was not
auspicious, his hostess finding him 'dull, dull, dull' and 'monot-
onous'. Exasperated by what was probably his paralysed formality, she adjudged him to be 'obviously very ignorant of England',
and in an effort to penetrate his reserve, tried the expedient of
talking French to him ('I don't think it was a great success', she
confided to her journal).

She was not alone in being perplexed by the apparent paradox
between the unconventional poetry and the impeccably conventional man who wrote it (Leonard Woolf was to make a similar
observation). Eliot was more liable to relax, however, once he felt
he knew the ground rules of a situation; rather than the opossum,
which shams death, his more appropriate emblem might have
been the chameleon, which merges with its immediate environment, whilst remaining itself: Clive Bell recalled of such gatherings, 'always the poet made himself inconspicuous by the
appropriateness of his costume'.[12] Bell was another of Russell's
introductions; and through him, Eliot would meet artists like
Roger Fry, and (in November 1918) Virginia and Leonard Woolf,
who were to publish his poetry on their Hogarth Press. In
mid-1915 Eliot had attended the Thursday night gatherings of the
group associated with the early Imagists, but later on he also
moved in the circles which revolved around Garsington and
Bloomsbury, whose personnel overlapped to some extent.

In December 1917, at a charity poetry reading in Lady Sybil
Colefax's drawing-room, Eliot met amongst his fellow-performers
the Sitwell siblings, who were in their own minor way engaged in
literary revolt; and despite his lack of enthusiasm for their poetry
(he would not consider appearing in Edith's *Wheels*), Eliot became
friendly with them. He and his wife used to meet with Edith,
Osbert and Sacheverell in London tea-shops, in 1918 and 1919.
Here, then, was yet another variation of milieu. On one hand,
Eliot's socio-literary versatility could inspire admiration: Anthony

Powell records his excitement on first seeing Eliot (in 1927 or 1928), 'a figure whom the Sitwells, Bloomsbury, even Wyndham Lewis, treated with respect'. But on the other, it fuelled suspicions such as those Lytton Strachey hinted at in a letter of June 1921, where he described Eliot – 'very sad and seedy' – appearing at a poetry-reading organised by the Sitwells and Arnold Bennett: 'Why, oh why, does Eliot have any truck with such coagulations? I fear it indicates that there's something seriously wrong with him'.[13] Eliot's connections with Bloomsbury and the Sitwells were despised by Pound and Lewis, seen by the former as an 'arse-blarsted lot' and by the latter (who was chronically hard-up) as 'millionaire Bohemia'.

Contacts accumulated, and Eliot knew what they were worth; Richard Aldington would later accuse him of having set out to cultivate the right people. There is an element of truth in this, insofar as Eliot manifested an awareness of structures of influence, and saw the necessity of using them; others – including Aldington – were attempting to do much the same, and it seems not to have involved Eliot in any compromise of principle. What we see here is not, I think, a relentless social climber, who discarded outworn acquaintances (there is much evidence to suggest that Eliot was a loyal friend); but a man who wished not to be exclusively as-sociated with any single sect, and who realised the importance – as Pound did not, or could not accomplish – of a broad base from which to launch a career.

If Pound introduced Eliot to *Poetry* and the *Little Review* in America, and to *Blast* and the *Egoist* in Britain, the line of contacts established through Russell opened other avenues. Middleton Murry, who had been briefly involved with D.H. Lawrence and Katherine Mansfield in the *Blue Review*, invited him to become an assistant editor of the *Athenaeum* early in 1919, when Murry took over the editorship; and although Eliot declined this offer because it did not seem financially secure, he became a regular contributor, some of the pieces he wrote being reprinted in *The Sacred Wood*. Moreover, his contributions to the *Athenaeum* caught the eye of the editor of the *TLS*, Bruce Richmond, and led (after a personal introduction arranged by Aldington, which Eliot jeopardised by appearing with a beard grown on holiday in France) to his con-tributing occasional leading articles. As with his pieces for Murry, some of these would achieve permanence in his collections of criticism.

Even if Eliot was not confined solely to Pound's sphere of

influence, that influence was significant. When Richard Aldington enlisted in the army, Pound – assisted by John Quinn's money – persuaded Harriet Weaver to appoint Eliot to the vacant assistant editorship of the *Egoist*, in June 1917. Whereas Eliot's work in the *New Statesman* and the *International Journal of Ethics* (mostly book reviews) was important to him as a source of income rather than a source of reputation, his editorial accession to the pages of the *Egoist* gave him greater scope. In his regular articles, Eliot offered a series of lively reflections on contemporary poetry and studies in contemporary criticism, culminating in what was probably his most influential essay, 'Tradition and the Individual Talent', published in two parts at the end of 1919, and republished in *The Sacred Wood* the following year. The appearance of this essay coincided with the closure of the magazine, and left Eliot without an organ in which he had a controlling voice; but by this stage he was contributing to the *Athenaeum*, and although he told Quinn that there he was 'a sort of white boy' who wrote reviews rather than editorials, he also acknowledged that these brought him 'a certain notoriety which I should never have got from the *Egoist*' (L 315). He would in 1959 look back on the period of Murry's tenure at the *Athenaeum* and Richmond's at the *TLS* as 'the high summer of literary journalism' in his life-time.

Eliot might sport a beard when he wrote for little magazines, but for the cultural organ of *The Times* he was immaculately shaven. If in the *Egoist* (May 1918) he could declare, 'what we want is to disturb and alarm the public', when writing for Richmond he assumed the anonymous and urbane scholarliness that mantled a reviewer for the *TLS*, with only an intermittent acerbity to alarm his public. Again, this is the strategy of the chameleon rather than the guile of a hypocrite; and again we need to remember that these aspects of Eliot were simultaneous, not consecutive. Pound's perception that Eliot had modernised himself 'on his own' alerts us to the independence, which led him to avoid the factionalism which restricted the effectiveness of men like Pound and Lewis. When Eliot called on Pound in September 1914 he was very much the junior figure; but in January 1920 he would express his concern to John Quinn that 'there is now no organ of any importance in which [Pound] can express himself', with the consequence that 'he is becoming forgotten' (L 358). The period of Pound's sponsorship ended, and gradually the scales tipped the other way, with Eliot tactfully attempting to repay this debt to his increasingly isolated compatriot, as his own prestige increased. In this same letter, Eliot saw that Pound had damaged himself by a 'lack of tact'; it was doubtless a matter of both wisdom and temperament on his part, that he should avoid Pound's error.

If 1916 had been a nightmarish year for Eliot, 1917 was better. Having given up school-teaching, he spent the first months attempting to support himself and his wife by his pen, without conspicuous success; but on 19 March, thanks to the influence of a well-placed friend of the Haigh-Woods, he started work in the Colonial and Foreign Department of Lloyds Bank, initially in a temporary capacity, but as it would turn out, for nearly nine years. This phase of Eliot's existence was much misunderstood; especially by Pound, who regarded it as 'criminal waste', and devised schemes to free him from such shackles. I.A. Richards has left a memorable recollection of visiting Eliot in his office in the City, below the pavement glass trampled by insistent feet, whence Richards tried to lure him to the light and air of the newly-founded English faculty at Cambridge: but as ever, Eliot preferred not to. The fact was, that although he implied (in a letter to Lytton Strachey of 1919) that his job consigned him to 'sojourning among the termites' (L 299), it was less a source of imprisonment than a source of freedom. It freed him, most immediately, from financial uncertainty (in 1922 he was paid more than £500, a far from negligible salary; there would be a widow's pension for Vivien should he die); the bank turned out to be an accommodating employer, allowing him extended periods of sick leave at the time he was composing *The Waste Land*. His job had its interest for him, and in addition to providing the originals for 'Stetson' and the 'Bradford millionaire', imposed a routine which, if partly deadening, was also a source of order in a life sensitive to chaos; and even its termitic numbness might have had value, for a man who once said he liked playing patience because it was the nearest thing to being dead.

It is also a fact that, 1916 having been a non-productive year for poetry, in 1917 he began to compose again, almost exactly coincident with the start of his job: he wrote to his mother on 11 April that he had been doing some writing 'mostly in French' (L 175), and Pound mentioned the fact to Joyce in a letter of the same month. Pound continued his exertions to find publishers for Eliot's poetry; he had bullied Harriet Monroe into printing 'Prufrock' in June 1915, followed by more poems in October of that year and

September 1916. Alfred Kreymborg's *Others* had taken 'Portrait of a Lady' in September 1915; but it was not until Pound – again backed by Quinn – became foreign editor of the *Little Review* in May 1917 that a reliable American outlet was found, where Eliot's prose sketch 'Eeldrop and Appleplex', his French poems, and his earlier quatrain poems would be published. Meanwhile, again thanks to Pound, Eliot's poems came out in book form. Pound's *Catholic Anthology* was published by Elkin Mathews in November 1915; setting out to be a non-partisan survey of poetry from Yeats to the Imagists, it contained 'Prufrock', 'Portrait of a Lady', and three lesser poems by Eliot, and was intended to do for him what *Des Imagistes* had been meant to do for H.D. and Aldington. As well as securing Eliot the *Egoist* appointment in June 1917, Pound – unknown to him – arranged a subsidy for the Egoist Press to print Eliot's first volume of poems, *Prufrock and Other Observations*, which was published that month.

Neither volume prospered in the market-place: in spite of the inclusion of Yeats the anthology was not successful, and it took until 1922 to clear the 500 copies of *Prufrock*. The war was understandably engrossing the attention of most people, but nevertheless there were those who took notice; sometimes the notice was essentially hostile, as was Arthur Waugh's reaction to the anthology in the *Quarterly Review*, and sometimes it was enthusiastic, as Clive Bell's, distributing copies of *Prufrock* amongst the houseguests at Garsington. Both enthusiastic and hostile reactions had in common that they were for the most part responses to poems which had been written well before Eliot came to England; by the time *Prufrock* appeared, he was emerging from a period of creative dormancy into a different phase of his poetry: which reminds us that it was characteristic of Eliot as a poet that he did not write much, and that he seldom repeated himself.

What was repeated, and what was also characteristic, was his 'writer's block'. The episode drawing to its close in early 1917 seems to have lasted more or less from the time of his marriage, and was alleviated by his composition of poems in French – 'curiously enough it has taken me that way', as he put it to his mother. The adjective 'curious' would recur to Eliot forty years later, when he was asked about his French poems in an interview; recalling that at the time he feared that he had 'dried up completely' and was 'rather desperate', he had discovered it was possible to compose in French. Looking back, he supposed that because he took it less seriously, the pressure was lessened; so he wrote in French for a while, until he 'suddenly began writing in English again and lost all desire to go on with French'.[14] Ottoline Morrell's odd impulse to talk French to Eliot when English conversation became sticky seems to have been sound; and Eliot's own explanation goes some way to support the analysis offered by a psychiatrist (whose advice about a later block was sought without his consent), that Eliot's problem was an intolerance of the less-than-perfect, which inhibited his creative flow. 'He thinks he's God' was his verdict; Conrad Aiken relayed this to Eliot who, stalled in the writing of *The Waste Land*, was outraged by the invasion of his privacy.

However curious, Eliot's swerve into French in four published and two unpublished poems is partly attributable to the fact that for a while this had been for him the language of literary authenticity, the language of Laforgue and Baudelaire (and of congenial thinkers like Maurras and theorists like Remy de Gourmont). Quite apart from the many specific echoes of poets, French nuances can sometimes be detected in his use of English: 'descending at a small hotel' puns upon a French idiom (*descendre à un hôtel*), and when Eliot's streetlamp 'beats like a fatalistic drum', the image derives – also punningly – from the French for streetlamp (*réverbère*). In a letter to his brother in 1919 he wrote of the 'relief' of speaking a foreign language (L 330); and when composing in French, the very 'foreignness' of that voice may have been a means of achieving his 'best mode oblique' (the phrase comes from the 1909 poem 'Nocturne', CCP 601), the lofty if satirical perspective met with in the poems he went on to write in English. There, his employment of the quatrain stanza – like his use of French – established a liberating distance by requiring him to focus on his structure and his medium, in a formal playfulness independent of any originating 'inspiration'.

In fact, both his poems in French and his seven quatrain poems may be seen to constitute a 'swerve' into a conscious and manipulated poetry, different in kind from the fragmented spontaneity of his strongest poems to date. There was an external context for this as well as an internal one, relating to the debate about contemporary poetry consequent upon Amy Lowell's Imagist anthologies, which appeared annually from 1915 to 1917. Pound, as we have seen, was somewhat alienated from this group, feeling it to betray principles of clarity and economy. Lowell's first two collections contained prefaces, in which she offered definitions of 'imagist' poetry and of 'free-verse' or *vers libre*; and it is probable that Eliot intended a reply to Lowell when he published his 'Reflections on *Vers Libre*' in the *New Statesman* (March 1917). In this, he stressed the need for restraints of craftsmanship, controversially asserted that '*vers libre* does not exist', and that 'there is no freedom in art'. In his pamphlet *Ezra Pound: His Metric and Poetry*, published anonymously in New York in November, Eliot continued to emphasise the merits of structure and to doubt the freedom of free verse, implicitly reaffirming the assurance he offered in the *New Statesman* that 'formal rhymed verse will certainly not lose its place'.

He was in the fortunate position of being able to fulfil his own prophecy. In discussions with Pound, which were quite possibly concurrent with the writing of his article, the two had decided that (and here we switch to Pound's account) 'the dilutation of *vers libre*, Amygism, Lee Mastersism, general floppiness had gone too far and that some counter-current must be set going'.[15] The remedy for this was 'rhyme and regular strophes'; more specifically, the model was to be Théophile Gautier, to whose *Émaux et Camées* Pound introduced Eliot at this period. As Eliot recalled, 'the form gave impetus to the content'; they studied the poems, asking themselves, 'Have I anything to say in which this form will be useful?': a procedure which led to Pound's *Hugh Selwyn Mauberley* and Eliot's seven quatrain poems, the first of which – 'The Hippopotamus' – was published in July 1917. In his correspondence, Eliot discriminated between light poems like this and 'Whispers of Immortality', and the seriousness of 'Burbank . . .' and 'Sweeney among the Nightingales' (cf. L 311). It was his habit to disparage recent work, so it is all the more surprising that he should declare to his brother early in 1920 that he considered these two to be 'among the best that I have ever done' (L 363).

The poetry Eliot was writing in 1917 and 1918 is not his best, no matter what he himself thought. It was, nonetheless, valuable to him as an exercise in the precise use of language and form; and it also inaugurated a period of collaboration with Ezra Pound (which was to culminate in Pound's creative editing of *The Waste Land* from the manuscripts which Eliot showed to him). Both the French and English poems of these years were discussed with Pound, whose suggestions seem to have been fertile (for instance, changing 'était' to 'pendant' and 'oubliant' to oubliait', in lines 25–6 of 'Dans le

Restaurant', and 'droppings' to 'siftings' in 'Sweeney . . . Night-ingales'). Eliot's adoption of a distinctive new style also enables us to gauge his growing influence, from those who either imitated or parodied it. The quatrain poems were for the most part published in the *Little Review*, although the Hogarth Press (Leonard and Virginia Woolf) published four in its pamphlet edition of seven of Eliot's poems, issued as *Poems* (1919). In December 1918 Pound wrote to Marianne Moore that he was rejecting imitations of Eliot for the *Little Review*, and a year later the magazine *Coterie* published a parody by Robert Nichols of Eliot's quatrain style; other poets followed suit, but it could be argued that even here Eliot was ahead of the game, since his poem 'A Cooking Egg', published in *Coterie* the previous May, has about it an air of self-parody (and a 'cooking egg' is one on the verge of staleness). Osbert Sitwell started writing quatrains – and to Eliot's chagrin came to be better known than himself for doing so – but what is striking in both parodists and imitators is how very much less deft their use of form and language is than Eliot's.

In any case, Eliot had again moved forward, and was no longer writing quatrains; with the composition of 'Gerontion', he entered upon his next phase. Although later he implied that he had started to write this poem in 1917, it is clear that the bulk of the writing took place in the summer of 1919; 'half-finished' in June, it was eventually revised for the press in August, while he was on holiday in France (part of the time he stayed with Pound in the Dordogne, so it was probably then that it was finalised). In January 1922 Eliot would ask Pound whether the poem might stand 'as a prelude' to *The Waste Land*, which suggests that he felt the two to be connected; and his first reference to *The Waste Land* is found in a letter to John Quinn on 5 November 1919, not long after finishing 'Gerontion'. This had not been published prior to its appearance at the beginning of *Ara Vos Prec* (February 1920; published the same month in New York as *Poems by T.S. Eliot*).

In the introduction to the Faber edition of Pound's *Selected Poems*, Eliot declared that his own chief stylistic influences had been 'Laforgue together with the later Elizabethan drama'; and although he claimed these to have been influencing him from the beginning, it is perhaps not until 'Gerontion' that the presence of Elizabethan and Jacobean dramatists (on whom he had been lec-turing at Southall) is clearly detectable in the movement of his verse, rather than thematically or allusively, as in previous poems.

Formally, the poem resembles earlier works like 'Prufrock' and 'Portrait of a Lady' in its length and construction; but whereas those were presentations of a self in a psychological or emotional context, 'Gerontion' portrays a self in rhetorical and historical context. Abandoning the overcharged allusiveness of the quatrain poems, it appears to embark on an overtly confessional mode – 'I would meet you upon this honestly' – but its rhetoric of directness is deceptive; its epigraph from *Measure for Measure* comes from the scene in which the duke, disguised as a friar, gives sham spiritual guidance to one condemned for fornication. If at first the poem strikes us as a dramatic monologue, similar to Browning's, we soon see that it is not concerned to portray the interior of a character, so much as to depict a predicament or to evoke an epoch. Its thematic resemblance is to 'Burbank', with 'Antwerp', 'Brussels', 'London' and 'Limoges' suggesting the international setting.

The poem was written in the aftermath of the Great War – a period that might perhaps be termed the 'little peace', in view of its sense of lost directions and disappointed expectations. Eliot had seen friends like Aldington and Lewis enlist – and when first he met Herbert Read, the latter had been in uniform. With the entry of the USA into the conflict in 1917, Eliot had himself attempted to secure an appointment in his country's forces, but circumstances and his medical history conspired to frustrate his efforts, and he returned to his job at the bank. Whether there is in consequence a personal note to the declaration in 'Gerontion' is impossible to know; but – as in 'Prufrock' – Eliot was a connoisseur of the character on the edge of action, rather than at its centre:

> I was neither at the hot gates
> Nor fought in the warm rain
> Nor knee deep in the salt marsh, heaving a cutlass,
> Bitten by flies, fought.

His sullen negatives obtrude upon a curiously detailed evocation of long-forgotten wars ('hot gates' translates Thermopylae); like the eunuch in *Antony and Cleopatra* who retains his 'fierce affections' and can 'think what Venus did with Mars', this old man can imagine valour.

Indeed, military and amatory prowess are associated in the

poem, which is replete with innuendo; the lines already quoted are susceptible of sexual interpretation – and such suggestiveness is also a feature of those dramatists whose work seems to have been most influential here. The poem's last fourteen lines, with their urgently propulsive run-ons and collapsing grammar, ending in a verbless one-and-a-half line summary, enact a sexual crescendo and diminuendo. It ends in the unproductive dryness with which it had begun, and in between we have encountered, paradoxically, the memorably energetic presentation of states of apathy and indirection. The speaker has memories which are not of his own past, inhabits a house which he does not own, calls up individuals who have no apparent association with each other or with him, and implies a variety of failures of nerve, faith, honesty and passion. His cosmos is perpetually on the brink of dissolving into chaos, and what sounds like straight talk finally evades analysis: 'Gives too soon / Into weak hands, what's thought can be dispensed with / Till the refusal propagates a fear'. Lines such as these have a force which does not depend on our making sense of them.

'Gerontion' is an obscure poem, but unlike the quatrains its obscurity does not result in mannered aridity; the abstract precision of its references gives them the inexplicable logic of images from dreams or nightmares – the compulsiveness, for example, of 'Hakagawa, bowing among the Titians'. The creative resourcefulness of its language achieves a dense and persuasive texture. Examination of the first fifteen lines shows that what initially looks like dramatic blank verse is also powerfully haunted by elements of strong-stress and alliterative poetry. Echoic combinations of adjective and noun accumulate ('old man', 'dry month', 'hot gates', 'warm rain', 'salt marsh', 'dull head'), interspersed with other devices, such as the repeated assonances of long vowels, the play on 'w' sounds and sibilants in lines 8 and 9, and alliterations. Structural repetition of words and phrases – always a feature of Eliot's poetry – are handled with masterly subtlety: the first 'Nor fought' suggests a second, but then the 'nor' and the 'fought' are separated by three clauses; and it should also be noted how the insertion of 'heaving a cutlass' unexpectedly extends the line and prevents rhythmic predictability. It is a virtuoso demonstration of just what strategies of control can operate beneath an apparently unstructured surface; very few English or American poets this century have been capable of so wide-ranging an exploitation of the capacities of words; and the remarkable fact is that Eliot's sensuous response to language subserves a vision which is basically ascetic.

The poem which Eliot had in mind in November 1919 as his next project was initially called 'He do the police in different voices' – although at what stage this title emerged is unclear. Nor is it clear how quickly he began to write it or how far he got with it in the following months; on 18 December 1919 he told his mother that it was his new year's resolution 'to write a long poem I have had on my mind for a long time and to prepare a small prose book from my lecture [sic] on poetry' (L 351). It seems likely, however, that he suffered a recurrence of his block; for the second part of his resolution bore the quicker fruit. He had earlier been contemplating the inclusion of some critical prose in the American edition of his poetry, but this had come to nothing; by 10 May 1920 he was reporting to Quinn his success in placing his volume of essays with Methuen. Consisting of an assemblage and partial revision of articles and reviews he had published in periodicals, this was ready for the printer on 9 August; he enlisted the help of Pound and of Vivien in correcting the proofs after his return from a holiday in France with Wyndham Lewis, and *The Sacred Wood* was published on 4 November 1920. Together with the publication of his poems eight months before, Eliot was now represented as a poet and a critic by a reasonably substantial body of material.

The critical response to Eliot's poetry had been mixed. The first notice taken had been Arthur Waugh's review of Pound's *Catholic Anthology*, in the distinctly unrevolutionary *Quarterly Review*; responding adversely to what he saw as this 'very stronghold of literary rebellion', he damned all the contributors for misdirected 'cleverness', and noticed Eliot only to the extent of quoting some lines from 'Prufrock' to exemplify 'banality'. His closing suggestion was that these poets might be valuable, if they served as a deterrent to others. Pound, ever the publicist, twisted Waugh's remarks into a more direct insult against himself and Eliot, and used this as an excuse to issue a spirited defence of Eliot's poetry in the *Egoist* (June 1917). This, by no accident, was the same month in which *Prufrock and Other Observations* appeared; and in the *TLS* on 21 June a brief review dismissed this volume as 'purely analytical' poetry, and its author as 'frequently inarticulate' ('his "poems" will hardly be read by many with enjoyment'). Early in July a review in *Literary*

World revived the charge of 'too much cleverness', and in the *New Statesman* (August 1917) Eliot was damned with faint praise: his verse, whilst 'unrecognisable as poetry at present' was 'decidedly amusing', and 'The Boston Evening Transcript' was quoted as 'Mr Eliot's highest flight'. At greater length than all these put together, the same month Pound wrote a combative piece extolling Eliot in *Poetry*; indeed, the notices in American magazines such as the *Dial* (where Conrad Aiken admired Eliot as 'an exceptionally acute technician'), the *Little Review* and *Poetry* (where in addition to Pound, Marianne Moore sounded a note of praise) were more favourable: probably because of Pound's influence.[16]

The Hogarth Press *Poems* (London 1919) caused the *TLS* reviewer – faced by the French poems and some quatrains – to continue the critique of Eliot's 'cleverness', and the *Athenaeum* to continue the 'analytical' criticism by deploring in Eliot the 'attitude . . . of the scientist', which it felt ran counter to his true gift as a poet. With the appearance of *Ara Vos Prec*, Middleton Murry in the same magazine contributed a review which was admiring in the Latin sense of the word, but which beneath its tortuous metaphors seems to make the similar point, that Eliot's poetry is a chameleon colouring, within which true feelings are only intermittently discoverable. Murry's review had the merit, at least, of noticing 'Gerontion'; whereas the *TLS* reviewer on 18 March 1920 referred to no poem which had not appeared in the first volume. This piece takes Eliot to task for his 'new Byronism', an affected world-weariness; again, there is his pernicious 'cleverness' – 'his verse is full of derisive reminiscences of poets who have wearied him' – and the reviewer is patently exasperated by what he takes to be Eliot's negative response to everything.

Even in these unenthusiastic reviews there is, however, a distinct sense that Eliot is a force to be reckoned with; rarely is the tone completely dismissive. Louis Untermeyer, writing in the *Freeman* on 30 June 1920, assesses Eliot's influence as 'exceedingly limited', but nonetheless 'indisputable', and notes how other poets have adopted his quatrain style. Desmond MacCarthy opened a long and favourable review in the *New Statesman* (8 January 1921) with the assertion that 'when two people are discussing modern poetry together the name of T.S. Eliot is sure to crop up', and goes on to consider why even those of the old guard who despise new-fangled poetry cannot simply ignore this writer. William Carlos Williams would explain this by his assertion (published in the *Little Review* in May 1919), 'it is because Eliot is a subtle conformist'; in Williams's view, Eliot's continuous literariness betrayed the true revolution that would democratise the language and the act of poetry. Williams's reaction had about it a conscious perversity; most of Eliot's contemporaries – Marianne Moore, E.E. Cummings and of course Pound and Aiken – responded appreciatively.

On the whole, however, the tone of the reviews was to recognise the talent; those who were enthusiasts applauded the achievements, those who were not dwelt on the limitations – with the common charge being that of an arid cleverness and a wearying pose of weariness on Eliot's part. Reviews of *The Sacred Wood* pursued some of the same themes; the *TLS* (2 December 1920) reproached Eliot for 'a malice the more insidious because unconscious' toward writers he did not admire. 'Tradition and the Individual Talent' was seen as the 'central essay' of the collection, which exemplified criticism as 'science rather than art'; in spite of which, Eliot was subject to 'certain perversities, instinctive rather than rational'. In the *London Mercury* the following February, Eliot was praised for his specific observations ('his essay on Ben Jonson is wholly admirable'), but was faulted for failing to offer a definition of good criticism, as well as for neglecting larger questions ('What is poetry?', or 'What is poetry for?'), in the exercise of his 'critical method of dissection and analysis'.

Neither of Eliot's books was instantaneously successful, to judge from these reactions, although neither went unappreciated; but each was to have consequences for his career, because even if the general reader or the diehard reviewer did not immediately warm to this new voice, some of those who did were well-placed to advance his reputation. This leads toward the interaction of Eliot's career with the Universities, which will be discussed in the following chapter, along with the issues raised by his writing and the responses to it. In the period covered by this one, Eliot advanced from anonymity to the possession of a distinctive voice; in fact, he stood on the brink of his success. Writing in April 1919 to Professor Woods at Harvard, who was encouraging him to return to America, Eliot asserted that he was 'getting to know and be known by all the intelligent or important people in letters' (L 285); and in a letter to his mother the previous month he assured her that by a 'small and select public' he was regarded as 'the best living critic, as well as the best living poet, in England' (L 280). He went on to tell her, 'I really think that I have far more *influence* on English letters than any other American has ever had, unless it be Henry James'.

These are breath-taking claims, coming before he had published either *Ara Vos Prec* or *The Sacred Wood*; and to his mother he acknowledged his own conceit in making them. As well as conceit, however, we see something of his ambition glinting here; and if such claims were not strictly justified at the time he made them, they soon would be. An added reason for making them at this stage was, of course, to fend off pressure to return to America, and during these years he had accomplished the greater part of his transformation from an American. At the end of the year, Pound quit London in disgust, and urged Wyndham Lewis and Eliot to follow suit; but Eliot knew that Pound's initial advice to settle was sounder than his subsequent advice to leave. As Conrad Aiken had observed in a letter written to America that summer, 'Tom Eliot is here for life'; and so he was.

NOTES

1. See Eliot's introduction to *Literary Essays of Ezra Pound* (London, 1954).
2. Ezra Pound, 'Harold Monro', *Criterion*, XI, 45 (1932), 590.
3. C.K. Stead, *The New Poetic: Yeats to Eliot* (London, 1964).
4. Quoted in the introduction to *Imagist Poetry*, ed. Jones (Harmondsworth, 1972), p. 16.
5. *The Letters of Ezra Pound*, ed. Paige (London, 1951), p. 80.
6. *Paris Review*, p. 82.
7. Her remark is quoted by Peter du Sautoy, in 'T.S. Eliot: Personal Reminiscences', *Southern Review*, 21, 4 (1985), 949.
8. *Autobiography of Bertrand Russell* (one vol.; London, 1975), pp. 278, 280, 410.
9. Ibid., p. 242.
10. See Ronald Schuchard, 'T.S. Eliot as an Extension Lecturer, 1916–1919', *Review of English Studies*, XXV, 98 (1974), 163–73, and XXV, 99 (1974), 292–304. The syllabus from which I quote is at the University of Oxford (Department of External Studies).
11. The information in this paragraph derives from a letter Eliot sent (2 October 1959) to Harold Shearman, to mark the Jubilee of the extra-mural tutorial classes run by the University of London.
12. March, p. 18. Ottoline Morrell's memories, quoted in the previous paragraph, come from *Ottoline of Garsington*, ed. Gathorne-Hardy (London, 1974), pp. 101–2.

13. Anthony Powell, *Faces in My Time* (London, 1980), p. 190. Strachey's comments come from Michael Holroyd, *Lytton Strachey* (London, 1971), p. 440.
14. *Paris Review*, p. 85.
15. See note 2, above.
16. Significant reviews are gathered in Michael Grant's *T.S. Eliot: The Critical Heritage*, 2 vols (London, 1982). Hereafter cited as Grant.

4
1921–1925

These are the years in which *The Waste Land* was published and the *Criterion* founded; culminating in Eliot's joining the board of Faber and Gwyer, who issued his *Poems 1909–25* on 23 November 1925, the period witnessed his decisive emergence as the dominant figure in modern English letters. During these years, too, Eliot began his moves toward Anglicanism, and toward British citizenship (he alludes to his wish to become naturalised in a postcard to Richard Aldington of 15 October 1921). His public achievements accompanied a private life increasingly unhappy, punctuated by bouts of ill-health, depression and exhaustion; 1925 was also the year in which he seems first to have mooted to friends the possibility of a separation from his wife. Pound's absence from London was both the cause and the reflection of a change in the literary scene; socially, Eliot saw more of fellow-writers like the Woolfs and the Sitwells, although he took care to maintain a distance that left his independence uncompromised. In any case, he had no need of patronage, once the *Criterion* was started; by virtue of his talent and his position, he himself became the centre of a group of lesser writers associated with his magazine – such as Aldington, Flint and Herbert Read. He retained a working relationship with Wyndham Lewis, and published extracts from Lewis's *Apes of God* in the *Criterion*, to the probable discomfort of the Bloomsbury writers and the Sitwells, whom Lewis held up to ridicule.

By temperament, Eliot seems to have been a loner, regarding his associates with an affection that foundered on distrust: according to Conrad Aiken, in the winter of 1921–22 Eliot remarked with vehemence that 'literary people are shits', and at another time cautioned Aiken against revealing his best ideas in conversation in England, for they would assuredly be stolen. In letters written during this period, Aiken commented on how 'wary and guarded' Eliot seemed, holding him 'at arm's length' in spite of an apparently friendly manner. In the early years of Eliot's friendship with Virginia Woolf, she more than once recorded her feeling that he withheld himself or was not entirely honest with her. It's possible to ascribe this behaviour to an unctuous hypocrisy on Eliot's part, as some were inclined to do; but it might more fruitfully be seen as one symptom of a central problem which, for Eliot, was intellectual and spiritual as well as emotional, and had its issue in his writing as well as his personal relationships. This 'problem' was that of the difficulty of making public an intensely private sensibility, whose most authentic experiences, early and late, were not directly communicable, nor easy to share.

Apprehensions of 'the heart of light, the silence' or 'the still point of the turning world' were accompanied by the incapacity of language to describe them; but it was equally necessary to try to do so, because otherwise such incommunicable experiences are imprisoning and isolating. Yet the very act of producing such private or subconscious intuitions into the publicity of consciousness entailed potential falsification: the predicament of Lazarus in the drawing-room. In terms of social behaviour, the problem is how to remain 'yourself' in a context requiring you 'to prepare a face to meet the faces that you meet' – exacerbated in Eliot's case, one supposes, by the increasing contrast between his publicly-maintained decorum and the subversive turbulence of his domestic circumstances. Artistically, the problem is how to provide a coherent structure for a poetics of fragmentary glimpses; and intellectually, the difficulty is how the part belongs to the whole without ceasing to be a separate entity: how the individual talent incorporates itself to the tradition. In religious terms, the question is that of how the soul is reconciled to God.

These matters are reflected in the poetry and the criticism which Eliot had published up to this point (including the three essays published separately in 1921, and later issued as *Homage to John Dryden* (1924), as well as *The Sacred Wood*). Confronted by Eliot's poems, many early reviewers had commented on their difficulty and their 'cleverness', evidenced in a literary allusiveness that practically became his hallmark; and to some degree a sense of Eliot's 'difficulty' continues. The obscurity of his 'meaning', together with the recondite nature of many of his literary allusions, have led some to conclude that this is a game to be played by the intelligentsia alone – with the equal conclusion that, if you can play the game of reading Eliot's poems, then you are entitled to consider yourself a member of that élite. It is clear that a certain coterie spirit infused early admirers, particularly those in the universities: if you liked Eliot, you were 'in' the secret, and could number yourself amongst the initiate. The attractiveness of many of the Modernist writers to the academy was – and is – that their texts seemed to necessitate a skilled interpreter: Eliot's poetry offered professors the satisfying opportunity to display their learning by identifying his quotations. In fact, 'source hunting' came to be seen as the necessary preliminary to reading an Eliot poem: his allusions were traced and explained, and his erudition applauded by those who in the process inwardly congratulated themselves on being sufficiently erudite to do the job.

There is a degree of intellectual snobbishness in Eliot's poetry, as in his criticism; the unattributed quotations create an atmosphere of scholarly display whose function is, in part, deterrent: dare we question a man who seems to know so much more than we do? Eliot confessed that the depth of his learning was less than he let it appear, particularly in his criticism, where it served the strategic purpose of endowing his opinions with greater weight. It seems a radical mistake on the part of many critics and readers, to assume that his poems can only be approached by identifying his allusions – without which they cannot be properly appreciated. Not all of Eliot's echoes seem to have been consciously controlled; nor can we be sure that his use of a quotation is evidence that the work from which it comes is thematically relevant, since some of these associations are obscurely personal. In his 1920 essay 'Philip Massinger', Eliot addressed the issue of literary borrowing (his word was 'theft'), asserting that 'the good poet welds his theft into a whole of feeling which is unique, utterly different from that from which it was torn' (SE 206).

We have seen that one account offered of Eliot's allusions was that they represent 'derisive reminiscences of poets who have wearied him'. The *TLS* reviewer was perhaps not entirely wrong to diagnose an element of mockery, but he mistook its target: it is not the dead poets who are derided, so much as a present age that can no longer rise to their level. Emotional, cultural and spiritual decay are the habitual motifs of Eliot's writing, and the echoes which inhabit it serve to evoke 'the vanished power of the usual reign'. It does not matter, on the whole, whether we can accurately assign such evocations to their original settings, so long as we register the poetry as haunted by parodic diminutions of greater voices. The sense of separation, from a past which was coherent and a scale of action potentially heroic, can be observed in personae such as Prufrock and Gerontion, who acknowledge their own littleness and measure it against unattainable ideals of conduct: Prufrock knows that he is not Prince Hamlet, and Gerontion vividly describes the battles he has not fought.

In his review of *Ara Vos Prec*, Desmond MacCarthy suggested that it was Eliot's 'weakness' that 'he seems rather to have felt the glory of life through literature'.[1] The literary self-consciousness of Eliot's poetry is notable, and its sense of a rich but squandered heritage goes hand in hand with a perception of the inadequacy of available experience: Eliot was an intensely modern poet who intensely disliked the modern world. It can, however, be argued that his literary references amount to more than evasion or inert nostalgia, but are an effort to establish the present relevance of past writers, as well as an attempt to rescue the modern self from imprisonment in the fortuitous jumble of purely personal experience. To set an allusion to a seventeenth-century writer resonating in the context of a contemporary poem is partially to reinterpret that writer, by striking light from an unexpected facet; but it is also partially to reinterpret the experience in question, by showing its affinities with what has gone before. Although the major effect of the echoes of previous literature in Eliot's earlier poetry is to suggest ironic disjunction, when the words of a dead writer refract a modern experience that experience may also be redeemed from its isolated contemporaneity, becoming representative and 'impersonal'.

In 1928, in his introduction to Pound's *Selected Poems*, Eliot asserted that 'the poem which is absolutely original is absolutely bad; it is, in the bad sense, "subjective" with no relation to the world to which it appeals'. This makes clear a prevalent concern of the earlier criticism, that literary value has more to do with conformity than with deviance. But it is important that what is conformed to is a living principle, not merely received practice; and although great writers of the past offer a standard for judging literature, they do not necessarily offer a model for producing it. Moreover, in Eliot's view these same great writers are not museum pieces but a vital force, in that each age will discover in them its particular preoccupations; and the measure of their greatness will be their adaptability to this necessary work of reinterpretation. 'Each generation must translate for itself', he goes on to assert in his introduction to Pound, and 'translation' applies equally to literature written in one's own language, but in a different age: in his essay on Andrew Marvell (1921) he affirmed that 'to bring the poet back to life' was 'the great, the perennial, task of criticism'.

The task is perennial because according to Eliot great literature needs perpetually to be rediscovered in terms of the successive ages which read it. In this way it can be seen that the conformity referred to above is not simply a one-way process of making the present conform to the past, but the equally important process of making the past conformable to the present; which brings us squarely into the area of 'Tradition and the Individual Talent' (1919). In this, the most celebrated of his critical essays, Eliot addresses himself to defining the correct relationship between the contemporary writer and his precursors. He attacks the prejudice which values a poet simply in terms of his difference from his predecessors, and asserts the necessity for an 'historical sense', defined as a perception not only of 'the pastness of the past, but of its presence'. His major point is that great works do not exist as an unchanging catalogue, to which the only possible response is passive reverence; he claims that there is a kind of mutual accommodation:

> The existing monuments form an ideal order among themselves, which is modified by the introduction of the new (the really new) work of art among them. The existing order is complete before the new work arrives; for order to persist after the supervention of novelty, the *whole* existing order must be, if ever so slightly, altered.
>
> (SE 15)

The point is not, of course, that previous achievements are in themselves changed by new additions; what does change is our perception of them, as the perspective in which they are viewed alters. *Oedipus the King* remains itself, but we may read it differently in the backward light of, say, *King Lear*. There is no point in attempting to reproduce within ourselves the response to Sophocles of his contemporary Athenian audience, because 'the conscious present is an awareness of the past in a way and to an extent which the past's awareness of itself cannot show' (SE 16). The masterpieces from different periods of history must be revived as living tissue; this, as Eliot asserts in his introduction to *The Sacred Wood*, is an important part of the business of the critic, 'to see literature steadily and to see it whole: and this is eminently to see it *not* as consecrated by time, but to see beyond time; to see the best work of our time and the best work of twenty-five hundred years ago with the same eyes'. This note is struck repeatedly in *The Sacred Wood*, whether Eliot is asserting that to accept Aristotle 'in a canonical spirit . . . is to lose the whole living force of him' (SW 10), or whether he argues that to read Jonson well 'does not so much require the power of putting ourselves into seventeenth-century London as it requires the power of setting Jonson in our London' (SE 148).

If the present must accommodate the dead writer, so must the literary canon enfold the good contemporary author. Eliot seeks to establish a theory of 'tradition' firm enough to assert the standards of the past, but flexible enough to adjust itself to the new. Clearly, he is concerned to reconcile two aspects of his own sensibility, which combined desire for the assurance of an external authority with a highly original, somewhat erratic, creative temperament. If on the one hand he attempted to displace a 'canonical spirit' that affirmed the achievements of classic writers simply to disqualify the modern writer, on the other, in arguing the importance of tradition, he is also set against an overvaluation of 'originality', rooted in the notion that a poem expresses the unique personality of its writer. He is in reaction, then, against excesses of 'Classicism' and excesses of 'Romanticism'; although increasingly it seemed to him that the latter posed the greater threat, and required corrective action.

Eliot fiercely attacked the subjective, purely personal attribution of value. As we have seen, critics commented on the scientific tone of his essays; and this appearance of dispassionate exactitude was one that he cultivated in his prose, and attempted to extend to his poetry. 'Tradition and the Individual Talent' notoriously stresses the impersonality of the artistic process, insisting that poetry has nothing to do with the expression of emotion, and comparing the poet's mind to a chemical catalyst, or a 'receptacle' within which reactions occur. The poet's personality, the originality which merely differentiates him from other writers, is what isolates and makes him marginal; only by the features which incorporate him into the tradition does his work attain lasting significance. The act of composition, far from being an expression of a complex individuality, seems instead to foreshadow that 'condition of complete simplicity / (Costing not less than everything)' which Eliot would write about much later:

What happens is a continual surrender of himself as he is at the moment to something which is more valuable. The progress of an artist is a continual self-sacrifice, a continual extinction of personality.

(SE 17)

Two things are noteworthy here: the religious suggestiveness of the description, and the force of that rather shocking final phrase – intended to remind us, perhaps, that in the sacred wood dark and pre-Christian mysteries are enacted. Whether his governing metaphor was drawn from science or from elsewhere, Eliot constantly stressed the unaccountable nature of poetic creation. His introduction to Pound defines a masterpiece as resulting from the confluence between an 'unconscious, subterranean' development in the writer, and his conscious application to technique: 'an accumulation of experience has crystallized to form material of art, and years of work have prepared an adequate medium'. In *The Use of Poetry and the Use of Criticism* (1933), composition is expressed in terms of the removal of an obstruction, 'the sudden relief from an intolerable burden' (p. 145). Twenty years later, in 'The Three Voices of Poetry', obstetric and pathological metaphors recur: the poet 'is oppressed by a burden which he must bring to birth in order to obtain relief. Or, to change the figure of speech, he is haunted by a demon, a demon against which he feels powerless, . . . and the words, the poem he makes, are a kind of form of exorcism of this demon' (OPP 98).

This may seem rather a romantic, if not necromantic, account. But these sources for the poem lie below the structures of thought and feeling that constitute a 'personality'; in his essay on 'The Metaphysical Poets' (1921), Eliot rebuked those who looked into their hearts and wrote for 'not looking deep enough': 'one must look into the cerebral cortex, the nervous system, and the digestive tracts' (SE 290). Accidents of character pertinent to the poet as an individual are transcended in the true work of art, as he argued in his essay on 'Shakespeare and the Stoicism of Seneca' (1927):

Shakespeare, too, was occupied with the struggle – which alone constitutes life for a poet – to transmute his personal and private agonies into something rich and strange, something universal and impersonal.

(SE 137)

Through all this runs Eliot's sense of the insufficiency of the single self: vulnerable to inexplicable interior forces (in the digestive tract, for example), isolated and potentially anarchic unless regulated from without. This is as much a moral perception as a psychological or sociological observation; operating as a principle in his criticism, it led him always to prefer the orthodox writer to the eccentric, as in this differentiation of Blake from Dante in *The Sacred Wood*: 'What his genius required, and what it sadly lacked, was a framework of accepted and traditional ideas which would have prevented him from indulging in a philosophy of his own . . . The concentration resulting from a framework of mythology and theology and philosophy is one of the reasons why Dante is a classic, and Blake only a poet of genius' (SE 322).

If the creative impulse needed rescue from the arbitrariness of selfhood, so too did the critical impulse. This is the burden of Eliot's essay on 'The Function of Criticism' (SE 23–34), which he published in the *Criterion* in October 1923, and which we consider here because of its explicit links with 'Tradition and the Individual Talent'. Elaborating on the earlier piece, it proposes 'an unconscious community' between 'the true artists of any time', which requires conscious definition (sneering, meanwhile, at 'the second-rate artist', anxious to preserve 'the trifling differences which are his distinction', and therefore unable to 'surrender himself to any common action'). This theory of necessary self-effacement is logically extended to the task of literary criticism, which is defined as being ideally an endeavour toward 'the common pursuit of true judgment'. This seldom actually happens, Eliot notices, and he associates the problem with 'Romanticism', using as his exemplar Middleton Murry; whereas Eliot, as a loosely-defined 'Classicist', believes 'that men cannot get on without giving allegiance to something outside themselves', Murry's view is that the important thing is what he calls 'the inner voice'. Suggesting that the difference between a classicist position and a romantic is 'the difference between the complete and the fragmentary, the adult and the immature, the orderly and the chaotic', Eliot is rather scathing about Murry's formula: 'why have principles, when one has the inner voice?'.

The need to make conscious what is unconscious, to render collective what is individual, comes from Eliot's distrust of undisciplined subjectivity. The main thrust of his critical enterprise is well represented by the quotation from Remy de Gourmont he used as an epigraph in *The Sacred Wood*: '*Ériger en lois ses impressions personnelles, c'est le grand effort d'un homme s'il est sincère*' ['To establish his personal impressions as laws; this is the great effort of a man who is sincere']. It was only by enlarging personal impressions into precepts which were generally valid, that one could rise above the unaccountability of the inner voice and enter into intellectual community. This, however, raises questions concerning the compatibility between Eliot's theory of criticism and his practice of poetry; for although in 'The Function of Criticism' he stressed the 'critical labour' involved in the production of a good poem, it seems nonetheless that the fragmented spontaneity of the 'inner voice' has a strong resemblance to what was for Eliot the originating impulse of a poem. Is the legislative exactitude of the criticism easily reconciled with the mysterious sources of the poetry?

That there was a difference, Eliot himself acknowledged in his essay on Joyce written in the same year. Returning to definitions of classicism, he stated that it was 'much easier to be a classicist in literary criticism than in creative art – because in criticism you are responsible only for what you want, and in creation you are responsible for what you can do with material which you must simply accept'.[2] Some of his readers, too, felt that there was a contradiction: in a letter to Herbert Read which the latter assigns to 1924, Eliot declared himself unconcerned by 'the apparent inconsistency – which has been made the most of – between my prose and my verse'.[3] In fact, Eliot may well have been right in feeling the inconsistency to be apparent rather than real. As we have seen, both good poetry and good criticism involve rising above defects of personality, whether by transmuting personal anguish into something rich and strange, or by establishing personal impressions as authentic principles. Moreover, elsewhere Eliot made it clear that self-surrender lay at the root of good criticism as well as good poetry; this is implicit in his remarks on the fertilising nature of literary influence, but is most strongly expressed in a letter of 1935 to Stephen Spender, where he stated that 'you don't really criticise any author to whom you have never surrendered yourself'.[4] Both poetry and criticism originate in a deep-seated urge; both represent the subsequent elaboration of this initial impulse, the drawing upward into consciousness which is effected by an attachment to externals. In the case of the poem, this is the 'critical labour' involved in wrestling with its words and meanings; and in the case of criticism, this is the attention to the literary artifact which attempts to make the responses it provokes objectively demonstrable. Each endeavour aims outward from the self toward a community.

Notions of wholeness and community pervade Eliot's thinking; especially his thinking about literature, which seemed to offer a means of rectifying the disintegrated nature of contemporary life. In a post-war Europe permanently scarred by the recent cataclysm, Eliot advanced his concept that there was something called 'the mind of Europe', which stretched from Homer onward through Dante and Shakespeare, and would stretch even further to include contemporary writers – provided they possessed 'the historical sense'. An assertion of the persistence of an ideal continuum would have had its attractions in that shell-shocked climate, whatever scepticism might at first attach to the notion that Europe had a 'mind' left. Much had been destroyed between 1914 and 1918: the enormous loss of life and squandering of resources had been accompanied by a weakening or disappearance of many assumptions about the values of 'civilisation'. Studying the cultural and psychological effects in literature, in *The Great War and Modern Memory* (1975), Paul Fussell has shown how that conflict came to be endowed with a semi-mythic status, a blood-letting that separates the complications of modern consciousness from an era of innocence. This was a gradual development, of course; but little as Eliot would have subscribed to a myth of 'innocence', it can be seen how congruent some of his ideas were, with a period in which many men felt disappointed with the present, and severed from the past.

As well as registering feelings of triviality and severance, Eliot affirmed the possibility of significant wholeness. In 1921, in 'The Metaphysical Poets' (SE 281–91), he declared that 'it appears likely that poets in our civilization, as it exists at present, must be *difficult*' – which, as well as justifying his own verse, fed into the modern age's sense of its complex difference from others. But in the same essay, recognising that 'the ordinary man's experience is chaotic, irregular, fragmentary', he asserted the capacity of a poet like Donne to 'amalgamate disparate experience', and see it whole. In fact, we can see Eliot at this time promulgating myths both of schism and of reconciliation. Our experience is fragmentary because, unlike Donne and his fellows, we are the victims of disjunction; our fallen state, however, is not attributable to the Great War, but to 'something which had happened to the mind of England', a 'dissociation of sensibility' which set in with the poetry of Milton and Dryden in the late seventeenth century. This wound to the collective psyche, 'from which we have never recovered', drove a wedge between 'thought' and 'feeling' in poetry, and produced a succession of poets who thought and poets who felt, but seldom both together. Arguing that the metaphysical poets were 'trying to find the verbal equivalent for states of mind and feeling', Eliot implied that the contemporary writer, needing to make a complex response to his complex fate as a modern, might have to resort to a tactic of dislocation to force thought and feeling back together.

Eliot's criticism had overt and covert purposes. Overtly, it was concerned with the 'correction of taste' and the establishment of 'true judgment', with rescuing literary appreciation from unattributable caprice by formulating principles and instituting method. This was not to consist in the mere imposition of inert criteria, however; since really – as he observed of Aristotle – 'there is no method except to be very intelligent', it becomes a matter of 'intelligence itself swiftly operating the analysis of sensation to the point of principle and definition' (SW 11). Eliot aimed at the restitution of intelligence to the acts of poetry and criticism – doubtless with reproaches of his own 'cleverness' in mind. This overt purpose was carried out with what looked like magisterial erudition, enlivened by incisive wit. It was successful to the extent that Eliot's essays, whilst not actually 'rediscovering' writers like Donne and Marvell, gave an influential slant to an incipient debate, and certainly made the Elizabethan and Jacobean writers fashionable in a new way. Eliot's appearance of forensic impartiality survived the fact that he almost invariably focused on aspects of these writers of most immediate relevance to himself. His covert purpose, to which he confessed a good deal later, and which is more apparent to us in retrospect, was a natural consequence of the overflowing into one another of his creative and his critical preoccupations: his criticism was a means of encouraging an intellectual climate which would be receptive to the kind of literature he himself valued, and which he and his associates were writing. In this, he was to be unprecedentedly successful; not necessarily in overcoming all opposition to the work of Pound, Lewis, Joyce and himself, but in putting into circulation terminology and critical concepts which were particularly favourable to a discussion of his own verse.

It is hardly to be doubted that Eliot's essays did much to mitigate the threat posed by his poetry; partly by suggesting ways of

approaching it, and partly by the reassurance offered that, whatever unaccountable difficulties were posed by his strange poems,
they were the product of a mind demonstrably methodical in the
sphere of criticism. In this, the posture of scholarliness was important, serving also to demonstrate that however new and iconoclas-
tic this modern young writer might seem, he was not in any simple
way a rebel: in spite of flashes which scorched some respected
reputations, he asserted the importance of the past, and made it
clear that it was possible – indeed, necessary – to embrace the
avant-garde without abandoning the classics. But his criticism was
also provocative and subversive; however improbable his theory of
'dissociation of sensibility' is as literary history, it was a notion
which challenged a response – as with his comments on the
'artistic failure' of *Hamlet*. No professor would have been so rash,
or so daring, as to propound such notions.

Those who were professors at the time Eliot published his early
volumes were not, on the whole, appreciative. But of greater
importance was the fact that clever undergraduates and junior
lecturers – those who would in time become professors – were
made converts. I.A. Richards has recorded his excitement on
buying his copy of *Ara Vos Prec* in 1920, when a newly-appointed
lecturer in English at Cambridge; going on to comment, 'I don't
recall being, in those early days, much concerned with his criticism
– no, only with the poetry and almost at once with the idea that he
would be *the one hope* for the then brand-new English Tripos'.[5]
Richards's attempts to entice Eliot from the counting-house to the
senior common-room failed, but show how early, and how sym-
biotic, was the relationship between Eliot and the universities. A
different picture is painted of Oxford by F.W. Bateson, then an
undergraduate, in his recollection that 'we were hardly aware of
Eliot the poet, whereas we were very much aware of Eliot the
critic. *The Sacred Wood* was almost our sacred book'.[6] Whether
Cambridge's interest in practice and Oxford's in theory define the
difference between these institutions is a nice point; but it shows
how Eliot's influence could be disseminated through one of his
activities, if the other failed.

After *The Waste Land* even Oxford undergraduates heard about
the poetry, and by the later 1920s the criticism had established
itself at Cambridge; James Reeves recalled in 1948 that 'when I
went up to Cambridge twenty years ago, I was handed as it were,
in much the same spirit, two little books, the one in prose, the

other in verse. They were *The Sacred Wood* and *Poems 1909–25*. Those who played the part of sidesmen were not, it should perhaps be said, my tutors but my fellow undergraduates. Eliot was not at this time "officially" recognised'.[7] Reeve's final observation needs qualification; although there were of course those who resisted, Eliot's poetry had already been treated by I. A. Richards in the second edition of *Principles of Literary Criticism* (1926), and in that year Eliot had given the Clark Lectures at Cambridge, sponsored by Trinity College. This is hardly the appearance of one academically *persona non grata*. Eliot's reputation was certainly more securely established at Cambridge: at roughly the same period it was still necessary for an Oxford English don (Neville Coghill) to learn about Eliot's poetry from an undergraduate (W. H. Auden); but we can see how Eliot's attractiveness can hardly have been diminished by the undergraduate reader's belief that here was an intensely important writer, whose existence was still a secret from the hide-bound fogey to whom he submitted his weekly essay.

In the early 1920s, while his following in the universities was beginning, Eliot continued the life of a banker under the London pavement. Richards was not the only one to try to rescue him from this: Ezra Pound was involved in two abortive schemes designed to provide Eliot with a sufficiently-secure financial base, on which he could afford to quit the bank. In June 1920 Pound had protested in a letter to Quinn that it was 'a crime against literature' to allow Eliot to languish at his desk, when he should have been writing poems. Their efforts failed, however, and the idea was set aside. From the outside, it must have seemed that Eliot needed help; for in 1921, dogged by his own ill-health and that of his wife, as well as writing for the *TLS* and the *Dial* (run by his friend Scofield Thayer, through whom he had met Vivien), he was struggling with what would become *The Waste Land*, and was laying plans for the *Criterion*. Although the gestation of each involved him in frustration and self-doubt, these two projects were to prove of great significance in advancing his reputation as poet and arbiter of taste.

1921 was a crucial year for Eliot, which is worth examining in detail. Politically and economically, Britain was in trouble, with high unemployment and a coalition government not obviously capable of rectifying matters; through his work in the bank, Eliot was doubtless well-placed to appreciate the seriousness of this. Domestically, life was difficult: Vivien's father had fallen ill in the previous year, and although he recovered, the strain involved in nursing him led to her collapse in March and April, and in May she went to convalesce by the sea. In this month, the poem 'Song to the Opherian' was published in Wyndham Lewis's magazine *Tyro*, under the pseudonym 'Gus Krutsch', possibly because prose by Eliot appeared in the same issue. Eliot's letter to Pound (January 1922) shows that at one stage he considered incorporating this poem with *The Waste Land*, but thematically and emotionally it is part of the elongated and changing sequence which eventually stabilised as 'The Hollow Men'. In June Eliot was visited by his widowed mother, his sister Marian, and, for part of the stay, his brother Henry – with whom he attended a performance by the Russian Ballet of Stravinsky's *Rite of Spring*.

Although the visit was made in response to Eliot's own suggestion, and although he was anxious to be with his mother, whom he had not seen since his somewhat shame-faced return to the USA after his marriage, it was a tense period. Not only did it involve the Eliots in the upheaval of vacating their flat in favour of their visitors, for Eliot it comprised as well the awkwardness of having to confront his spiritual estrangement from family and country; with the added difficulty of knowing that his mother blamed and resented his wife for his expatriation, and that his wife blamed and resented his mother for their financial problems. Eliot had wondered, in advance of his mother's visit, whether it all might be rather a strain for a septuagenarian; but in the event he found her 'terrifyingly energetic', and the person most obviously suffering from stress at the end of it was himself.

As well as writing 'London Letters' for the American *Dial* (in which he commented on aspects of the British music-hall, the planned demolition of some City churches, and Cubism), he wrote the three important essays for the *TLS*: 'Andrew Marvell' in March, 'John Dryden' in June and 'The Metaphysical Poets' in September; it is probable that he completed each assignment roughly a month before publication, and in the cases of the two later essays, he expressed immediate dissatisfaction with them in letters written shortly afterward. In addition to these demands made by his literary journalism and his family, he was engaged, during the summer, in negotiations toward the setting-up of a new magazine. This required protracted discussions with the financial backer,

Lady Rothermere, whose husband (the first Viscount Rothermere) was at that time proprietor of the *Daily Mirror*; the contact seems to have been made through Scofield Thayer, who had hoped that Lady Rothermere might fund the *Dial* as well as a British venture (she did not). Although, as we have seen, it had long been the ambition of Pound and Eliot to control a serious periodical, Eliot was quickly made aware of the drawbacks of such a position: not only were these negotiations fatiguing, for Lady Rothermere had no intention of offering her editor a blank cheque; but also, under the terms of his contract with Lloyds, he was not permitted to take additional paid employment, and in consequence derived no financial benefit from his time-consuming editorial duties.

Meanwhile, what of the poem he had told John Quinn he had 'in mind' in November 1919? Writing to Quinn on 9 May 1921, Eliot again refers to his 'long poem', some of which by this time is out of his mind and 'partly on paper': he was anxious to get it finished. This letter is one in which he speaks, somewhat slightingly, of *The Sacred Wood*; and he implies that the completion of this project delayed his attending to the poem (L 451). It is more likely, however, given the unpredictable nature of his bursts of composition, that his book of essays gave him something on which to concentrate energies that were not yet ready to focus on poetry. Using his own metaphor, we might say that various experiences needed to crystallise before they were ready for the poem, and that although it seems probable that 1920 was a year of writer's block, he was nonetheless 'living through' his material. Incidental encounters during the course of his work at the bank, the meeting with James Joyce in the summer of 1920, and the séances held by the mystic P.D. Ouspensky (financed by Lady Rothermere) which Eliot attended in the autumn of that year, would form such crystals - aided, in the case of Joyce, by the fact that Eliot was reading the 'latter part' of *Ulysses* in manuscript in the first half of 1921. He pronounced it 'truly magnificent' in his letter to Quinn.

With the belated discovery and publication of the original manuscripts, from which *The Waste Land* was reduced to the form in which we now know it, scholars have advanced various theories about the date and order of its composition. With the exception of certain incorporated fragments which may have been composed even before 1914, the bulk of the poem was written in 1921; the questions centre on where Eliot was when he wrote the parts from which it was assembled, and on the sequence in which he wrote them. Although it seems unlikely that the facts can ever be certainly established, there has emerged what looks like the most plausible account; to appreciate it, we need to know what was happening to Eliot during the year.

He was negotiating about his projected magazine during the summer, while his mother was visiting. In July he wrote to Ottoline Morrell, stressing the fatiguing nature of these discussions, and telling her he had found it necessary to recall Vivien from the country to help him with the ensuing work. This, together with another letter to her of June 1922, in which he says he has kept Lady Rothermere waiting a whole year for 'her review' (as he calls it), leads us to suppose that the *Criterion* had been intended to appear a good deal earlier. If Eliot had been anxious to finish his long poem in May, it seems unlikely that he would have been able to accomplish very much during his family's visit – before their arrival, he complained to Quinn about the lack of the extended periods of concentration necessary for composition, and the various disruptions of the visit can hardly have been conducive to his work. The complicated and difficult business with Lady Rothermere was obviously an added burden, which adversely affected both his health and his wife's; towards the end of August 1921 his family left England, and it is probable that in the late summer and autumn Eliot had to confront the fact that his two cherished projects, the poem and the magazine, were stalled.

In September his symptoms of ill-health and unease so worried his wife that she insisted he see a nerve specialist, whose diagnosis – surprising to Eliot – was that he needed a three months' rest-cure, following a strict regimen of seclusion and mental inactivity; and that he should embark on this as soon as possible. After consulting with his employers, leave of absence was arranged from 12 October, and Eliot left for Margate, accompanied at first by Vivien. During this period he concluded that his problem was not a physiological case of 'nerves', but a kind of emotional disorder, for which he used the term *'aboulie'*; responding to the recommendations of friends, he decided to go to Lausanne, and put himself in the hands of a Dr Vittoz. Returning for a week to London, he left the country on 18 November, stopping in Paris on the way to leave Vivien with the Pounds (she also stayed in a sanitarium). He was due back at the bank on 12 January, and on his return early that month he stopped with Pound in Paris, and showed him what he had accomplished.

In a letter to John Quinn of 25 June 1922, Eliot announced that he had written a long poem 'mostly when I was at Lausanne for treatment last winter' (L 530). It has for some while been supposed that the greater part of *The Waste Land* was composed in Switzerland; and with the publication of the facsimile of the original manuscript, some scholars have suggested that 'The Fire Sermon' was the first part of the poem to have been written, prompted to this by the different typewriters and paper used at various stages. The most convincing account, however, as offered by C.K. Stead, is that Eliot was wrong to suggest that most of the poem had been composed in Switzerland, and that in fact the greater part of it had been written before he left for the continent.[8] The vital shaping of the disparate mass, the excavation of the poem we know as *The Waste Land* from the sprawling series Eliot showed to Pound, took place in January 1922, with Pound able to announce to Eliot, in a letter written on 24 January, that 'the thing now runs from "April . . ." to "shantih" without a break'.

The probable facts are these: when Eliot told Quinn in May 1921 that his projected poem was partly on paper, it is likely that what he referred to were the parts of the manuscript headed 'He Do the Police In Different Voices', which he envisaged as the title for the whole poem. Part I, 'The Burial of the Dead', differs from 'The Burial of the Dead' as finally published principally in its starting with 53 lines of verse describing a night on the town, apparently in Boston, after which we encounter 'April is the cruellest month'. Part II, initially entitled 'In the Cage' but changed by Eliot to 'A Game of Chess', is broadly similar to the section as published. It incorporates lines and images from a poem 'The Death of the Duchess', which obviously preceded it. Precisely when these were written is uncertain; Stead makes the commonsensical assumption that the allusion to 'April' may indicate the month of composition; but there is apparently a letter of Wyndham Lewis's dated 7 February 1921, in which he talks of having been shown by Eliot a long new poem in four parts (what these four parts could have been, at that stage, is not obvious).[9] 'In the Cage' seems to have been composed when Eliot was apart from his wife, for after commenting enthusiastically on the typescript, she asks him to send her back the copy she has marked; this might indicate the period of her convalescence in the country.

'The Fire Sermon' as originally conceived was markedly different from what has survived, and was also different in style from what preceded it. It started with a set of rhyming couplets for 70 lines, mockingly depicting the morning activities of a twittering woman of social and intellectual fashion, Fresca; she is treated with sexual disgust. At some stage, on the verso of one of these typed sheets, Eliot has pencilled a first draft of what would later become the opening ten lines of the section ('The river's tent is broken . . .'). The unedifying couplets were followed, in the draft, by what was predominantly blank verse, much of which survived into the final version; this also contained a sententious denunciation of the inhabitants of London ('phantasmal gnomes'), unhesitatingly rejected by Pound when he was shown it. The section then continued in sneering quatrains, describing the loveless seduction of the typist by the house agent's clerk, as witnessed by Tiresias. On a sheet of paper, on the bottom half of which Eliot has written a first draft of his apostrophe to the gnomes of London, he had (presumably earlier) pencilled the first draft of his invocation of the city and of St Magnus Martyr (ll. 259–65 as published).

It has been argued that Eliot's use of heroic couplets and the heroic stanza, together with the moral stance taken, is attributable to his reading of Dryden; he did this during May 1921, for the essay which became 'John Dryden'; it is probable that a reading of Dryden led him to read Pope as well, whose influence is also detectable. If, then, we can assign these lines to the period immediately before his family arrived to visit (in June), then we can suppose that when he went to Margate, he had with him over 400 lines of typescript, together with some material still in manuscript. At Margate Eliot was meant to live quietly; but he did a small amount of composing. In a letter to Sidney Schiff provisionally dated 4 November 1921 he tells of having done 'a rough draft of part of Part III' (L 484); and it seems almost certain that this refers to the lines with which the section closes, beginning with 'The river sweats' (in the manuscript, the Thames-daughters outline their predicaments at slightly greater length).

It is hardly likely that Eliot would refer to 'Part III' unless the two previous parts were in existence; so it seems safe to conclude that when he left for Paris, he had with him the material from which the first three parts of his poem would be condensed. It is difficult to believe that he did not discuss this with Pound on the outward as well as the homeward journey. Whether or not he did, it now becomes clear that what was written at Lausanne was Parts IV, 'Death by Water', and V, 'What the Thunder Said'. If 'The Fire

Sermon' was looking rather a mess, 'Death by Water' as originally set forth in Eliot's fair-hand was a different kind of failure, attributable to over-organisation rather than the reverse. It comprises a long account of an ill-fated sea-voyage, which one feels is meant to conduce to a sense of awe and dread, but which is notable for an absence of intensity; of the 92 lines, only the final eight, which derived from the closing lines of 'Dans le Restaurant', were retained. The ponderousness of the original 'Death by Water' suggests the difficulty Eliot had with it; by contrast, 'What the Thunder Said' was a miracle of ease: 'OK from here on I think', Pound commented at the beginning of the manuscript, and offered only the slightest emendations. Something had happened in Lausanne, after the labour of Part IV, that enabled Eliot to relax the kind of unproductive control evident in 'Death by Water' (and in parts of 'The Fire Sermon'). The apparent effortlessness of this phase of composition – Eliot's own revisions were slight – seems to corroborate his notions that poetry involved a surrender of the self.

Two other people besides Eliot were involved in the making of the poem: his wife and Ezra Pound. It has become a commonplace of criticism that the tense, uneasy hopelessness of the couple who talk to each other in 'A Game of Chess' is drawn directly from the circumstances of Eliot's own unhappy and disintegrating marriage. Looking back from the 1960s, Eliot would attribute the state of mind out of which the poem came to his marriage (L xvii); but it is also clear from contemporary correspondence that Vivien's comments were valued by her husband: 'must wait for Vivien's opinion as to whether it is printable' (L 484). At her instigation he included two lines and omitted one, and they were close enough at this period for him to need her help with the *Criterion*, and for him to wish her to accompany him to Margate. A letter to his brother from Lausanne (13 December 1921) emphasised his reliance on her: '[Vivien] has had to do so much *thinking* for me' (L 493).

Pound's influence was decisive, as Eliot consistently acknowledged. His ear for the accurate word and the authentic cadence and his eye for the sharper image operate throughout. As he offered no comments on the first part of 'He Do the Police in Different Voices', we assume that Eliot had already decided to drop the opening scene. Pound's help was essential, however, in organising 'The Fire Sermon'; where he informed Eliot that the verse was simply not good enough, exploded 'b-ll-s' at the passage about 'phantasmal gnomes', and decimated the quatrains at the end to leave the encounter of the typist with her clerk less ob-trusively judged, if also less grammatically coherent. In Part IV, 'Death by Water', Pound's instantaneous conviction that all save the closing lines were unusable may have shaken Eliot's nerve, but it rescued his poem.

All the time Pound was diverting Eliot's poem from discursive-ness, whether due to an over-interpreted symbolic structure or to sententiousness, toward a greater concentration and immediacy – back, in short, toward the principles of imagism.[10] Wherever he detected too conscious an attitude on Eliot's part his editorial pencil was most active. Eliot usually assented to Pound's excisions, although he retained the lines about St Mary Woolnoth, among other small acts of salvage. But Pound's sense of a whole poem was stronger and clearer – even though when he mentioned it in the *New Age* of 30 March 1922, he described it as 'a very important sequence of poems'.[11] After Pound's initial clarification, Eliot was still wondering whether to use 'Gerontion' as a prelude, omit 'Death by Water', and incorporate other fragments. More tellingly still, when *The Waste Land* was to be first published, in the *Dial* in America and the *Criterion* in Britain, Eliot was prepared to con-template printing it in more than one instalment; but Pound's vociferous protest against this 'outrage' carried the day.[12] It is not without precedent that an editor should substantially determine the final shape of an author's manuscript, although it is rare in the case of poetry. Nonetheless, Pound's significant responsibility for the way *The Waste Land* turned out provokes two questions: the first is, how far does the actual process by which this poem was created and finished fit in with Eliot's theories about composition? And the second is, to what extent did the poem Pound discovered differ from the poem(s) Eliot had conceived?

Considering Eliot's emphasis on concepts of authority and re-sponsibility, and on the need for discriminating judgement, his reliance on Pound's determinations may seem strange. Yet a little reflection shows us that, in fact, what happened between the two poets corroborates much of Eliot's thinking. His model for the production of poetry, after all, was of an obscure and even painful stimulation occurring below the level of rational discourse: the writer's job was to elevate this, by dint of 'critical labour', from its dark origination into an accessible work of art. In their collabora-tion, Pound performs the labour of clarification and exposition which Eliot was himself unable to accomplish: in *The Waste Land*, the two necessary operations of inspiration and elaboration have separated, with Eliot creating and Pound constructing. But a further irony is that most of Pound's construction was concerned with laying bare the work's self-purposive creativity, and with eradicating those inert passages where Eliot's over-conscious direction had been detrimental to the spontaneous sources of his poem.

We might have expected a self-avowed 'classicist' to shoulder more directly the responsibility for his creation. But Eliot's was the awkward predicament of both recognising and distrusting the inner depths from which his poetry arose; he could not deny his poems, but he attempted to distance himself from their hidden forces by dissociating them from his personality, and by struggling to make these isolated intense moments conformable to a larger pattern. His insecurity can perhaps be seen, not only in his need for Pound's advice, but in his provision of notes for *The Waste Land*. Variously accounted for as a way of extending the poem to a more publishable length, as an effort to avert the charge of plagiarism, and as an erudite joke, the notes may also be a strategy whereby Eliot redeems his poem from its origins in the isolation of his psyche, and makes it respectable by making it explicable. Indeed, his habits of literary allusion, as well as perhaps suggesting the cultural acquisitiveness of a nervous American, may also be defensive: as if he were fearful of assuming full authorial responsibility for any impulse that could not be verified from an external source. His own originality was in many ways a threat; and it should be remembered that the importance of criticism as the establishment of a community of judgement, was that it gave a rational and impersonal account of processes that may be – in Wallace Stevens's phrase – 'extreme, fortuitous, personal'.

Our second question concerned the relationship between the poem Eliot wrote and the poem Pound discerned within it. It is debatable whether the singular noun is appropriate in Eliot's case, for despite his references to a 'long poem', it seems to have existed for him as series of fragments, whose inter-relatedness was not necessarily apparent. It was a characteristic of poems like 'The Hollow Men' and *Ash-Wednesday*, as well as *The Waste Land*, that they were assembled out of separate items. But this is not to say that the poem is a kind of automatic writing, coherent only in a mirage of retrospect: it is clear that when Eliot argued with Pound that the epigraph from Conrad's *Heart of Darkness* was 'somewhat elucidative' of *The Waste Land*, he had a notion of what his poem was 'about'; and even if we feel that his reference to Jessie Weston's *From Ritual to Romance* (which it is possible he had not fully read) has sent commentators on a wild-grail chase, readers do not on the whole feel that the poem is without internal direction.

But was Eliot's direction the same as Pound's? Some critics have argued, since the revelation of the original material, that Pound's intervention was in part regrettable; and when Eliot presented John Quinn with the manuscripts, Quinn commented that he would not have made all the cuts that Pound suggested. It is difficult, however, to believe that the excluded portions represent much of a loss. The opening scene of Boston night-life, with its curiously tentative colloquialism, attempts a mode which Eliot was to exploit much more successfully in *Sweeney Agonistes*; Eliot himself saw that it did not belong here. As for the passages Pound deleted, the couplets on Fresca and the original quatrains, in 'The Fire Sermon', are simply a much less compelling use of the resources of language than the rest of the poem; and the account of the ill-fated voyage removed from 'Death by Water' displays a well-wrought earnestness appropriate to a prize poem. Eliot was later to elaborate a theory of the necessity that a poem of any length should vary its intensity; this would be his practice in the Quartets. But it is doubtful that these duller stretches of *The Waste Land* are attributable to any tactic of variation; more likely, that they simply represent the periods when Eliot had been deserted by his muse.

It is probably fair to say that Pound's emendations worked against Eliot's conscious intentions, for it was precisely Eliot's strained assertiveness and over-formulated imaginings that he sought to extirpate. He had been unable to persuade his compatriot to omit the 'Hamlet' passage from 'Prufrock'; here he was surer of his ground, discerning that the 'true' poem was at variance with its author's conscious purpose. The original was a curious intermingling of the spontaneously right and the laboriously wrong; a loose assemblage, whose general themes could be discerned as the futility of people's lives, the barrenness of their relationships, the distastefulness of their bodies, and the corrupt inauthenticity of their experience. 'He Do the Police in Different Voices' was, in other words, attempting a critique of modern life: its acceptance of tawdry substitutes, its disconnection from the past, and its need for purgation. By removing the overt denunciations and by breaking up the regular verses, whose orderliness laid claim to an unearned authority, Pound diminished the element of assertiveness and encouraged a poem which was less a statement than it was an enactment, and more a confession than an indictment.

Pound adjudged the poem to be 'the justification of the "movement", of our modern experiment, since 1900'.[13] Eliot remained unsure enough to wish to append the defensive notes; but the attempts to establish an internal coherence through quests for the Holy Grail and the character of Tiresias lack conviction. For although there remain general themes, which embrace the decay of love and the futility of modern society, the collapse of values and the search for order, to attempt to articulate these in terms of an intellectual position at which the poem arrives, or a summary that it offers, is to try to reinstitute the poem as the tract Eliot mistakenly attempted to produce, which interfered with the poem that was urgently writing itself. The fact is that any 'meaning' derived from *The Waste Land*, and expressed as a paraphrase of Eliot's intentions or beliefs, is incomparably less interesting and productive than our experience of the poem itself.

The revelations offered by comparing the finished poem with the original material are twofold: we can see, for example, how 'rats' alley', that vista of futility, counterpoises the hopeful setting of 'the hyacinth garden' – a connection which Eliot subsequently obscured (Ts 11, 13). But if the drafts reveal minor coherences of this kind, their more significant revelation is of a major incoherence, making it apparent that Eliot himself did not know what his poem was: and that, furthermore, the stronger his conscious sense of what he wished to say, the less appropriate was the poetry he wrote. The poem as we have it is the result of opportunism rather than an overall design; and this means that it exists for us far more in our sense of what it is, than in our sense of what Eliot may have been trying to say in it. What, then, is our experience of *The Waste Land*? Most obviously in reading it, we respond to its disjunctions and dislocations; our sense is of its variety of modes and voices, together with our frustration at not quite achieving any resolution of its multiplicity. If only we could really understand what the thunder says, perhaps we could make sense of it all. But to 'make sense' of this poem is to do rather more than Eliot himself did, is to introduce a consistency of purpose and design that its very procedures refute. We should not attempt to make a coherent statement from a poem which is largely 'about' its own inability to make a coherent statement.

The poem is, of course, something of an echo chamber; various 'influences' may be discerned. The very fragmentariness of its structure may owe something to the *Satyricon* of Petronius (quoted as an epigraph); there are obvious allusions to Dante, and to Shakespeare; 'He Do the Police in Different Voices', coming from *Our Mutual Friend*, alerts us to the relevance of Dickens's novel, and its London of decay and corruption, its Thames that conceals corpses; also relevant is the London of Joseph Conrad; and what Eliot does for London in *The Waste Land* is analogous to what Joyce does for Dublin in *Ulysses*: to observe the contemporary city refracted through the lens of mythical association. But none of these, among the myriad influences and allusions which we could identify, forms or focuses the poem.

It provides a setting for many and disparate voices: a voice which declares – with appropriately Germanic inflexion – 'In the mountains, there you feel free', as well as the scriptural voice which offers us 'fear in a handful of dust'. It parades a variety of styles; there is the transition from the high, studied rhetoric with which 'A Game of Chess' opens, to the cockneyisms at its close. There is a strangeness in this collocation of different styles, similar to the *mélange* of reality, which contains both the 'inexplicable splendour' of St Magnus Martyr's Ionian allusions and an industrial cityscape of canals and gasworks. The poem offers a variety of languages: Latin, Greek, German, French, Italian and Sanskrit, as well as English; it is rather like turning a radio dial, and hearing disconnected snatches of speech – speech from different ages as well as different nations.

Such a metaphor suggests arbitrariness, yet there does appear to be what might be called a 'thematic drift' within the poem. Small items like repeated phrases, and the larger fact of its division into five implicitly progressive parts, suggest a purposive structure. Ideas of sleep giving way to waking, of dryness to rain; the concept of the city, both as London and as all cities, with its flowing river conducting to the wider sea and distant shores; the inference of a quest, of an enigma to be riddled, and of a purgation to be undergone as part of this, all operate upon the reader's willingness to collaborate – like Pound – in shaping the poem. But at the centre is the fact that the quest is indecisive, the purposiveness unfulfilled; the poem remains radically 'unclosed', like a deliberately obscured allegory. Whatever the overt influences upon it, its literary antecedents may be *The Rime of the Ancient Mariner* and 'Childe Roland to the Dark Tower Came', for like them it enacts a rite of passage both portentous and inconsequential. Does its variety of voice and style affirm cacophony or polyphony? The last line Eliot actually composed himself ('These fragments I have shored against my ruin') does not finally reveal whether the shoring or the ruination takes effect. Have these disparate experiences been amalgamated within the poem, or are they brokenly exhibited as the Ozymandian fragments of a failed enterprise of integration? Do all these different voices resonating in the poem – including, we suppose, Eliot's own – amount to a chorus, or a babel?

The blending of an individual voice into an accumulating chorus is an appropriate image for the conjunction of an individual talent with tradition. 'He do the police in different voices' may denote the hope that 'different voices', despite their apparent fortuity, might in the end add up to 'the police' – a regulating and arbitrating body. But however much Eliot may have wished to be a poet such as Pope, imperiously disposing his meanings and affirming continuity between his endeavours and those of his great predecessors, his own predicament was that he lacked Pope's confident relation both to his own and to preceding ages. *The Waste Land* invokes the noble past primarily to express estrangement from it, and displays a fractured and inverse relation to the literary canon – figured not as 'monuments' arranged in an 'ideal order', so much as 'a heap of broken images'. Yet the sense of estrangement is not total: St Magnus Martyr, freighted with its sense of the past, persists in the poem; and the original drafts contain phrases which evoke the continuity of past in present.[14] There is, nonetheless, an air of the mournful inaccessibility of the past and its inexplicable splendours; we might aspire to be Antony and Cleopatra, but we're really Albert and Lil.

The magic heart of this poem lies in its incoherent coherence: its organising principle is not in any fixity of purpose or of meaning, but lies in the processes of transition, whereby one voice becomes another, one scene melts into another, one style replaces another. The note identifying Tiresias as 'the most important personage in the poem' is appropriate to the extent that, himself sexually metamorphosed, he presides in a poem of transformations: in which divans turn into beds, nymphs into good-time girls, the Thames into the Ganges, eyes into pearls, and consciousness into regenerative oblivion. It is this protean quality that Pound seems to have divined, a logic of the imagination that he sought to protect from the drably conceptual manifestations, born of Eliot's critical guilt at having produced so structureless and unaccountable a poem; he defended its liberating unfixedness against its author's efforts to impose a unifying – and therefore falsifying – cohesion.

Because *The Waste Land* is habitually read as a document of anguish, it is worth remarking that its procedures are more mysterious, and also more humorous, than such a view suggests. A certain kind of wit (using Eliot's own definition as 'the recognition, within an experience, of other kinds of experience which are possible') is present at the opening of 'The Fire Sermon', where the satirical exclusion of pastoral vision coexists with its elegiac presence, and a world of Arcadian possibility both is and is not admitted; there is a comicality in the scene with Madame Sosostris – less obtrusively managed than the conversations in the pub. 'Phlebas the Phoenician' is an incipiently fatuous alliteration, compounded by the addition of 'fortnight' and 'forgot'. Yet the point about these effects – which returns us to the definition of wit – is that none of them is blatant, none can be certainly defined as one thing, not another. The notes, too, have their sly humour: unilluminatingly cross-referencing lines 115 and 195, for example, or drily understating Eliot's personal reaction to St Mary Woolnoth's tolling in the hour of office drudgery.

Whatever its humour, when the poem was completed Eliot proceeded toward another nervous breakdown: as therapy, composing it had no lasting effect, because the problem it addressed could be solved only in the religious, not the literary, dimensions of his life. At this stage of his life, when (according to Spender) he was considering the possibility of Buddhism, a suitable religious synthesis had not presented itself. Eliot's dissatisfaction was such that only something which transcended the conditions of the actual world – as literature cannot – could allay it. *The Waste Land* is not in any real sense a Christian poem, despite its churches and chapels and biblical intonations; but it exhibits the conditions out of which Eliot's Christianity would grow. This is why at the first publication the note on 'shantih' described the Christian formula of 'the Peace which passeth understanding' as 'a feeble translation'; subsequently, it is given as 'our equivalent to this word'. Because it is a secular poem about a world which is contemplated as disordered, *The Waste Land* is itself unresolved, admitting to no redeeming higher meaning; and it is one of the major differences between it and *Four Quartets*, by which time Eliot's Christianity is evident, that these later poems are susceptible of analysis and paraphrase, of a separation of 'meaning' from 'experience'.

Eliot was often diffident about recently-completed work; but in spite of his uncertainty about the nature of this poem, once it was shaped he appears to have been free from doubts about its quality: writing to John Quinn on 25 June 1922 he described it as the best he had ever done. By June the following year, when he recited the poem to Leonard and Virginia Woolf, who were to publish it in England, he seems to have given a memorable and secure performance: 'Eliot dined last Sunday & read his poem,' she wrote in her Journal, 'he sang it & chanted it [&] rhythmed it'.[15] Before then, he had had to encounter the problems of its American publication, about which he was writing to Quinn in his June letter. Having initially been satisfied by the price offered by the *Dial*, he became enraged to discover how much more Thayer had paid George Moore for an insignificant short story. Moreover, as the poem was to appear as a book, as well as in a magazine, the issue of priority of publication arose. In December through Quinn's mediation matters were arranged: whereby the *Dial* agreed to award Eliot's poem its annual prize of $2000, and to buy 350 copies of the book when it was published (with the addition of the notes) one month after its appearance in the magazine. *The Waste Land* appeared in the *Criterion* in October and the *Dial* in November 1922; Boni and Liveright published it in New York on 15 December 1922, and the Hogarth Press issued it in London on 12 September 1923.

Quinn – who insisted on buying the original manuscripts rather than accepting them as a gift – reported to Eliot that the poem had surprised Horace Liveright by selling well, and going quickly into a second impression. Its appearance had, however, been skilfully stage-managed: the *Dial* announced its award in the same month it was published as a book. In the same issue there was a weighty review by Edmund Wilson, in which he hailed Eliot as 'one of our authentic poets', and welcomed his 'complicated' poem as an analysis of 'the starvation of a whole generation'. Not all reviewers were as appreciative; but controversy is no foe to sales, and the debate which ensued about this very strange poem with notes (Pound thought these played an important part in capturing people's attention) began to establish it as a matter on which it was necessary to have an opinion. Given the nature of *The Waste Land*, it was to be expected that there should be some antagonistic reviews: nor is it surprising that in the United States Louis Untermeyer dismissed it as 'a pompous parade of erudition', and in Britain J. C. Squire announced himself unable to make head or tail of it. But even these adverse reviews could hardly fail to suggest this was an unusual poem; and when the *Manchester Guardian* pronounced it to be a 'mad medley', this may have made more impression on its readers than tepid praise would have done.

The *TLS*, having noticed the poem as 'of exceptional importance' in a brief review of the first issue of the *Criterion*, changed its mind (and its reviewer) by the time the Hogarth Press published the poem, when the writer (Edgell Rickword) took the poem to be evidence that Eliot's gift had gone 'awry' – a view which was also shared by a more sympathetic reader, Clive Bell. But of greater interest than these are the reactions of Eliot's peers. Pound obviously thought the poem was a triumph; and Conrad Aiken, who was perhaps the more perceptive reader in the end, reviewed it as 'unquestionably important, unquestionably brilliant'; adding that it succeeded 'by virtue of its incoherence, not of its plan' (Aiken had recognised fragments of earlier poems he had been shown). John Crowe Ransom, however, disliked the poem, which he rebuked for its disconnectedness and its irreverence toward the literature of the past (a charge which Allen Tate answered).[16] William Carlos Williams has recorded in his *Autobiography* his sense of desolation at the publication and success of *The Waste Land*, which he felt to have retarded his own endeavours at accessible poetry, by giving the poem back to the academies, as he put it. Against this view, it has to be said that not everybody in the academies wanted this poem, which by some was construed as an assault on established values: so we have the paradox of a poem being seen simultaneously, by different readers, as an act of revolution and of conservative retrogression.

Even unappreciative reviews acknowledged Eliot to be a figure in the forefront of modern English letters, a man whose work had to be attended to, whether one liked it or not: not only was he a poet and critic, he was by this time also the editor of a new quarterly. His public career seemed to be advancing successfully; but behind it lay a tense and unhappy private life. Some of this tension was due to the very pressures his success created, as may be seen in the case of the *Criterion*. Eliot had returned from his six-month leave of absence, in January 1922, with his poem written, but the review yet to appear, and Lady Rothermere waiting: this required urgent attention. He came back, also, to the same cycle of domestic difficulty with a wife whose ill-health provoked his own, and to the problems with his job at the bank, which offered a consoling security but required exasperating amounts of his time. It seems probable that Eliot would have undergone another serious crisis, had not Vivien prevailed upon her father to finance a summer holiday for him that year.

Pound, who had heard from Aldington about Eliot's renewed decline, set back in motion his earlier scheme of financial support, under the name *Bel Esprit*: as before, its aims were to secure enough pledged contributions over a sufficient period, to enable Eliot to leave the bank and devote himself to writing. He set about this energetically, without at first consulting Eliot; Ottoline Morrell and Virginia Woolf established the 'Eliot Fellowship' a little later, and the two proposals went forward together. The most visible result of all this was stress and irritation: Eliot had mixed feelings about being an object of charity, the proponents of the two schemes doubted each other's methods, and both were put out by Eliot's indecisiveness. A libellous article in the *Liverpool Daily Post*, virtually accusing Eliot of breach of promise toward his guarantors, exacerbated his unhappiness. The problem was that, however little he enjoyed the daily grind of banking, it paid him a secure salary and imposed a structure on his life, as well as offering security for Vivien; perhaps most importantly of all, he was financially independent. The prospect of having much more time to spend, presumably at home, can hardly have seemed unambiguously attractive; both schemes lapsed, and Eliot was to spend a little more time under the pavement.

Refreshed by his summer holiday, he returned to tackle the problems of the *Criterion*. It was his intention to produce a serious and truly European review; he engaged skilled, literate linguists like Aldington and Flint to write regular reviews of major foreign periodicals. Eliot's view of the project, expressed in his letters, alternated between a self-deprecating suggestion that it might, at most, accomplish a little good, and a belief that by this organ he could mould taste and reform errors. The scheme was hatched in great secrecy, with Eliot swearing his correspondents to silence; this can be partly attributed to his sense, expressed in a letter to Aldington of 13 July 1922, of the pleasure many would take at his failure: 'I am quite aware how obnoxious I am to perhaps the larger part of the literary world of London and that there will be a great many jackals swarming about waiting for my bones' (L 541). If he failed, he supposed that he would 'have to retire to obscurity or Paris like Ezra'.

As things turned out, his magazine did not fail. It would for a while achieve an influence out of proportion to the number of subscribers – which at its peak did not reach 1000. At the beginning, Eliot's editorship was anonymous, because he wished to avoid any possible repercussions at the bank. His 'anonymity' was partial: amongst the literary world it was an open secret who was editing the *Criterion*, and whose judgement its style and content reflected. At first, however, there was no obvious editorial policy: the *TLS* reviewer, observing that in the first number *The Waste Land* was published alongside contributions from literary elder statesmen such as George Saintsbury and Sturge Moore, concluded that the journal did not represent any particular opinion, so much as that it was the organ for 'those who are genuinely interested in good literature'. Here already we can see the difference between Eliot's decision not to alienate the old school, and the editorial policies of men like Pound and Lewis, who would not have consented to any compromise.

The first issues of the *Criterion*, then, neither announced nor embodied a party line; in them were to be found critical essays and creative writing, from the pens of such as Hermann Hesse, Roger Fry, Luigi Pirandello, Julien Benda, Virginia Woolf, Herbert Read, Paul Valéry, W.B. Yeats, E.M. Forster and Richard Aldington: all of whom were represented in the first volume. From the beginning there was a discernible international flavour, and the earlier issues contained a higher proportion of literary material than later was the case. A process of gradual definition of its aims took place. In the fourth issue (July 1923) Eliot published a brief note, signed with his initials, on 'The Function of a Literary Review'. This he defined as 'to maintain the autonomy and disinterestedness of literature, and at the same time to exhibit the relations of literature (. . .) to all the other activities which, together with literature, are the components of life'. Such a note, asserting the difficult balance of separation and connection central to Eliot's thinking, was hardly a clarion-call; and in October of that year a flyer was inserted into the magazine, which offered a less defensive view:

> The *Criterion* aims at the examination of first principles in criticism, at the valuation of the new, and the revaluation of old

works of literature according to principles, and the illustration of these principles in creative writing. It aims at the affirmation and development of tradition. It aims at determining the relation of literature to other humane pursuits. It aims at the assertion of order and discipline, and the maintenance of order and discipline in literary taste.[17]

This sounds several Eliotian notes; and that the 'tradition' to be affirmed was no provincial English affair, was shown by the section on 'Foreign Reviews' which appeared from the third number onward, consisting of short notices of the major foreign periodicals. All this underlined the internationalist tendency, and it is worth remarking on the irony that *The Waste Land* should first appear in the *Criterion*: for if the journal's function was to affirm a fundamental unity in 'the mind of Europe', the poem as surely suggests its disintegration and collapse.

Initially the effect of editorship seemed to be adverse, provoking a crisis about which he complained in a letter to Quinn of 12 March 1923, when he roundly declared, 'I wish to heaven I had never taken up the *Criterion*' (Ts xxvi). Its demands on his time – without equivalent financial rewards – made it seem ever more impossible to combine these activities with his regular job. Thanks to J.M. Keynes, he had the offer of the post of Literary Editor of the *Nation*; but the salary (£500) was less than he earned at Lloyds, and the job was only guaranteed for six months. Not for the first time, Eliot exasperated his friends by seeming to dither: then he turned down the offer, and Leonard Woolf was appointed instead. In fact, 1923 was another intense year for Eliot: Vivien was very ill; the necessity and the difficulty of leaving the bank pressed upon him, for he needed the money to meet medical expenses. But if his journal added to the stress, he well knew its importance to his career, offering as it did a position of influence; those who attended the weekly *Criterion* lunches at a pub and the monthly dinners at a restaurant, were to remember his unemphatic but unchallenged presidence, and his occasional instructions to reviewers to sink a hatchet into an overblown reputation.

It was becoming ever more apparent that, whatever its financial benefits, banking must give way. Eliot contemplated setting up another review as a means of making money (and by leaving the bank he could be paid for what he did on the *Criterion*); but in the event, if his editorship provoked the crisis, it was also the means to its solution. In July 1925 came the first problem, when Lady

Rothermere, reaching the end of her three-year contract to underwrite the venture, indicated her unwillingness to continue as sole backer. Negotiations then took place with the newly-formed publishing-house of.Faber and Gwyer, to whose chairman, Geoffrey Faber, Eliot had been recommended by both Bruce Richmond and Charles Whibley. The upshot was that the firm entered into a five-year agreement with Lady Rothermere, whereby they bore half the costs of the magazine; Eliot was to continue as the sole editor. In addition, in November 1925 he became a director of Faber and Gwyer; they had at first been looking only for a part-time appointment, but Eliot had impressed Faber sufficiently, that he invited him to join the board. In this way, Eliot was released from the toils of banking; but without the cost of having to relinquish an office routine which would henceforth, as in the past, be an important part of his life.

Faber and Gwyer was small and inexperienced; but like the *Criterion* it offered Eliot the opportunity to exert an influence on the literary scene, which grew with his prestige. The effects were mutually beneficial, in fact; thanks largely to Eliot's presence on its board, Faber and Faber (the name was changed in 1929) would for a considerable period become the pre-eminent publishers of poetry in Britain. The sequence of events which led to his incorporation on the board of directors illustrates how correct Eliot was to have regarded it as necessary to cultivate the right people; people whose advice given in the eminent seclusion of clubroom or senior common-room constituted a network of power. Another introduction made during this period would be significant for the course of his life: some time in 1923 Richard Cobden-Sanderson, who published the *Criterion*, introduced Eliot to William Force Stead. Stead was a former diplomat who had subsequently taken holy orders; and it was he who encouraged Eliot to explore more deeply the writing of seventeenth-century Anglicans, in particular that of Lancelot Andrewes, Bishop of Winchester. This development would lead to his baptism and confirmation in the Church of England.

The next book Eliot published after *The Waste Land* was *Homage to John Dryden*, issued by the Hogarth Press in October 1924. It was perhaps a measure of the slackening of his activity in this department that, when Leonard and Virginia Woolf suggested a volume of criticism, he should be obliged to revert to three essays published in the *TLS* in 1921. Even so, it was not a bad decision: in book form, the essays were to have a considerable influence – as well as teasing the educated reading public with the notion that the author of *The Waste Land* could admire a poet like Dryden. For those who were themselves to become influential critics, such as F.R. Leavis, the book confirmed the impression created by *The Sacred Wood*, that here was a serious and discriminating voice. For several generations, it would be impossible for a discussion of Donne or Marvell to proceed without some allusion to Eliot's essays.

His creative writing had taken a new turn. In 1923 he had been engaged on what turned out to be an abortive project; the production of a kind of verse drama whose rhythms would be informed by something of the urgency of a beating drum. In September 1924 he discussed this at the Reform Club with Arnold Bennett; a writer whom he consulted, probably, because he trusted Bennett's feel for low-life effects. This project, which can be seen to have its roots in *The Waste Land*, and which prefigured the interest in drama which dominated the latter part of Eliot's writing career, nevertheless led nowhere. What survives, published as *Sweeny Agonistes* in 1932, remains for us a tantalising glimpse along a passage Eliot did not take, toward a door he never fully opened. Many have regretted that he turned away from the nervous vigour of this experiment, toward the measured urbanity of his later work.

Eliot was, in fact, already moving away from *The Waste Land* – 'a thing of the past so far as I am concerned' (L 596). In this letter to Aldington of November 1922 Eliot asserted he was 'feeling toward a new form and style'; and this probably referred to his dramatic experiment. But his profounder movement, as became clear, was toward what he would define as orthodoxy, and a more disciplined and monitored inner life. The intensities of *Sweeney Agonistes*, its sardonic glints of violence revealed and then suppressed, could have little place in such a development. The poetry he wrote during this period continued the sporadic creation of the parts of a poem yet to be assembled. At the beginning of 1925 the *Criterion* published 'Three Poems' by Thomas Eliot (for once emphasising his apostolic name): 'Eyes I dare not meet in dreams', 'Eyes that I last saw in tears', and 'The eyes are not here'; the last two became Parts II and IV of 'The Hollow Men'. In March that year the *Dial* published as 'The Hollow Men' three poems: 'We are the hollow men', 'Eyes I dare not meet in dreams', and 'The eyes are not here'. Not until the publication of *Poems 1909–1925* did 'The Hollow Men' emerge in its final form of five parts, with epigraphs. This volume had been published by Faber and Gwyer on 23 November; at the end of the following month Conrad Aiken remarked in a letter that it had already sold 700 copies. Eliot had indeed arrived.

NOTES

1. 'New Poets', *New Statesman*, XVI (January 1921); in Grant.
2. '"Ulysses", Order, and Myth', in *Selected Prose of T.S. Eliot*, ed. Kermode, (London, 1975), p. 177. This selection also contains the early essay 'Reflections on *Vers Libre*'.
3. Tate, p. 21.
4. Ibid., p. 55.
5. Ibid., pp. 2–3.
6. Quoted in Bernard Bergonzi, *T.S. Eliot* (London, 1972), p. 56.
7. March, p. 38.
8. C.K. Stead, *Pound, Yeats, Eliot, and the Modern Movement* (London, 1986), especially pp. 359–63. Hereafter cited as Stead.
9. See Ackroyd, pp. 110, 345.
10. This is argued by Stead.
11. See Noel Stock, *Life of Ezra Pound* (Harmondsworth, 1974), p. 309.
12. See Pound's letter of January 1931 to Harriet Monroe, in *Letters*, ed. Paige, p. 310.
13. Ibid., p. 248.
14. I have in mind phrases such as 'I have seen and see' (Ts 31), and 'I have heard and hear' & 'the walls / Of Magnus Martyr stood, and stand' (Ts 37).
15. VWD II, p. 178.
16. These and other reviews are gathered in Grant, vol. I.
17. Quoted in Margolis, pp. 39–40.

5

1926–1934

This period could be viewed with equal plausibility as one of crisis or of consolidation. In these years, Eliot took three important steps affecting his private life, which were to have profound consequences for him as a writer: he was baptised and confirmed into the Church of England; he adopted British citizenship; and he separated, finally and absolutely, from his wife. Momentous as each of these decisions was, they in fact make apparent an impetus which had been growing throughout the preceding period. Eliot had already begun his move toward Christianity, and emotionally if not yet administratively had settled that his future lay in Britain; the difficulties of his marriage to Vivien had already begun to seem terminal. These were not sudden ruptures with his past, but were to some degree the formalisation of his future; and in terms of his career, his reputation grew, the *Criterion* continued, and Faber and Gwyer became more solidly established. Few seriously disputed that Eliot was a major figure, automatically to be bracketed with Joyce and (less a matter of consensus) Pound and Lawrence, as a seminal figure in modern literature.

Such a view of consolidation, however, errs in the other direction, by making matters seem too straightforward. Although by 1934 Eliot's was a voice which commanded attention, his status as a kind of founding father had its drawbacks. There had risen up a new generation of poets – chief among them W.H. Auden – whose voices were not always in harmony with his; and to some readers these writers seemed to be more exciting representatives of the contemporary. As Eliot's personal development began to be reflected in his writing and his public career, there were those amongst his devotees who were caught unprepared by his conversion, which had the appearance of suddenness to them. Inevitably, given the time-lag between composition and publication, and given the time-lag between publication and general acceptance, readers were acclimatising themselves to *The Waste Land*, at a time when Eliot had moved toward a different kind of poetry,

103

and was working from different premises.

So although the years from 1926 to 1934 continue the developments of previous years, they nonetheless seemed to some observers to mark a schism or a change of direction. Eliot did begin to write a new kind of poetry; and the nature of the change was most sharply illustrated in 1934, when London saw the first performances of two contrasting theatrical experiments by Eliot: *Sweeney Agonistes* and *The Rock*. The first commemorated a direction Eliot failed to take, after the publication of *The Waste Land*; the second indicated the course on which he was embarked. As it happens, these two pieces in a sense begin and end the period with which we are concerned: for *Sweeney Agonistes*, although written earlier, was first published (as 'Fragment of a Prologue' and 'Fragment of an Agon') in the *Criterion*, in October 1926 and January 1927; *The Rock* was published by Faber and Faber at the end of May 1934. There is a considerable difference between them, as the following extracts show:

> When you're alone in the middle of the night and
>   you wake in a sweat and a hell of a fright
> When you're alone in the middle of the bed and
>   you wake like someone hit you in the head
> You've had a cream of a nightmare dream and
>   you've got the hoo-ha's coming to you.
> Hoo hoo hoo
> You dreamt you waked up at seven o'clock and it's
>   foggy and it's damp and it's dawn and it's dark
> And you wait for a knock and the turning of a lock
>   for you know the hangman's waiting for you.
> And perhaps you're alive
> And perhaps you're dead
> Hoo ha ha
> Hoo ha ha
>
> 　　　　　　　　　(*Sweeney Agonistes*, CPP 125–6)

> And now you live dispersed on ribbon roads,
> And no man knows or cares who is his neighbour
> Unless his neighbour makes too much disturbance,
> But all dash to and fro in motor cars,
> Familiar with the roads and settled nowhere.
> Nor does the family even move about together,

But every son would have his motor cycle,
And daughters ride away on casual pillions.

(*The Rock*)

The lines from *The Rock* (CPP 152–3) entirely lack the rhythmic
urgency transmitted by the earlier work: a deficiency only partly
explained by the fact that Eliot was writing for a chorus (the lines
from *Sweeney* are also spoken in unison). Given the differing
immediacy of these passages, we are inclined to suspect that in the
first Eliot is talking of something he knows about, but that the
parsonical inflexions of the second show him addressing a topic on
which he has opinions rather than experience (and does he intend
these daughters straddling 'casual pillions' to be humorously
smutty?). Both deal with conditions of loneliness, but we find
ourselves intimately compelled by the 'you' of the first passage,
whereas the 'you' of the second implicates us in nothing very
pressing, and quickly loses its specificity in generalised evocations
of 'no man', 'all', and 'the family'.

In addition to this contrast in the very language, the circumstances of each performance in 1934 could hardly have been more
different: *Sweeney Agonistes*, with its handful of characters, was
played before a small audience in a room without a stage, by
Rupert Doone's Group Theatre. *The Rock*, with its large cast, its
elaborate set and scene-changes, and its orchestra, ran for two
weeks at Sadlers Wells, playing to a house of 1500 each night. Yet
little as this comparison suggests it, *The Rock* represented an artistic
renewal for Eliot, an emergence from the doldrums amid which his
creative impulse had become becalmed.

There was little obvious sign of such a fallow period, in 1926. *Poems
1909–1925* was selling well; his journal, renamed the *New Criterion*
to denote the changed management, set out to clarify its aims. A
mark of Eliot's reputation was that he had been invited by Trinity
College, Cambridge, to deliver the Clark Lectures for that year (the
following year E.M. Forster was to give them, which became his
book *Aspects of the Novel*). There is a photograph, taken in 1926 by
his brother Henry outside the premises of Faber and Gwyer, in
which Eliot appears jaunty, even dandyish: in a double-breasted
suit whose upper pocket spills a handkerchief, spats on his feet
and a bowler on his head, the new director leans onto his walking-
cane, his gaze direct from the shadow of his hat-brim, while a shaft

of sunlight casts into relief an enigmatical smile.[1]

Perhaps the enigma outweighs the smile. The very completeness of Eliot's appearance here, with every accessory in place, reminds us of the degree to which his clothing was costume, announcing or defining a role. From Virginia Woolf's early quip about expecting Eliot 'in a four-piece suit', to Herbert Read's remarks about the rather strange, large-check knee-breeches which Eliot affected early on, friends noted the significance of Eliot's dress. He himself endowed Prufrock with some of his own clothes-consciousness, alert to the meaning of a correctly-pinned neck-tie, or to the gesture of white flannel trousers. In an age more formal than our own, Eliot seems to have stood out as more formal than most; and such formality can of course be a highly-developed defence-mechanism, a desire to be impregnably correct.

The suspicion that his immaculate poise concealed a less finely-balanced interior was felt by various of Eliot's friends. Conrad Aiken had expressed in a letter of 1922 his opinion that Eliot 'cried out for analysis', and in a letter of January 1926 he told of Eliot's strange reply to a note of congratulation on *Poems 1909–1925*, which Aiken had sent him from hospital in London: the response had been a page torn from the *Midwives Gazette*, with phrases referring to types of vaginal discharge underlined. Aiken took this as another symptom of the ferocity he sensed lying within his fellow-countryman's composed demeanour. There were others who thought that Eliot's calm concealed a hidden force: Virginia Woolf, shortly after meeting him for the first time, was writing in her diary that 'the odd thing about Eliot is that his eyes are lively & youthful when the cast of his face & the shape of his sentences is formal & even heavy' (September 1920); and she confirmed her sense of tension and paradox in an entry later that year:

> A mouth twisted & shut; not a single line free & easy; all caught, pressed, inhibited; but great driving power some where – & my word what concentration of the eye when he argues!

As intimacy between them grew, Virginia Woolf would lose her sense of Eliot's hidden dangerousness; but she never seems to have lost her sense of a degree of artifice in his self-presentation, nor of the conflict of forces within him: in November 1934 she was noting in him 'the wild eye still; but all rocky, yellow, riven, & constricted'.[2]

The increasingly unhappy circumstances of Eliot's marriage must have added to the posed brittleness of his demeanour in front of other people. Yet he kept up his faith in his wife's abilities to the extent of letting her contribute pseudonymously to the *Criterion* up until 1925: she wrote commentaries, stories, and the occasional poem, using names whose initials were 'F.M.'. What is even odder than that these light (but not unaccomplished) pieces should appear in a publication aspiring to a heavyweight reputation, is the fact that some of her contributions quite obviously touch on her relations with her husband, the editor. Perhaps most obvious is Fanny Marlow's 'Fête Galante' in July 1925, with its description of an 'American financier' who is also a 'marvellous' if unprolific poet. The character Sibylla, seeing him leaning 'with exaggerated grace' against the fireplace at a social occasion, is 'struck afresh by his strange appearance':

The heavy slumbering white face, thickly powdered; the long hooded eyes, unseeing, leaden-heavy; the huge protuberant nose, and the somehow inadequate sullen mouth, the lips a little reddened. His head was exceptionally large, and not well shaped; the hair thin, and plastered tightly down.[3]

– 'What is wrong, what is missing?', she asks herself.

These curious items can only have appeared with Eliot's active collusion, so it should not be supposed that they are intimate confessions; there must have been an element of games-playing involved. Nonetheless, it was a strange game to play, given that no matter what the element of caricature in the above description, it contains details (such as Eliot's use of cosmetics) which are verified from other contemporary sources. The portrait hints at a certain languid menace attaching to this character; and perhaps the fact that pieces such as this were essentially 'in-jokes' recognisable by a privileged few reminds us, not only that Eliot was a practical joker, but that practical joking and the adoption of deliberate disguises are also exercises of a power which is by no means necessarily benevolent or ingenuous.

This is because such behaviour can be a form of aggression, which masquerades as playfulness. In the case of Eliot's strange missive to Aiken, it is not clear whether this was a snub, an outburst of sexual revulsion, or a comment by Eliot on his own poetry – the difficult obstetrics of poetic creativity is a metaphor we

encounter in his critical writing. Some commentators have diagnosed an incipient hysteria in Eliot's verse, whenever it touches on
female sexuality; and there is some evidence outside his writing
that he suffered from an extreme physical squeamishness. Leonard
Woolf tells the story of taking a walk in the country with his wife
and Eliot; Woolf dropped behind to urinate, and when he explained this on catching up with the others, Eliot, shocked, asserted that not only could he not himself have done this, he
certainly would not have confessed so openly as Woolf had done.
Apparently, he could not bring himself to shave in front of his wife
(which suggests he must have conceived of Sweeney, happily
shaving naked while his sexual partner has her fit, as his own polar
opposite).

Talking with Virginia Woolf in 1921, Eliot rebutted the critics'
charge that he was 'learned and cold'; and she commented to
herself that coldness was probably a sore point with him. It is also
probable that the questions 'what is wrong, what is missing?' must
have occurred, in various guises, to Eliot himself. *Poems 1909–1925*
contains many examples of men who have lost their passion, from
Prufrock through Gerontion and the ungenerative relationships in
The Waste Land, to 'The Hollow Men', whose predicament seems
partly to comprise erotic failure: in which reproachful eyes are
avoided, and trembling tenderness with 'lips that would kiss' is
baulked of its human object. But this erotic aspect is really part of
the larger issue of authenticity; and these hollow men, in their
pitiable immobility, are inauthentic not only in their love-life, but
in every other area of life as well, reduced to the condition of
ciphers:

> Shape without form, shade without colour,
> Paralysed force, gesture without motion.

As Eliot was to observe in his essay on Baudelaire (1930), 'the
worst that can be said of most of our malefactors, from statesmen
to thieves, is that they are not men enough to be damned' (SE 429).

Considering the question 'what is missing?', we might propose
the answer 'love'; but it becomes increasingly apparent that, for
Eliot, that term needed qualification. It could not simply stand for
emotional relationship between humans; it required a larger context, which he was coming to see as essentially religious. If the
passionate impulse of the hollow men lacks human requital, so the

'broken stone' to which they offer their prayers instead suggests a religious impulse that lacks an adequate object or expression (like the 'heap of broken images' in *The Waste Land* of which, it is reminiscent). The poem's final section embarks on and then interrupts the doxology of the Lord's Prayer, and ends instead with a nursery rhyme jingle. The hollow men have not yet found their passion: they have no focus of intensity which could rescue them from their own meaninglessness. Lives such as theirs will amount to no more than the debris of papers which posthumously await 'the lean solicitor'. Eliot was, however, moving toward a position from which, no less convinced than before of the hollowness of life and of 'the void' within it, he could conceive of how it might be redeemed from its inauthenticity:

> Shadow of its own shadows, spectre in its own gloom,
> Leaving disordered papers in a dusty room;
> Living first in the silence after the viaticum.
>
> (CPP 107)

Interviewed by the *New York Times* in 1953 Eliot was to recall that after writing 'The Hollow Men' (or, it might more accurately be expressed, after coming to a final decision on which poems to include in the sequence and in which order), he thought that he had probably come to an end of his poetry. This feeling is a phenomenon we shall often notice in his career; but on the whole it was not apparent to most of those who were buying copies of *Poems 1909–25* – although Allen Tate's review in the *New Republic* noted that 'The Hollow Men' marked the end of a phase, and wondered about the possibility that Eliot had 'nothing more to say in poetry'. Most of the reviews were at least respectful; even J.C. Squire in his *London Mercury* (March 1926) granted Eliot 'certain powers of intellect and craftsmanship', before declaring 'why on earth he bothers to write at all is difficult to conceive'. It was perhaps as predictable that Squire should dislike the book, as that I.A. Richards (*New Statesman*) and Leonard Woolf (*Nation*) should review it favourably; Edgell Rickword (*Calendar of Modern Letters*) admitted to the influence Eliot now had, but tried to define those aspects in which the poems were deficient. Efforts were also made to place Eliot: Edmund Wilson argued for an American lineage and affinities with James and Hawthorne; perhaps more interestingly, J. Middleton Murry saw Eliot as an 'incomplete romantic', aligned both with traditionalists and modernists – 'Mr Charles Whibley on his one arm and Miss Gertrude Stein on the other'. Murry forecast that Eliot's resolution of his search for authority would be through one of two contrasting acts of faith: either to 'trust himself', or to 'join the Catholic Church'.[4]

His hope was that Eliot would take the first path, but his second guess proved nearer the mark. In Murry's presentation of Eliot's dilemma, we find ourselves again contemplating the strange fusion in him of the conformist and the iconoclast; and these two aspects are illustrated by two articles he wrote anonymously in 1926 for the *TLS*. The first, published on 4 March, was a review of Sir Arthur Quiller Couch's *Oxford Book of English Prose*. Here indeed was an emblem of the English literary establishment; and it was a hippopotamus for which Eliot had a lance, arguing that no critical principles underlay its selection of items, and implying that the nearer it drew to contemporary writing, the less reliable it became. He made his point by contrasting a passage included in the anthology, in which Lytton Strachey described the death of Queen Victoria, with a passage from *Ulysses* in which Joyce presented Stephen Dedalus strolling on the seashore. Joyce was not represented in the anthology, but Eliot insisted that the comparison showed him to be a truer master of prose: the monarch's death-bed was instantly forgettable, whereas 'merely to read of Stephen Dedalus walking on the beach is to have come into contact with the vibrating reflex of an actual experience'. Strachey, who had in earlier days been a distant friend of Eliot, is reported to have acknowledged the justice of the comparison with some distress.

If his championship of Joyce showed Eliot operating in Modernist mode, his advocacy of another writer, seven months later, seems to reveal a contrary aspect. In September, to mark the tercentenary of the death of Lancelot Andrewes, Bishop of Winchester, Eliot wrote an essay asserting him to have been a vital, formative figure in the creation of a distinctive and intellectually respectable Church of England. He saw Andrewes as representing the *via media* of Anglicanism and, notably, argued that his sermons and devotional writings were superior to those of Donne: because in Donne we have the voice of one who is first and foremost a 'personality', whereas in Andrewes we hear 'the voice of a man who has a formed visible Church behind him, who speaks with the old authority and the new culture'. For Eliot, Andrewes truly represented the spirit of the age, and the influence which defined the Church of England as a national community of faith rather than a sect.

In these 1926 pieces in the *TLS*, then, we observe Eliot both subverting the Establishment (so far as this is represented by the Oxford view of literary history), and endorsing it (so far as it is represented by an established Church). Yet on reflection the contrast is less stark than may at first appear. In the earlier piece, a hint of Eliot's future direction may be seen in his approving quotation of a description of the martyrdom of Becket (from Caxton's edition of *The Golden Legend*); and we remember that his fondness for Wren's City churches, so evident in *The Waste Land*, was in large part a consequence of their being monuments to the Church of England. Moreover, both Andrewes and Joyce are to a degree founding fathers of their respective movements; and if Joyce is valued for his exactitude of language, so too is the Andrewes who 'takes a word and derives the world from it'. Both men showed an ascetic devotion to their callings, and each displayed a cosmopolitan scholarliness that prevented any lapse into the narrow provincialism Eliot especially despised.

In each essay, Eliot was concerned with defining the spirit of a movement: modern prose in all its vigour is to be found in the writing of Joyce, not Strachey; the best of Anglicanism is to be found in Andrewes, with his merit of 'relevant intensity', rather than in Donne, whose intensity is suspected of acknowledging no context other than the self. So although it might be tempting, considering these pieces, to regard Eliot's development in terms of a rejection of Joyce in favour of Andrewes, it is truer to say that he relegated Donne in favour of Andrewes; as Ronald Bush points out, this reverses the preference expressed by Eliot in a piece on 'The Preacher as Artist', written for the *Athenaeum* in 1919.[5] The Donne to whom 'a thought was an experience' had seemed to be one of the sponsorial figures in Eliot's early verse; but in 1926, not only in the essay on Andrewes, but also in his Clark Lectures earlier that year, Eliot had been concerned to analyse his dissatisfaction with Donne; and this seems to mark a significant shift in sensibility.

Between February and March Eliot gave eight lectures 'On the Metaphysical Poetry of the Seventeenth Century' in Cambridge, at the invitation of the Master and Fellows of Trinity College. Unlike other sets of lectures he was to deliver, this was not subsequently published, although some of the ideas reappeared in later writings. In them, Eliot criticises Donne as one 'imprisoned in the embrace of his own feelings', a writer who entertained ideas for their own sake rather than being committed to them as statements of truth. Set against such an attitude are the great poets of the thirteenth century, pre-eminently Dante, whose perceptions were at one with Thomist theology, and who valued human love (for example) in the context of its relation to divine love. Eliot later focuses a similar critique on Laforgue, suggesting that his inability to bring mature reflection to bear upon the experiences he writes of condemns him to the production of a 'poetry of adolescence', disparate and unintegrated with any larger schema. Thus, Donne and Laforgue, two early and important influences on Eliot's own poetry, and prominently used by him in his early criticism as yardsticks of value, found themselves weighed in a later balance, and found wanting.[6]

This should not be represented as an about-turn; but it does mark a shifting of the balance between various elements in Eliot's thought, with greater importance being attached to tradition, and greater scepticism being directed toward the individuality of talent. Dante, a truly European poet, was able to reproduce an order he perceived and affirmed; as Eliot remarked in his address on 'Shakespeare and the Stoicism of Seneca' (1927), 'Dante had behind him the system of St. Thomas, to which his poem corresponds point to point' (SE 135). By contrast, Donne's amalgamations of his disparate experiences may finally be specious or showy, and relate to nothing broader than the poem's own occasion; in a talk he later gave on Donne for the BBC, Eliot commented that Donne's poetry 'expresses no settled belief in anything'.[7] In his essay on Blake in *The Sacred Wood*, in the context of a discussion of the value to a nation and its writers of a 'continuous religious history', Eliot had noted 'the crankiness, the eccentricity, which frequently affects writers outside of the Latin traditions' (SE 321–2). Since writing this in 1920, Eliot had come to see that Christianity offered such continuity: to attempt to substitute for it a personal mythology, much as Blake did, or to use it to subserve the presentation of personality, as Donne did, was to risk being marginal, provincial, idiosyncratic; was – perhaps above all – to deny the writer the security of having 'behind' him some larger authenticating structure, whether 'the system of St. Thomas' in Dante's case, or 'a formed visible Church' in the case of Andrewes.

This obviously conduces to ideas about 'belief' and 'orthodoxy', with which Eliot increasingly concerned himself in a religious context rather than a literary one; whereby Anglo-Catholicism took over from 'the mind of Europe' as the incorporating entity. It was thus ironic that in a long footnote in his book *Science and Poetry* (1926), I.A. Richards should praise *The Waste Land* for expressing the disillusionment of a generation, and Eliot for 'effecting a complete severance between his poetry and *all* beliefs', at a time when the poet was lecturing at Richards's own university partly about the connections between poetry and belief. In January 1927, in a note on the subject published in the first number of Wyndham Lewis's new magazine *The Enemy*, Eliot declared, 'I cannot see that poetry can ever be separated from something which I should call belief'.

This is an aspect of the 'time-lag' already referred to, between what even an educated readership was able to assimilate, and what Eliot was actually writing. Moreover, the academy – or its avant-garde – had enthusiastically embraced Eliot as the type of poet and critic who most responded to its sense of its own function: a 'difficult' writer who peppered his work with obscure allusions to out-of-the-way texts obviously required professional explication. Eliot's learned scepticism and dark tones, his controlled subversion of surface meanings, his emphasis on seeing the poem as a poem and not some other thing, sponsored various critical initiatives. His poems encouraged psychological readings, on the basis of their apparently-suppressed 'true' utterance; they were tractable to approaches which highlighted 'ambiguity' (William Empson's influential *Seven Types of Ambiguity* (1930) used a passage from *The Waste Land*); and together with his prose they were enlisted by those who concentrated on the poem as a text in isolation, whether exemplified by Richards's advocacy of 'practical criticism', or by the 'New Critics' in the USA (chief amongst whom, perhaps, was Cleanth Brooks). But as well as the names of Richards, Empson and Brooks, we should add that of F.R. Leavis, whose concern with establishing a canon of English literature, and with the moral implications of the state of culture, reflected another facet of Eliot's writing. It has been noted that the rising arc of Eliot's career coincided with the establishment of 'English' as a discipline in the British universities, especially at Cambridge. This is best seen as symbiosis rather than collusion: none of the critics mentioned above pretended to like Eliot's writing because it served his turn, nor did Eliot consciously produce poems for university teachers and their students. Undeniably, however, the connection with the universities helped Eliot's career, even though it meant he was often identified with poems of a type he was no longer writing.

Another source of Eliot's influence was his journal (the *New Criterion* between January 1926 and January 1927, the *Monthly Criterion* from May 1927 to March 1928). Defining his 'Idea of a Literary Review' at the beginning of 1926, the editor hoped that in time to come it would be seen to have defined 'the development of the keenest sensibility and the clearest thought'. The editorial space afforded Eliot the chance to promote favoured views, such as the 'modern tendency' toward 'classicism' (January 1926), or 'the idea of a common culture of western Europe' (April 1926). As editor, he could and did suggest the attitude reviewers might take toward certain writers; in 1926 Carl Sandburg and Amy Lowell were suggested to be ripe for deflation, whereas Pound and Lewis were generally treated favourably. The editorship also endowed Eliot with certain powers of patronage, not only toward creative writers, but also toward the rising generation of literary critics whose work he accepted. Although Eliot recognised the need for dissent, which led him (for example) to publish an exchange of contrary views between himself and Middleton Murry, something of a house style did develop, one symptom of which was that contributors seemed quite frequently to insert overt or covert allusions to the editor's own writing in their pieces. Looked at now, there is an effect as of 'their master's voice' on encountering these catch-phrases.

Although an approving diagnosis of the 'classical' bent of modern sensibility, and a concern with 'a new European consciousness' (August 1927), can be seen to relate to ideas apparent in Eliot's early criticism, the *Criterion* was changing. Gradually the proportion of creative writing fell, as that of critical or theoretical contributions rose. A primary concern with literature began to be supplanted by attention to politics and economics – the editor commenting in November 1927 that 'politics has become too serious a matter to be left to politicians', and enforcing the need for intelligent men to become 'amateur economists', in recognition of 'an age in which politics and economics can no longer be kept wholly apart'. Such aspects, together with the debate about forms of right-wing politics met with in the pages of the magazine, reflect something of the temper of the times – as does Ezra Pound's increasing preoccupation, in his *Cantos* published in these years, with economic analysis. But they also reflect the change in Eliot, which would probably have surprised those of his readers who were devotees of the iconic, detached poem, or who valued *The Waste Land* as a document of comprehensive despair: they might have failed to recognise *their* author as the man who, contemplating what he defined as 'the political and economic anarchy of the present time', prescribed 'the necessity for a severe spiritual askesis and the discipline and development of the soul'.[8]

This was a path on which Eliot himself had already embarked; at the very end of the previous month, in conditions of considerable secrecy, he had been first baptized and on the following day confirmed in the Church of England. The decision had apparently been made in November of the previous year, and Eliot had been attending communion service for some months before then. However quickly he had grown disenchanted with the Unitarianism in which he had been raised, it seems that a religious impulse remained strong in him: it has even been suggested that he was tempted by Roman Catholicism while at Harvard, as well as by Buddhism at the time of *The Waste Land*. In the event, it was the Anglican communion which claimed him, and in particular its Anglo-Catholic branch, which sought for eventual reunification between the Churches of Rome and England.

In 'Shakespeare and the Stoicism of Seneca', Eliot spoke of the poet's struggle to transmute his 'personal and private' life into 'something universal and impersonal'. If poetry was one way of resolving the fortuitousness of personal experience, by incorporating it into what Yeats termed 'the artifice of eternity', then analogously the Christian faith embodied a profounder struggle to rise above the littleness and loneliness of self, toward an alignment of the soul with the divine principle – expressed by Dante in the words Eliot quoted, *'la sua voluntade è nostra pace'* ['His (God's) will is our peace']. Eliot's decision to become an Anglican rather than a Roman Catholic (as Murry had suggested) illustrates his commitment to England; further formalised by his adoption of British citizenship that year. The fact of its being an established Church, politically and historically intertwined with the state, was important: to be a Roman Catholic in England was to be a member of a sect. Moreover, although Anglo-Catholicism represented the most hierarchical aspect of the Church, and offered the nearest approach to the discipline which Murry supposed would attract Eliot to Roman Catholicism, as a Protestant theology it necessarily implied the responsibility of the believer to define his relationship with God; this resembles the ideal accommodation between the edifice of tradition and the individual talent, which is not a matter of passive conformity to an inert pattern.

Whether the secretive character of the church ceremonies in Oxfordshire was dictated by Eliot's own psychological necessities, or whether intended to forestall the opposition of agnostic friends, or whether the church door at Finstock was locked in order to spare the casual visitor the shock of seeing a grown man bending over the font (as has been asserted), we cannot tell. If he anticipated an adverse reaction from those who knew him, Eliot was not entirely wrong. Vivien is reported to have been against his conversion, and this would have driven another wedge between a couple already quite estranged. Pound was to dismiss the step as an 'irrelevant' solution to the problems of the age, and one of the strongest responses was that of Virginia Woolf; she learnt of Eliot's conversion in January 1928, and the following month was recounting the 'shameful and distressing interview' in a letter, judging Eliot to be 'dead to us all from this day forward'. She clearly regarded it as a retrogressive step, quite irreconcilable with the Modernist thrust Eliot had seemed to represent: 'I mean,' she exploded, 'there's something obscene in a living person sitting by the fire and believing in God'.[9] In the event, their friendship survived the shock.

The first indication for the general reader that the poet of *The Waste Land* and 'The Hollow Men' had turned an important corner came with the publication, in August 1927, of 'Journey of the Magi': the first poem Eliot had written since completing 'The Hollow Men'. His output during the latter part of 1925, 1926 and the greater part of 1927 had consisted – in addition to his work in the *Criterion* – of articles and reviews in the *TLS, Dial, Nation* and *Athenaeum*, and also the *Nouvelle Revue Française*. This amounted to quite a volume of prose, signifying both Eliot's industry and his sense that he might be written out as a poet. He had to some extent been keeping in practice as a poet by translating St John Perse's poem *Anabase* from the French, between 1926 and 1930; this left its mark on some of the poems he composed in this period. Not for the last time in his career, the stimulus to compose came from without. In what seems to have been a marketing strategy to promote the sales of poetry, Faber decided to issue a series of original short poems in pamphlet form, attractively presented with special artwork such as line drawings and woodcuts. Eliot was duly commissioned to produce one, and 'Journey of the Magi' resulted. The series was known as 'Ariel' poems, and Eliot's contributions to it have been gathered under that title in his *Collected Poems*.

His reanimation as a poet produced not only these poems, but led to the sequence that eventually formed itself as *Ash-Wednesday*. The strict order of publication was: 'Journey of the Magi'; 'Salutation' (which became poem II of *Ash-Wednesday*, and was published in December 1927 in the *Saturday Review of Literature*); 'Perch'io non spero' (which became poem I, and was published in the French magazine *Commerce* in spring 1928); 'A Song for Simeon' (September 1928); 'Som de l'Escalina' (which became poem III, *Commerce*, autumn 1929); 'Animula' (October 1929); *Ash-Wednesday* (April 1930); and 'Marina' (September 1930). In spite of the parallel composition of the two sets of poems, it is worthwhile treating the 'Ariel' poems first and separately (excluding 'Triumphal March', 1931, and 'The Cultivation of Christmas Trees', 1954), because they can be seen to form a loose sequence, which starts with a journey and ends with an arrival.

Like 'Gerontion', 'Journey of the Magi' presents the voice of an unillusioned old man; but the involved dramatic syntax of the earlier poem has been replaced by a much simpler, more immediate voice, narrating through the sequential parataxis of 'and' and 'then'. It is the story of an uncompleted transition, told by an old man who knows what he has lost, but not what he has found. Apart from its quotation from Andrewes's nativity sermon, 'Magi' does not contain the dense, echoic allusiveness which had once been Eliot's trademark. Some of its images have a memorable quality, but it is notable that such allusion as it does contain is not specifically literary, but loosely biblical, such as the 'three trees', the dicing, and the 'pieces of silver'. Unlike this Magus, Simeon, the speaker of the next poem (biblically the utterer of the *nunc dimittis*), knows that he inhabits a Christian universe. A Jew rather than a pagan, Simeon darkly embraces the necessary suffering that history will unfold, in a 'tomorrow' to which he lays no personal claim.

Moving from one on the brink of death, 'Animula' deals with the soul's progress from birth (reversible terms, as the poems suggest).

Dante provides its first line, in translation, but the poem then comes up to date in its depiction of the world of the modern, middle-class Infant Child, surrounded by accessories such as etched silver trays, servants (note the plural), and the *Encyclopaedia Britannica*. These reassuring details are invoked, only to be dismissed as immaterial; and in its anticipation of life 'after the viaticum' (the last rites offered to the dying), the poem imaginatively crosses the threshold at which its two predecessors stop. 'Marina', the next (and most interesting), deals with an awakening, as of the soul in paradise freed from the 'unsubstantial' universe of death. As a poem of rebirth and restoration, it is a natural culmination to a series of poems about renunciation. It has a rhythmic interest and sensitivity which recalls an earlier Eliot – as do the Shakespearian allusion of its title and its provision of a learned Latin epigraph (although on investigation this does not seem particularly apposite, being the words of Hercules emerging to lucidity from the fury in which he has slaughtered his family). In such a light, it is perhaps fitting that the 'garboard strake' in 'Marina' was resurrected by Eliot from the seafaring passages excised by Pound from the manuscripts of *The Waste Land*.

Moving as they do from uncertainty to the brink of revelation these poems, albeit composed over four years, might just as easily have been assembled by Eliot into a sequence as some of the poems which actually were. It appears that they imply a spiritual progress on the part of their author, but Eliot seems to have felt the need of a more public and unambiguous statement: for when his volume of essays *For Lancelot Andrewes* was issued by Faber and Gwyer in November 1928, he took the opportunity to insert in the preface a resonant declaration. The book was subtitled 'Essays on Style and Order', and in his opening remarks Eliot explained that part of what lay behind it was a desire 'to disassociate myself from certain conclusions which have been drawn from my volume of essays, *The Sacred Wood*' (FLA ix). There seems to be a certain energy of repudiation directed against his former self; and there is also perhaps a suggestion that Eliot wished to disentangle himself from out-of-date notions about him held by certain admirers. When he goes on to define his 'general point of view', in a formulation which echoed Charles Maurras, as 'classicist in literature, royalist in politics, and anglo-catholic in religion', it looks like conscious provocation. Earlier in his critical career Eliot had wished to 'disturb and alarm' the reading public; it now seemed that he wished to shock those readers who had acclimatised themselves to his disturbing and alarmist vision, by promulgating these ideas of order.

If this were his intention, he succeeded – at least as far as the *TLS* reviewer was concerned. Assessing the volume on 2 December the same year (the promptness of this review itself an indication of Eliot's stature), he paid the usual tributes to what Eliot had accomplished, but confessed to 'increasing perturbation' as he read onward, astonished that such opinions should come from 'the author of *The Waste Land*'. Just as Virginia Woolf had presumed him 'lost to us forever', so this reviewer could only interpret Eliot's position as an exchange of 'modernism for mediaevalism'. There were eight essays in the volume, culled from Eliot's literary journalism from 1926 onward; although certain elements recur (such as avoidance of extremes, recommendation of the *via media*, advocacy of an established Church, and affirmation of the European idea; along with a manifestly Christian point of view), the pieces do not really generate a thematic unity.

Eliot's own suggestion in the preface, that he was offering a revision of his first book of criticism, is relevant here. For in March 1928 he had written a new preface for *The Sacred Wood*, which Methuen reissued that year; in it, he offered the perception that the unifying concern of that collection had been 'the integrity of poetry', defined in the dictum, 'when we are considering poetry we must consider it as poetry and not some other thing' (SW viii). Without wholly rejecting this view, Eliot asserts that he had now 'passed on' to the problem of 'the relation of poetry to the spiritual and social life of its time'; and it is this that is embodied in *For Lancelot Andrewes*, published eight months later. If readers of *The Sacred Wood* had carried away a sense of the great importance of poetry, the 1928 preface defined it as 'a superior amusement'; and this diminished sense of 'the integrity of poetry', shocking to purists, was evidenced in *For Lancelot Andrewes*, only three of whose essays were on primarily literary figures. In his preface to the later volume, further books were projected by Eliot, seeming to indicate an increasing intrusion into his literary criticism of the social and religious dimensions: 'The School of Donne', 'The Outline of Royalism', and 'The Principles of Modern Heresy' were offered as the titles of books 'in distant preparation'. In the event, only a version of the last of these was ever produced (*After Strange*

Gods, 1934); but the changed direction seemed clear. It is, for example, visible in Eliot's declaration in a letter to Herbert Read in 1930, *à propos* W.H. Auden, that 'I think that if a man's ethical and religious views and convictions are feeble or limited and incapable of development, then his technical development is restricted'.[10]

It was not an inflexible dogma that Eliot adhered to. This is made clear by his short study of Dante which Faber and Faber published in 1929, in the series *Poets on Poets*. In spite of a dedication to Charles Maurras, which might have boded a doctrinaire approach, the discipline of writing for a non-specialist audience, and the animation produced by Eliot's unfeigned enthusiasm for his subject, produced a relaxed appreciation rather than a stringent polemic. He seems to have kept before himself the circumstances of his own initial encounter with Dante, and recalled the innocent surrender of an earlier self to this literary experience; remembering that one test of true poetry, as he puts it, is its capacity to communicate before it is understood. Eliot did not forget the importance to a reader of this primary impulse of unaccountable excitement; the particular eminence of Dante lay in his ability to evoke this impulse within an overarching structure which, although capable of elucidation and assuredly connected with a religious view independent of his poem, did not therefore substitute an authenticating philosophy for the immediacy of the creative imagination. Dante moved outward from an intense personal experience to achieve a poem that is the highest possible expression of European culture as an unfragmented whole. Here again Eliot addressed himself to the question of poetry and belief, arguing that it was not necessary for a reader to believe as Dante did in the theology behind the *Divine Comedy*, although it clearly was necessary for a reader to give it a degree of credence; the distinction he offered, was between 'philosophical belief', which is not essential, and 'poetic assent', which is a conditional commitment to the literary work (SE 257).

That Dante had been much on Eliot's mind is also clear from *Ash-Wednesday*. When he showed a draft of the sequence to Leonard and Virginia Woolf, which at that stage consisted of five sections, the titles of four of them were quotations from Dante (the exception being the first, whose title came from the poem of Cavalcanti echoed in its opening line). Why he at last decided against these titles is not known; perhaps he felt it would be too reminiscent of the allusive poetry he used to write. *Ash-Wednesday* is manifestly a different kind of poem. It was published in 1930, with a dedication to his wife; but it seems unlikely that Vivien collaborated on this venture as she had with *The Waste Land*: she was increasingly disturbed, and had been spending time in various sanatoria, where her husband occasionally joined her. The instability of the marriage was reflected in a quick succession of moves the couple made from flat to flat during this period. So unpredictable was her behaviour becoming that Eliot, the master of preserved appearances, risked embarrassment and even direct humiliation on social occasions they attended together. The natural outcome was that such engagements, proffering invitations to disaster, were shunned by Eliot, with the consequence that Vivien's suspicions about her exclusion from his life became more extreme. Even friends acquainted with his wife's condition, such as the Woolfs, could not always be exposed to it.

There is indeed no matrimonial feel to *Ash-Wednesday*; the women it invokes are Virgins, Holy Mothers, or associated figures. But there is a sense of a life being summed up: a confrontation of waste and hopelessness that gradually engenders a slow pulse of renewal; and the title, of course, alludes to the first day of Lent, the period of fasting and penitence that precedes Easter in the Christian calendar. The first poem's rhythms, established by its variable line-lengths and the fall of the rhymes, enact a mind contemplating but resisting action. Just as cruel April provoked unwilling wakefulness, or as the Hollow Men clung to their state of un-being, the speaker here renounces 'the blessèd face', and solicits the benison of amnesia:

> And I pray that I may forget
> These matters that with myself I too much discuss
> Too much explain
> Because I do not hope to turn again

But even as it appears resigned to immobility, expecting nothing from this world or the next, the poem ends quoting the close of the Hail Mary, the Roman Catholic prayer for intercession.

It seems that the 'three white leopards' at the beginning of the next poem (the first-written in the sequence) are the agents of a purifying if disintegrative change, like the sea for Phlebas in *The Waste Land*, inducing the right kind of 'forgetfulness'. If, too, there is a 'desert' here, it is not the ominous geography of spiritual aridity, but an emblematic location in which leopards, ladies, junipers and bones may be iconographically disposed. Contrasted with the contemporary 'Ariel' poems, this poetry is more rhythmically inventive and more challenging in its formulations: witness, in this second poem, the intrusion of the two-beat lines which invoke the 'Lady of Silences', as well as the strangeness both of its tone and its imagery. When an undergraduate at Oxford asked Eliot what he meant by the first line, the poet simply read it back to him (this was in 1928, when it had been published separately as 'Salutation'). In his study of Dante the following year, Eliot – commenting on the lion, the leopard, and the she-wolf which occur in the first canto of *Inferno* – asserted that 'for a competent poet, allegory means *clear visual images*. And clear visual images are given much more intensity by having a meaning – we do not need to know what that meaning is, but in our awareness of the image we must be aware that the meaning is there too' (SE 242–3). This might have been a less intimidating response to the earlier enquirer, who really only wanted to be reassured that he was not reading nonsense verse; in essence, the reply would have been that he need only accord the image poetic assent, not philosophical belief. With the poem set in *Ash-Wednesday*, it becomes clear to us, not necessarily what the leopards 'mean' precisely, but that the poem as a whole represents a stage of spiritual progress, in which the demands of the body are to be transcended.

The third poem, with its imagery of ascending a staircase and encountering temptations to be mastered, reinforces this sense of a spiritual journey, in which the pleasures of the visible world, however enchantingly portrayed, must be renounced. Thus in language and imagery of considerable sensuous appeal Eliot paradoxically preaches his sermon of ascesis: the 'jewelled unicorns' and the 'gilded hearse' are there to be rejected. The collapse of the sequence into the learned quibbles, puns and popular song double-rhymes that disfigure poem V is remarkable, in view of what has gone before. Suddenly we have plenitude of meaning and poverty of images; and it is difficult to conceive that the text could command 'poetic assent' in the absence of any 'philosophical belief' in its religious message. Yet as suddenly, in the closing poem, Eliot recaptures the subtler resonances of his voice, and the curious compulsion of the imagery derived from his New England days: the 'granite shore', 'bent golden-rod', and 'whirling plover', which are strangely pastoral items in the poetic effects of this eminently urban sensibility, and which gratefully evoke a nature it is the poem's business, theologically, to rise beyond. Unlike the thwarted prayer with which 'The Hollow Men' had almost ended, this sequence ends with a direct quotation from the Roman Catholic mass.

Ash-Wednesday looks both forward and back: back, to the drama-tised first-person 'confessional' narratives that had characterised Eliot's verse from the beginning; and forward, in its more overt identification of the 'I' of the poem with the poet himself, and in its philosophical (or theological) closure. The American poet and critic Allen Tate saw the progress as one from irony to humility. Instead of the furtively conditional glimpses of Prufrock's inner life or the baroque confessionalism of 'Gerontion', *Ash-Wednesday* establishes a tone of meditational directness and comparative 'sincerity'. Less concerned with the dramatics of self than with the impulse of devotion, the poem's voice merges, not as in *The Waste Land* into a cacophonically disparate series of echoes, but into the simple adequacy of the litany. Although *Ash-Wednesday* has an air of irreducible mysticism, in which its leopards, ladies and juniper-trees are inexplicably just what they are, there is behind its move-ment a finally unifying synthesis – evidenced, for instance, when in the last section the definition of life on earth as a 'dreamcrossed twilight between birth and dying' is revised to a 'time of tension between dying and birth'.

Writing about Eliot in 1928, E.M. Forster commented on his stand-ing with the young, deriving in particular from the prestige of *The Waste Land*: 'He is the most important author of their day, his influence is enormous'.[11] Eliot's long poem, already 'a thing of the past' for its author in 1922, continued to seem highly contemporary to its readership; but if they appreciated it as an anatomy of despair and disillusionment, this was a phase beyond which Eliot had progressed. Christianity offered him a resolution for his feelings about the emptiness of life, by stressing the greater significance of the afterlife. This was a position in which he could continue to indulge a degree of congenial contempt for modern life, without yielding to despair: for whatever the panorama of futility that met his eye, the prospect was ultimately redeemable. Indeed, however meaningless present experience might appear, by virtue of its connection with the hereafter it had its own necessity, and could not be rejected as a field of exertion. Time was a preparation for timelessness, and the correct attitude toward everyday reality lay in learning how 'to care and not to care'.

Ash-Wednesday is probably Eliot's most inward-looking poem, and the one in which his new faith was most unambiguously presented: it finally cannot be read as a secular poem. His Christianity did not, however, mean that he went into a mystical and comfortable retreat, and he resented those who supposed that this was so. Eliot's theology included the concept of Hell; and when he wrote of the *Cantos* that Pound's 'is a Hell for the *other people* (. . .), not for oneself and one's friends' (ASG 43), he was implying a profound distinction between the two of them. His religion also defined the terms of his engagement with this world, and one consequence of the constitutional link between the English Church and the English state was that the Church, in Eliot's view, should be a social and political force. It was to do this more by subversion than by acquiescence, and in his essay 'Thoughts after Lambeth' (1931) he rejoiced that 'the orthodox faith of England is at last relieved from its burden of respectability' (SE 368–9); as he saw it, 'respectability' was now attaching itself to contemporary creeds of communism, or of humanism, or of fashionable despair.

This essay throws some light on why Eliot joined the Anglican communion, and on his attitude toward the Church of England as an institution. Discussing the differences on a point of doctrine between Roman Catholicism and Anglicanism, Eliot suggested that 'the Roman Church must profess to be fixed, while the Anglican Church must profess to take account of changed conditions'. This vision of an adjustable continuity would clearly be attractive; for here as elsewhere in the piece we encounter his reformulation in religious terms of issues which are parallel to questions he had formerly raised in his literary criticism:

> What in England is the right balance between individual liberty and discipline? – between individual responsibility and obedience? – active co-operation and passive reception?
>
> (SE 376)

Anglicanism enshrined a spirit of flexibility which left room for manoeuvre, in the establishment and adjustment of such 'balance'. His own attitude toward the Church of England was not that of the uncritically obedient convert: in this essay he pokes gentle fun at the more fatuous pronouncements of its bishops.

The questions posed above clearly have a political dimension. If one phase of Eliot's religion was to be seen in the self-examination of *Ash-Wednesday*, a further development was in the application of the insights gained to a sphere wider than the private conscience. In his creative writing, one consequence would be his move toward the theatre, with its possibility of a collective experience. In his criticism and literary journalism, it confirmed an increasing tendency toward social and political pronouncement. This had been observable in the *Criterion* (for whose financing Faber's became solely responsible, on Lady Rothermere's withdrawal at the end of 1927); an interest in the unity of European culture came to involve a notion of what a European polity should be. The editorial commentary for March 1928, for example, advanced the notion that Britain, by dint partly of being an imperial power, could form a bridge between the 'Latin and Germanic' cultural elements. Although continuing to find room for new literature, publishing W.H. Auden's 'Paid on Both Sides' in January 1930, the emphasis shifted toward political, economic, social and religious matters.

It does not seem in retrospect that Eliot was a particularly acute political commentator or analyst with regard to his adopted country; possibly because he was too apt to let what he wanted it to be interfere with his perception of what it was. George Orwell fumed about the 'snootiness' of the *Criterion*, referring in particular to an editorial of January 1932 in which, eyeing the problem of unemployment, Eliot toyed with his duty to employ more servants, who could profit from the 'cultured and devout atmosphere' at home. This verges on the laughable, as does the Commentary from October 1931 (vol. XI), in which the city-dwelling editor extolled agriculture as 'the foundation for the Good Life in any society'. Conceding the low wages and hard work of life on the land, the argument was advanced that 'genuine patriotism' is possible only in a society 'in which people have local attachments to their small domains and small community, and remain, generation after generation, in the same place' (here we sense the influence of Maurras).

This is mere wishful thinking, related in spite of disclaimers to a pastoral ideal that was not especially relevant to political or social realities; Eliot's blindness to certain areas of English life was also to be seen in his underestimation of the strength of the non-conformist faith in which a writer like Lawrence was raised. His views about the innate wholesomeness of old-style organic communities were also in conflict with the enthusiasm for the machine and for industrially-transformed society discernible in many younger writers, who were currently coming into fashion. Amongst the likes of Auden, Spender, Day Lewis and MacNeice there prevailed a loosely Marxist orientation, ideologically committed to a vision of change inspired by what they imagined to be happening in Stalin's Russia; this involved the transformation of precisely those archetypes of rustic stability which Eliot was extolling.

Eliot's politics were, of course, of the Right rather than the Left, and his imagination was more compelled by the solitary leader than the triumphant masses. At the beginning of the decade he was experimenting with the idea of a sequence of four poems connected with the figure of Coriolanus; the first of these, 'Triumphal March', was published by Faber in April 1931 as an 'Ariel' poem, and the second, 'Difficulties of a Statesman', was published in *Commerce* that winter. In common with more than one of Eliot's literary projects, the grander design came to nothing, and what survives, entitled 'Coriolan', was eventually consigned by the author to the 'Unfinished Poems' section of his collected volume. The poems display a certain fascination with the idea of a masterly figure, and an apparent contempt for the unexalted onlooker (Cyril), as well as for the public world of 'select committees and sub-committees' (of which Eliot would in time become a dutiful, if suffering, member). 'Difficulties of a Statesman' also touches on a theme derived from *Coriolanus*, of the problems faced by the son of a noble family – 'Here is the row of family portraits, dingy busts, all looking remarkably Roman, / Remarkably like each other' – expressed as a thwarted longing for closeness with his mother. Eliot's own formidable mother had died in September 1929, and his reaction had been, Vivien noted in her Journal, 'most terrible'.

Two aspects of 'Coriolan' are noteworthy. It represents a departure from *Ash-Wednesday*, whose confessional intimacy and resonant imagery here give way to sardonic humour and a strong sense of the banal falsifications of a world opposing visionary possibility and emotional fulfilment. Insofar as the attempt to find a new style and subject remained incomplete, it was unsuccessful; but like *Sweeney Agonistes* this was a challenging experiment, which reminds us of Eliot's constant concern to break new ground. Also, in being unfinished, the abandoned sequence marks another crisis in Eliot's creativity, a point at which he supposed himself to be written out as a poet. The next verse he published would be the group of poems 'Five-Finger Exercises' in the *Criterion* (January 1933); although a certain darkness of tone pervades these light verses, the title seems an accurate description of what they are – and the smallness of their intention contrasts with the larger project for 'Coriolan', from which he had turned away.

In the midst of its fatuous bustle of a public occasion 'Triumphal March' invokes 'the still point of the turning world'; and the son in 'Difficulties of a Statesman' yearns for 'a still moment', a spiritual homecoming. This offers a contrast to the spirit of homelessness or deracination which we associate with the major 'Modernist' writers, who were notably expatriates. *Ulysses* replaces actual Dublin with Joyce's imagined city, and the list of locations in which it was composed ('Paris – Trieste – Zurich') suggests the haphazardness of place. Eliot's earlier poetry, with its unreal cities and its displaced persons (Fräulein von Kulp and Hakagawa), evokes this mood as strongly as any; but although in his expatriation and his cultural cosmopolitanism his career conforms to type, it can be seen that this was more truly an effort at re-racination: his identification with England, its literature and its Church, constructed something to which to belong. Although at times he seems to imagine 'England', outside London, as consisting of a suburbia of golfing agnostics beyond which lay green fields and a church-going peasantry, Eliot could represent it to himself as a meaningful geography, imbued with history. His earlier poems had implied the fortuity of place ('Jerusalem Athens Alexandria / Vienna London'), his later effort would be to explore the 'grace dissolved in place' ('Marina'): this is most clearly seen in the locational settings of his 'Landscape' poems and, more weightily, of the Quartets.

It is not surprising that Eliot should have been attempting political satire (his own projection for 'Coriolan') at the beginning of the 1930s: the country was in a mess. In December 1930 unemployment stood at 2.5 million; the following year Britain was forced off the gold standard and a National Government under Ramsay MacDonald was brought into being, to confront the deepening Depression. In the *Criterion*, Eliot was scathing about the succession of general elections. 'Coriolan' implies something of the fraudulence of political appearances; but in its implication of the private pain within the public mask it may (as so often with his poetry) be making a point of personal relevance. Eliot was not directly affected by the political and economic crisis; his was a position of unquestioned eminence in the world of letters – underscored in 1932 by the publication of his *Selected Essays*. Nevertheless, these were probably the unhappiest years of his life.

In his foreword to the posthumous *Collected Poems* of Harold Monro, written in 1932, Eliot declared that 'the compensations for being a poet are grossly exaggerated; and they dwindle as one becomes older, and the shadows lengthen and the solitude becomes harder to endure'. This has the ring of a personal declaration (Stephen Spender quoted it in his review of the volume in the *Criterion*), and however much Eliot tended to relish his own gloom the expression seems sincere. Externally, however, few could have supposed this. Such had been his success, and such his reputation, that Richard Aldington could publish a 'novel' *Stepping Heavenward* (1931), which was a recognisable lampoon of Eliot. Other indications were seen, in the beginning trickle of what would in time become a flood of critical studies of the poetry. He was invited by his old University, Harvard, to take up the Charles Eliot Norton professorship for the academic year 1932–33, and by the University of Virginia to deliver the Page–Barbour lectures in 1933; under the terms of appointment, both sets of lectures were published in book form, respectively as *The Use of Poetry and the Use of Criticism* (1933), and *After Strange Gods* (1934).

Eliot's standing was considerable; but there were also indications that his eminence was that of a respected senior rather than a living force. It was a fitting augury that the *Criterion* should publish its first contribution from W.H. Auden in January 1930, for in many ways the coming decade was to be dominated by his poetic voice, rather than Eliot's. In 1932 anthologies of contemporary poetry were published whose titles (*New Voices, New Signatures*) implicitly identified Eliot with the old; indeed, Michael Roberts in his introduction to *New Signatures* rejected the doctrine of difficult poetry, associated with Eliot. The literary magazine *Scrutiny*, started in Cambridge in 1932, paid its tribute to the *Criterion* and to Eliot's endeavours, but asserted with increasing force that Eliot's journal failed to exact the highest standards from its contributors. One of the main forces behind *Scrutiny*, F.R. Leavis, was heavily in Eliot's debt intellectually, and published his enthusiasm in *New Bearings in English Poetry* (1932); but as time progressed he found himself obliged to take a less unreservedly admiring tone.

It is clear to us in retrospect that after its initial momentum the *Criterion* had settled down into a rather sedative kind of worthiness. Although Eliot was consistent in his championing of Pound and Lewis, and did what he could to further the cause of Joyce, and although he was a sponsorial figure to the rising generation of writers by virtue of his editorship and his position at Faber's, the circles in which he moved were no longer those of excitable literary innovators, but of the English upper-middle class. When in 1931 James Joyce and his wife Nora were invited to a dinner-party given by the Eliots, in addition to witnessing some odd behaviour on the part of Vivien, they would have listened to Mrs Geoffrey Faber discoursing on the difficulty of moving her servants between her various establishments (one wonders what Nora Joyce, a former hotel chambermaid, would have made of this). A degree of remoteness from everyday reality is discernible in many of Eliot's editorial commentaries, possibly a consequence of his mixing with unrepresentative men.

It may also have been a consequence of his extraordinarily tense private life. Aldington's book had deeply offended Eliot because of its allusions to his marriage, which had become unworkable. Virginia Woolf, Edith Sitwell, Ottoline Morrell, Osbert Sitwell and Conrad Aiken have all given glimpses of Vivien's behaviour and of the Eliots' domestic life which compel the conclusion that the situation was beyond repair, and harmful to both parties. There was no question of Vivien making a move; but for Eliot to do so required just the kind of decisive action he found most difficult. The invitation from Harvard, which Eliot accepted against her wishes, gave him the opportunity for an extended absence. He left England in September 1932, and by March the following year had decided on a separation from his wife as the only possible way forward: he instructed his solicitor to set matters in motion, and sent him a letter to be given to Vivien.

The last time Eliot had been in the United States he was an American citizen, and both his parents were alive; he had come to try to justify to them a course of life of which they disapproved. Now, he was a celebrity, returning in apparent triumph, with no censorious parents to confront – although there were those, of course, who resented his renunciation of American citizenship. In addition to Harvard and Virginia, Eliot visited other campuses, notably in California, where he visited Emily Hale, with whom he had entered into a renewed correspondence (this visit may have lain behind his declaration in a letter to Ottoline Morrell (14 March 1933), that he had been very happy, for him). He wrote his Harvard lectures while he was in America, rather than having prepared them beforehand; *The Use of Poetry and the Use of Criticism*, published in November 1933 after his return, is a book which perhaps promises more than it delivers. It fails to be a coherent historical account of its subject, although it does so with magisterial assurance; its value lies most in what it suggests about Eliot's own writing. There is an audible glumness in his declaration that 'poetry is not a career, but a mug's game' (UPUC 154), as in his final self-association with the 'sad ghost of Coleridge'. But as well as such hints of termination, there are also pointers toward the future, as when he contemplates the theatre as 'the most direct means of social "usefulness" for poetry' (153).

After Strange Gods, published the following February and consisting of the lectures delivered at the University of Virginia, has become notorious as the book in which Eliot appeared to make anti-Semitic remarks, and which he refused to allow to be reissued. Subtitled 'A Primer of Modern Heresy', its tone and stance may owe something to the right-wing provincialism Eliot was appealing to in his audience of young Southern gentlemen – in spite of the fact that the book offers itself as an attack on provincialism. It is an intemperate, ill-spirited performance, whose intellectual unhealthiness is best evidenced by its keenness to diagnose sickness in others: above all in D.H. Lawrence. Wishing to subvert the lax thinking of his modern society 'worm-eaten with Liberalism', Eliot adopted categories of 'heresy' and 'orthodoxy' which have more force than clarity. Behind his thinking, again, is a vision of a homogeneous society, communally knit within its 'tradition'; 'unity of religious background' was especially prized, and this led to his notorious remark that large numbers of 'free-thinking Jews' were therefore undesirable. When a correspondent, much later, challenged him on this point, Eliot insisted that the emphasis fell on 'free-thinking' (that is, *orthodox* Jews would be no problem); but 1933 was an especially bad year in which to offer people an excuse to anathematise Jews, or to entertain notions of racial purity.

After Strange Gods contained some highly irresponsible formulations, which Eliot came later to acknowledge as the product of his own sickness. Although the months in America, widely in demand, confirmed his importance as a man of letters, he returned to England in June 1933 with no clear forward path. His decision to separate from Vivien conferred some sense of freedom, but this for Eliot was an ambiguous quality: in letters to his spiritual advisers he stressed his need for discipline. There was no question of a divorce (which she would almost certainly have contested): Eliot regarded his decision to marry as absolute, however mistaken. His main concern after his arrival was to keep out of Vivien's way: he knew from friends that she was frantic, anxious to believe that it was all a terrible mistake, and the two of them victims of a dark intrigue; his whereabouts were known to very few indeed. In fact, he spent most of the first months of his new life in Surrey, staying near the home of his friend and colleague from Faber's, Frank Morley, an American. He enjoyed the sun, and wrote some of the poems which would form part of *Old Possum's Book of Practical Cats*. More significantly, he had a luncheon-meeting with E. Martin Browne, whom he had first met in 1930 at a week-end with the Bishop of Chichester, for whose diocese Browne was the newly-appointed Director of Religious Drama. In 1933 Browne was working with the Reverend Webb-Odell, Director of an Anglican fund whose purpose was to raise money for the building and endowment of forty-five new churches, to serve the rapidly-expanding suburbs of north London. The means by which this was to be done was by performing a pageant, depicting the history of the Church in England; Browne had an idea for the scenario, which was intended to be spectacular; he asked Eliot if he would be prepared to write the choruses (not the dialogue), and Eliot accepted. When he told Leonard and Virginia Woolf of the scheme to build new churches, Leonard asked 'why?' – 'and Tom merely chuckled' reported Virginia.[12]

When Eliot visited her soon after his return, Virginia Woolf had been struck by the release of energy in him, by his desire to live again. Writing his choruses for Browne's pageant gave him an immediate objective, and, in writing verse to be declaimed by a group, a technical problem to solve. As we saw at the beginning of this chapter, *The Rock*, which ran for two weeks at the end of May 1934, was a success insofar as it attracted substantial audiences; reviewers were politely deferential toward Eliot's contribution. Read today, the choruses are intermittently alive as poetry; but for the most part the liturgical resonances are heavy, and the humour, where apparent, leaden. Its chief merit was to have provided Eliot with a stimulus to write again.

Virginia Woolf, who had been 'disappointed' by reading *The Rock*, reported that Roger Fry had left a performance 'in a rage'; she commented that 'poor old Tom' seemed to be 'petrifying into a priest'.[13] Since the end of 1933 Eliot had indeed been living in the presbytery of St Stephen's Church, Gloucester Road, where in 1934 he became Vicar's Warden. He inhabited a fairly bleak room, and competed for the bathroom with curates. The sense of release he had felt the previous year seems to have been fitful, and he appears to have sensed that his work on *The Rock* had not been as good as he had wished. He was now in a position to solicit from his friends and acquaintances on behalf of other poets (such as George Barker) the kind of financial help which, in earlier years, had been attempted for himself. He settled into a life of spiritual ascesis, and felt that he had reached an end, rather than a beginning. In July 1934 he wrote to Bonamy Dobree, 'I don't think my poetry is any good: not The Rock anyway, it isn't; nothing but a brilliant future behind me'.[14]

NOTES

1. This photograph is in Ackroyd, and in Ronald Bush, *T.S. Eliot: A Study in Character and Style* (Oxford, 1984); hereafter cited as Bush.
2. VWD II, pp. 67, 77; VWD IV, pp. 262–3.
3. *Criterion*, III, 12 (1925), 558–9.
4. All reviews mentioned are reprinted in Grant, vol. I.
5. See Bush, p. 109.
6. *Ibid.*, pp. 83–5, for a summary of the Clark Lectures. In a letter to Mary Hutchinson of July 1919, Eliot judged Laforgue as 'inferior' to Corbière (L 317).
7. *Listener*, 19 March 1930 (502).
8. *Criterion* July 1927, 69, 73.
9. *The Letters of Virginia Woolf*, ed. Nicolson, 6 vols (London, 1975 onwards), III, pp. 457–8. Hereafter cited as VWL.
10. In Humphrey Carpenter, *W.H. Auden: a Biography* (London, 1981), p. 137.
11. Forster's remarks on Eliot are reprinted in *Abinger Harvest*.
12. VWL V, p. 256.
13. Ibid., p. 315.
14. Tate, p. 79.

6

1935–1945

Dr Johnson was much possessed by death, and talking about it with Boswell supposed that afterwards he himself would probably be damned; when asked what he meant, he 'passionately and loudly' replied, 'Sent to Hell, Sir, and punished everlastingly'. Eliot must have had this incident in mind when he reviewed Middleton Murry's book on Shakespeare (*Criterion* XV, July 1936). For he took Murry to task for implying that our age no longer worried about hell-fires, and insisted that there were still those who would be 'as amazed as Dr Johnson' by such a contention, and some who would be 'as terrified, not by death, but by what may come after'. Doubtless he counted himself such a one; in June 1930 he had declared to Paul Elmer More, in the course of a correspondence on religious matters, that he had been 'really shocked' by More's refusal to believe that God made Hell. In the same letter, Eliot asserted that he personally lived 'in daily terror of eternity'. It was in this perspective he commented on the right of Rudyard Kipling to a place in Poets' Corner, in the previous issue of the *Criterion*: 'burial in [Westminster] Abbey,' he observed, 'can be of no value to the affrighted soul on the way to its last judgement'.[1]

In February 1935, after what seems to have been an uncharacteristically open conversation with Eliot on the importance to him of belief in immortality, Virginia Woolf set down in her journal her opinion that he was a 'religious soul' and 'an unhappy man'. Although she became a little more tolerant of his Christianity, for her his religion and his unhappiness were connected; nor did it seem that he derived much satisfaction from what he had accomplished as a man of letters. Indeed, as his comments on Kipling suggest, there were more important matters to engross a writer than the state of his reputation. Eliot's concern for Hell can be related to aspects of his earlier work, in which he had been compelled by notions of the heart of darkness underlying ordinary life; and it seems that as early as 1919 he had shocked Pound by a declaration that he was 'afraid of the life after death'.[2] Earlier poems had portrayed Lazarus in drawing-rooms, and the work of this period has its own unsettling presences, as when the chorus in *Murder in the Cathedral* declares, 'the Lords of Hell are here', or when the Eumenides stand alongside more prosaic *dramatis personae* in the cast-list of *The Family Reunion*. In the essay 'Religion and Literature' (1935), Eliot argued that the whole of modern literature had been 'corrupted' by 'Secularism', which he defined as its failure to appreciate 'the primacy of the supernatural over the natural life' (SE 398).

That word 'primacy' reinforces Stephen Spender's reminiscence of Eliot as 'hierarchical by temperament'; for it suggests an ordering in which what is below can only be justified by what is above, and visible haphazardness is redeemed by an unseen pattern that informs it. This is most clearly seen in a letter to Bonamy Dobree of 1936, in which Eliot expressed his doubt that 'ordinary human affections' could be the pathway to love of God, stating rather his belief 'that the love of God is capable of informing, intensifying and elevating' such affections – which without it could hardly be distinguished from 'the "natural" affections of animals'.[3] This owes something to Dante; it can also be seen as congruent with Eliot's earlier, essentially Symbolist, aesthetic: for to the Symbolist the object is valid insofar as it is the vessel of a 'higher' meaning. But meaning could come from below, as well: to set life in the perspective of Hell also enlarges the temporal by a sense of its eternal consequences. In his essay on Baudelaire (1930) Eliot had affirmed that it was better to do something worthy of damnation than to be a moral neuter. If it is part of man's glory that he is capable of damnation, as of salvation, then the way up and the way down may indeed be the same, and Christ is as likely to be a tiger, as a lamb.

The way down had certainly fascinated Eliot from early on: in the obscure prose piece 'Eeldrop and Appleplex' (1917), Eeldrop considers the case of a man who has murdered his mistress 'in Gopsum Street'; he asserts that 'the important fact is that for the man the act is eternal', that he is 'already dead', 'already in a different world from ours'.[4] The idea is picked up again in Sweeney's obsession with 'doing a girl in' and its consequences. Reconciling eternity with 'Gopsum Street', the milk-man with the hang-man, is the particular problem of one who crosses the frontier (as it is put in 'Eeldrop and Appleplex' and *The Family Reunion*): what it is to be part of, yet separate from; in two simultaneous modes of existence. Becket the martyr, the 'I' of *Burnt Norton*, and the fugitive Harry in *The Family Reunion*, are all implicated in a similar perplexity, as Eliot considered the problem in a more religious light, in the three major works he produced up to the beginning of the Second World War.

It might have been supposed that a man with Eliot's attitude toward the things of this world would withdraw from them into a contemplative privacy: for if the moral predicament of the murderer had interested him from early on, so had the figure of the saint. Sceptical as he was about the reality of public affairs, however, he increasingly involved himself in thinking and writing about society. Even *The Rock* was undertaken to address a contemporary need, and his concern with the drama at this period grew out of his desire to be socially useful, by reaching a wider audience. We may not think much of *The Rock*, but the necessity of writing its choruses made Eliot start composing again, and led on to other things. Having seen a performance of the pageant, George Bell, the Bishop of Chichester with whom Eliot had spent a weekend back in 1930, asked Eliot if he would be interested in writing a piece to be performed in the Chapter House of Canterbury Cathedral, as part of the Canterbury Festival of 1935. Eliot accepted, making it a condition that the director should again be Martin Browne (who would in the event direct all his plays). In the *Criterion* of June 1928 Eliot had criticised John Masefield's verse drama *The Coming of Christ*, also performed at Canterbury, for being dull as poetry and inconsequential as theology; now he had an opportunity to do better.

Bell had commissioned the piece in the summer of 1934, and by the winter Eliot was at work; the only stipulation was that there should be some connection with Canterbury. Given Eliot's abiding fascination with martyrs, it was natural that he should turn to the subject of Thomas à Becket (a description of whose assassination he had quoted in the *TLS* in 1926); moreover, the story of the former Lord Chancellor who was created Archbishop, thereby becoming obliged to resolve for himself the conflict between two different orders of experience, had an obvious interest for him. In spite of this, however, the composition was not an easy process; partly due to the static nature of the plot, which is much more to do with what is happening inside Becket, than with what happens to him. There were also problems of stagecraft which Eliot had to contend with; he was a diffident playwright, and discussed early drafts with younger (and much less eminent) men, Rupert Doone and Martin Browne, responding as he could to criticisms that it was too abstract, and making grateful use of their suggestions. The title, neatly combining Eliot's low interests with his high, came from Browne's wife; the play was in a state of constant revision, up until the first performance.

This took place at Canterbury on 15 June 1935, with the actor Robert Speaight playing Becket. The festival audiences received it well, and it was encouragingly reviewed; the commercial theatre became interested. Ashley Dukes negotiated for the transfer of the production to his Mercury Theatre in London, where it opened at the beginning of November 1935 for a seven-month run, during which it was seen by some 20 000 people. Then, after a tour of the provinces, it transferred to the larger Duchess Theatre in London (30 October 1936), where it did well enough to merit a further run at the Old Vic. At the beginning of its London run *The Times* had hailed it as a 'great play', and it was broadcast by the BBC in January 1936. By going into the theatre Eliot had clearly achieved his object, of reaching more people than he could by his poetry alone. His play was a success.

It did not do well in the United States, however, when the transfer was attempted, which may suggest that Eliot's name drew less well in his old country than in his adopted one. This seems to be borne out by the publishing figures for the period, given by Donald Gallup in his *Bibliography*: in the mid-thirties the print-runs of Eliot's work were higher in Britain than in America (where he was published by Harcourt, Brace and Company), in spite of what must have been the potentially larger transatlantic market. This was the case with *The Use of Poetry and the Use of Criticism*, *After Strange Gods*, and *The Rock*; but *Murder in the Cathedral* offers the greatest contrast. In June 1935 Faber issued the play in a print-run of 3000, followed by a further 3000 in January 1936, 5000 in August 1937, and 4000 in September 1938, further supplementing this last by a cheaper 'Schools Edition' of 3000. In America, however, an initial print-run of 1500 (September 1935) was not augmented until June 1936, when 2000 were printed; there was then no further edition until 1963 (5000 copies).

Given its subject, it is perhaps surprising that *Murder in the Cathedral* took off in Britain; it would have been difficult to predict that a verse-drama dealing with martyrdom would generate much popular appeal. Its success may indicate Eliot's drawing-power, but some of his contemporaries would not be drawn: Virginia Woolf was repulsed by the evocations of pollution and corruption, and Ezra Pound, listening in Rapallo, eventually switched his radio off. Little as she liked the play, Virginia Woolf observed that its success reinvigorated Eliot, making him (as she remarked in a letter of 14 October 1935) intolerant of reviewers who dismissed him as an 'old fogey'. His own feeling was that he was just coming into his own, sure of his direction – which he told her was the writing of 'plays about modern life in verse'. Again we see his determination not to repeat himself: the opportunity had been there for him to produce another religious drama in a historical setting, but he preferred to break new ground. The line of development on which he had embarked was to lead to *The Family Reunion*; but before that there was another benefit to be derived from his play about Becket.

In the course of rehearsals, some lines given to one of the priests had been cut because they were not dramatically necessary, although good enough in themselves. With a little alteration they became the opening passage of *Burnt Norton*, the long poem which Eliot went on to write, briefly turning aside from drama. The name is that of a manor house in Gloucestershire, near Chipping Campden; it is a remote place, untenanted when Eliot visited it, most probably in September 1934, and most certainly in the company of Emily Hale. Eliot had kept in touch with her beyond his marriage, writing 'a nice letter' in 1919 (L 305); but at some stage their correspondence lapsed, to be reopened in 1927 when, working at a college in Milwaukee, Emily had written to ask his advice on the teaching of modern literature. Their initial letters were 'formal', according to Lyndall Gordon, but then the correspondence deepened. In 1930 they had arranged to meet for the first time since Eliot's Harvard days, in England; and in the winter of 1932–33 Eliot had crossed from Massachusetts to California in order to spend several weeks with Emily, who was teaching there at Scripps College. Later, when she visited England, Eliot introduced her to friends such as Virginia Woolf and Ottoline Morrell. She was in England at the time of the visit to Burnt Norton, staying alongside her aunt and uncle, who rented a house at Chipping Campden during successive summers in the mid-thirties (she had been virtually brought up by them; like her dead father, the Reverend Perkins was a Unitarian minister).

Eliot's relationship with Emily Hale became publicly known as late as 1974, and has since then been the subject of much speculation; particularly fuelled by the revelation that more than a thousand letters from Eliot to her are deposited in Princeton University Library, and under the terms of her bequest may not be inspected until fifty years after her death (which took place in 1969).[5] How much will be revealed when the box is opened we can only guess; but through his widow we have Eliot's declaration that he had been in love with Emily Hale in 1914, and through Lyndall Gordon's researches we can be reasonably sure that, a quarter of a century and more later, she would have been ready to marry him. The relevance of this to our present discussion is that Eliot visited the empty house and its deserted gardens at a time of his life when he had broken with the past, but was not yet settled into a clear future. Having at length extricated himself from an unhappy marriage (to the extent of separation, but not of divorce), he had with him at Burnt Norton a woman with whom he was once in love, many years before in America, and who was still a focus for his emotions. All these circumstances make it hardly surprising if, as he strolled through the gardens with her, he was struck by a contrast between the life he might have led and the life he actually had led.

Along with the gardens themselves, Eliot later cited two other influences on *Burnt Norton*: the beginning of *Alice in Wonderland*, and a story of Kipling's called 'They' (1904). The first is a book ostensibly for children, presenting impossibly altered states of being; the second is a strange tale whose narrator, rooted in the commonsense world of things mechanical, stumbles in his motor-car across a mysterious and remote Sussex mansion, inhabited by a blind mistress whose yearning for the children she has never had attracts the ghosts of dead children; these surround her, and tantalise her with half-apprehensions of their presence. The narrator, who has recently lost a child of his own, can see the ghosts, but she cannot; and the final feeling seems to be that whereas his real grief and pain are modifiable by the processes of time, she will remain trapped in her unanswerable longing. Another literary influence behind *Burnt Norton* was Henry James's short story 'The Jolly Corner', in which an American in late middle age returns to New York from a life spent abroad; in the echoing emptiness of the family property he has come to inspect, he encounters the ghost of the self he might have been, had he not left America. The story ends with some emphasis on the necessity of his 'accepting' the apparition, in spite of its marked difference from what he has in fact become. The tale was in Eliot's mind at this time: one of the characters in *The Family Reunion* alludes to it semi-directly, in a passage highly echoic of the first part of *Burnt Norton*.

Unlike Eliot's previous long poems, *Burnt Norton* appears to have taken shape quickly. It seems safe to suppose that he would not have embarked on such composition until after *Murder in the Cathedral* was well off his hands (June 1935), and the poem was first published in his *Collected Poems 1909–1935*, issued on 2 April 1936. With the exception of the lines cut from the play, it was not created from fragments originally conceived as separate entities; it differs from sequences such as 'The Hollow Men' or *Ash-Wednesday*, both of which had component poems published in magazines, before their form was finalised in a book. Unlike the dramas which preceded it, the poem was not written to commission; and although there would be an obvious attraction in including a significant new piece in his envisaged collected volume, it is doubtful that by itself this would have been enough. We may suppose that *Burnt Norton* was the product of an inner necessity; and if the precise nature of this necessity is difficult to establish, that seems appropriate in a poem concerned with how to relate instants of transcendent intuition to ordinary living, and how intimations of timelessness can be fitted within experience of time.

When he was at work on *Little Gidding* six years later, Eliot wrote to his friend John Hayward (to whom he submitted drafts of the later three Quartets for comment) that he felt the poem was lacking in 'some acute personal reminiscence (never to be explicated, of course, but to give power from well below the surface)'.[6] We infer from this that such an element was present in its three predecessors; and in the case of *Burnt Norton*, this acute reminiscence is presumably the inexplicable 'moment in the rose-garden' which initiates and in a sense contains the entire poem. This moment appears to involve a feeling of personal release from time. In *Murder in the Cathedral*, where the opening lines occurred in their earliest version, Archbishop Becket was being tempted by alternative lives he could have led; and in that context the lines functioned as a rejection of 'what might have been', and an affirmation of the chosen path. In *Burnt Norton*, however, the sense of there being only 'one end, which is always present' is less strictly enforced, as the dogmatic rhythms of its beginning give way to the illicit questing instigated by the mercurial thrush. The poem's title would have been almost impenetrably obscure to contemporary readers, unless they had a detailed gazetteer to hand. Its past participle 'burnt' hints at an unalterable destruction; but this is revised in the poem, which colludes with possible renewals, and summons up the selves which could have taken shape, the children who might have been born. Are such glimpses 'deception', or do they communicate a superior 'reality'? The poem's impulse may have been private, but the struggle is to make that impulse public; and this is the point of the epigraph from Heraclitus which Eliot affixed, about there being one 'logos' common to all, in spite of a man's supposing that his individual notion of it is unique.

Earlier in his career he had described himself, in conversation, as one who wrote about the Thames but thought about the Mississippi. If such a comment implied a potential tension between his American origins and his English adoption, it should also be recalled that his very Americanness contained – as he saw it – conflicting influences of South and North. The time of the composition of *Burnt Norton*, and its originating incident in the visit with Emily Hale, provided the circumstances for a heightened awareness of 'the imperatives of "is and seems" / And may and may not, desire and control' ('Animula'). *Burnt Norton* is a poem much concerned with ideas about a hidden pattern in events, and the relation between this inner pattern and the individual conscious will which seeks to shape its own life. Eliot had been meditating on these matters, as is clear from a curiously personal intrusion near the end of his essay on John Marston; discussing the play *Sophonisba*, Eliot detected 'an underlying serenity' beneath its surface ferocity, 'a pattern behind the pattern' of the characters' conscious choices. Expanding on this in an essayist's aside, Eliot described it as 'the kind of pattern which we perceive in our own lives only at rare moments of inattention and detachment, drowsing in sunlight' (SE 232). This piece was first published in the *TLS* on 26 July 1934; and almost simultaneously Eliot was making the first of his visits to Emily Hale, recently arrived from Boston.

Lyndall Gordon has argued for the importance of Emily Hale, as an unspoken dedicatee or addressee of much of Eliot's writing from 1927 onwards. The fact that she, a woman whom he had formerly loved, was with him in the rose-garden at Burnt Norton and formed part of the complex of feelings aroused there, might seem to make her central to the poem. Yet it is notable how *Burnt*

Norton declines the gambit of emotional urgency: 'abstention from movement', freedom from the practical desires of boarhounds or boars, are its truer territory. If Emily Hale offered the potentiality for human love, even the tempting possibility of return to America, in doing so she may also have presented a problem, perhaps a Beckettian temptation to revert to a foresworn world of 'appetency'. Gordon's account suggests her tolerant, compassionate, but withal bemused frustration at Eliot's apparent refusal to come to any clear decision about the future course of their relationship; she had apparently resigned her teaching job in the USA in order to spend an extended period in Britain, in the thwarted expectation that matters would be resolved.

Making up his mind, of course, was what Eliot had so disastrously done with Vivien; moreover, making up one's mind might well obscure the true pattern revealed in moments of inattention and detachment. *Burnt Norton* is in some ways a masterpiece of evasion: if the moment in the rose-garden is 'quick now, here, now, always', then it is purged of consequence, in an eternity of involition. The will, by contrast, exerts itself ridiculously in a world of 'waste sad time'. The 'shaft of sunlight' may not penetrate and spur to action, so much as conduce to a clairvoyant torpor. It can be seen how questions of action or suffering, and of the right world to choose, also inform *Murder in the Cathedral* and *The Family Reunion*, which were being completed or planned as *Burnt Norton* was written. Frank Morley, by then in New York, was sent a draft of *Burnt Norton* before publication, and since Emily Hale commented on earlier versions of *The Family Reunion*, it is not improbable that she too may have seen the poem in draft. If so, her reactions – as the reader most alert to its personal dimensions – would be interesting to know.

Personal resonances were of course largely inaudible to the wider readership, who received *Burnt Norton*, on its first publication as the significant new item in *Collected Poems 1909–35* (April 1936), with polite enthusiasm tempered by a degree of bafflement. Reviewers such as John Hayward, Edwin Muir and Peter Quennell praised it; but without particularly close engagement. This second collected volume marked a watershed in Eliot's career, and was taken by some as an opportunity to review his contribution to English letters, whether to mark his eminence or to anticipate his obsolescence. Whilst he was described in the *Sunday Times* as a 'major poet', Malcolm Cowley writing in the USA found it appropriate to have 'afterthoughts' about him, deciding that his earlier work seemed 'less cosmically important' than in 1925. Reviewing the book in *Scrutiny*, D.W. Harding defined the difference as relating to 'the change in attitude that has made Mr Eliot's work less *chic* now than it was ten years ago'. Nevertheless, Eliot's status was high: the month after *Collected Poems* was issued Virginia Woolf referred to him in a letter as 'now the titular head of English–American letters' – an estimate not wholly undercut by her sardonic inflexion, but perhaps also hinting that to occupy such a position was to be a spent force. Certainly, Eliot was no longer identified with the avant-garde, as he had been in 1926; a writer so consistently dismissive of the significance of the present was hardly likely to appeal to a decade, whose literary imaginings were much concerned with the expendability of the old order, and with its imminent replacement by a radically different future. As he well knew when he made his provocative declaration in the preface to *For Lancelot Andrewes*, his beliefs and attitudes were unfashionable, and continued to run against prevailing currents; in spite of which, his new *Collected Poems* sold healthily.

In his *Criterion* editorial of October 1933, Eliot had discriminated his own position from Pound's, explaining that whereas Pound approached public affairs 'primarily as an artist', he himself tended to do so 'from the point of view of a moralist'. The following year he confessed to Paul Elmer More in a letter that 'pure literary criticism has ceased to interest me', and this trend in his thinking was increasingly evident.[7] The other volume he published in 1936 (March) was *Essays Ancient and Modern*; its title made humorous allusion to the well-known hymn-book, and its 'modern' essays – the 'ancient' having been drawn from *For Lancelot Andrewes* – dealt with topics such as 'Religion and Literature', 'Catholicism and International Order', and 'Modern Education and the Classics'. There was very little pure literary criticism in sight, and there were those – best represented by F.R. Leavis and the other *Scrutiny* writers – who lamented the consequent decline in intellectual rigour which they detected in Eliot's criticism.

Where formerly he had been part of the London literary scene, with its little magazines, its intrigues and coteries, and its important and self-important innovators, he tended now to associate with groupings of predominantly Christian intellectuals. From 1934 he was one of the Chandos Group, a fortnightly dining club in which social matters were discussed within a Christian context. Another member, Philippe Mairet, had approached him for assistance with the *New English Weekly* after the death of its founder–editor A.R. Orage; the magazine promulgated the Social Credit theories of C.H. Douglas. For a while these interested Eliot because of their addition of a moral aspect to the science of economics (Pound was a more impassioned and ultimately less judicious devotee). He involved himself with the *NEW* in both editing and contributing capacities: the three later Quartets as well as early versions of *Notes Toward the Definition of Culture* were to have initial publication in its pages. Possibly more important as a shaping force in Eliot's social thinking was The Moot, a group of Christian intellectuals set up by J.H. Oldham in 1938, following the Oxford Conference of the previous year. This activity, as well, had a publishing outlet: in October 1939 Oldham started the *Christian News Letter*, and in 1940 Eliot, as guest editor, wrote the entire contents of three issues.

Activities such as these bore fruit in *The Idea of a Christian Society*, published in 1939 and based on lectures he gave at Cambridge. From a literary perspective this might look like a detour, but it nonetheless fitted with Eliot's own conception of his career. One of his reasons for going into the theatre had been the desire to be socially useful by reaching a wider audience; and there certainly was an audience for the Christian writing: *The Idea of a Christian Society*, which came out just after the outbreak of the Second World War, went through three editions in as many months. Perhaps more telling are the following figures: in January 1939 Eliot closed down the *Criterion*, which had run since October 1922 without ever attracting 1000 subscribers; whereas within three weeks of its wartime launching the *Christian News Letter* had a circulation of nearly 5000; as a professional publisher, Eliot might well have pondered this comparison. It was as a professional publisher at Faber and Faber that he continued to exert an influence on contemporary poetry, nurturing and encouraging several of the younger generation of writers; his office overlooking Russell Square became a place of pilgrimage for the literary aspirant. He took a keen and on occasions financially helpful interest in those whose talent he believed in, and is remembered as a tolerant but not uncritical publisher, who took pains with manuscripts. To the literary world he became known, with affectionate semi-sarcasm, as 'the Pope of Russell Square'; for to be published by Eliot at Faber's could be, for an emergent poet, the potential mark of apostolic succession.

From 1934, shortly after becoming Vicar's Warden, he lived in what Virginia Woolf described as the 'decorous ugliness' of the clergy house of St Stephen's, Kensington; moving from there in 1937 to a flat at 11 Emperor's Gate, which he shared with the Vicar, Father Eric Cheetham.[8] If at first these lodgings had provided an anonymous place of abode, safe from discovery by Vivien, he stayed on there when concealment was no longer necessary; perhaps because the extended temporariness of such dwelling corresponded to his sense that here and now do not greatly matter. But living virtually in the bosom of the Church, mixing with Christians of the upper-middle class, Eliot might seem to be wholly absorbed into the Establishment, in one of its forms. Virginia Woolf was inclined to think so, commenting in a letter of 1937 that 'Old Tom' had 'mounted into the oddest world of antique respectability'; and Conrad Aiken would look back on Eliot's career in terms of a surrender to 'the security in conformity, in joining and belonging'.[9] But if Eliot was an Establishment figure, this did not prevent him from subversive questioning – as, for example, in his pronouncements on the harm done by Milton to English poetry, in July 1936. And if he was a representative man, there was something of the accidental in this; he was obviously thinking of himself when he wrote, of Tennyson, that 'it happens now and then that a poet expresses the mood of his generation, at the same time that he is expressing a mood of his own which is quite remote from that of his generation'. He must, too, have had himself in mind when, in the same essay (initially titled 'In Memoriam' and published in 1936), he asserted that Tennyson the eminent Victorian was 'the most instinctive rebel against the society in which he was the most perfect conformist' (SE 337).

Eliot kept his seasons and rages, which are perhaps most evident in a work like *The Family Reunion*. It is interesting to note that, in a letter to Paul Elmer More of April 1936, Eliot named *Sweeney Agonistes* as his most original achievement.[10] At this time *Burnt Norton* had been published, but *The Family Reunion* was in progress, and there seems little doubt that in it he was trying to incorporate some of the elements of his earlier experiment. The country house setting and the potential murder mystery seem to signal a stock drama; but then to introduce supernatural agents of retribution, and to propose a notion of deep-seated guilt independent of an actual crime, was to extend the limits of the cosy genre.

The complacencies of this assured world are confronted by the more anguished (if also somewhat priggish) vision of Harry, the Fury-driven son; as a result of which its illusory social hierarchies are displaced by a profounder ordering, and the question becomes one – as the character Agatha puts it – of 'sin and expiation' rather than 'crime and punishment'. Here as elsewhere in his work Eliot brings considerable zest to the demolition of essentially bourgeois and secular visions of reality; the play is an attack upon 'normality': 'what you call the normal', declares Harry, 'Is merely the unreal and the unimportant'. In fact, the play's appurtenances of the everyday – its respectful servants, its dutifully unintelligent policeman, and its newspaper reports – are not concessions to codified stage conventions, but instead imply that what many people inhabit as 'real life' is an unconvincing comedy of manners.

Hidden presences, in *Burnt Norton* associated with hope, are more threateningly envisaged in this play as the avenging Furies – although at the end they have become the 'bright angels' of Harry's destiny, just as in the *Eumenides* of Aeschylus they are converted from their purpose of insensate vengeance. How far these recriminatory emissaries from a mysteriously vanished wife are the product of Eliot's complex of feelings about Vivien is a matter for conjecture, as is the degree to which feelings reinvigorated by Emily Hale fed into *Burnt Norton*. Vivien was certainly relentless in her pursuit of her husband (succeeding only once, at a *Sunday Times* book exhibition in November 1935); and by the time of the first performance of *The Family Reunion* she had been compulsorily confined in a private home for the mentally ill, where she was to spend the rest of her life (August 1938 to January 1947). It would be too simplistic to equate Harry's consuming guilt with Eliot's state of mind over his own wife; but there are elements in the play (a dominating mother and a displaced father, a constrained childhood, a furtive and subsequently unhappy marriage producing in Harry what Eliot described as 'a horror of women as of unclean creatures'), that offer points of comparison with the author's life.[11]

The play was a long time in composition: envisaged in a letter of February 1934, it has recently been suggested by Lyndall Gordon that Eliot drafted some of the scenes later that same year, before he was commissioned to do *Murder in the Cathedral*. His difficulty with it is implied by the various stages through which it progressed, right up until the first performance in March 1939[12]; and it was then that Eliot experienced a setback in his move toward the theatre. Whereas *The Rock* had been fairly well-received and certainly well-attended, and *Murder in the Cathedral* had been extremely successful, *The Family Reunion*, his long-gestated attempt to write a play about modern life in verse, received mixed reviews, failed to attract a substantial following, and closed after a run of five weeks. Virginia Woolf, who had noted how buoyant Eliot had seemed with the success of *Murder*, now observed how 'yellow and heavy-lidded' he was made by the knowledge that his next play had failed.

Within six months Britain would be at war with Germany; and leaving aside any faults in the play itself, this had not been the best time to place such an offering before the public. In September the previous year the policy of appeasement pursued by the British Government under Neville Chamberlain had culminated in the infamous – and, as it was to turn out, worthless – pact with Hitler in Munich; and if such desire to be let off the hook was at all representative of national sentiment, it could hardly be supposed that people would respond warmly to a play so austerely recommending the inevitability of suffering, so contemptuous of lives lived safely. Unlike his previous play, *The Family Reunion* did not triumph over an unpromising subject, and its failure is likely to have been a significant reversal for Eliot: in this drama he had tried to bring some of the unsettling savagery of his earlier and more daring work to bear upon his later thinking; he had tried not to be 'an old fogey', and he would not take such risks in the theatre again.

It is usually suggested that the reason he turned aside from drama to composing the three later Quartets was the difficulty of staging plays in wartime Britain. This was the account Eliot himself offered, but as Gordon points out, *Murder in the Cathedral* was revived throughout the war in various improvised theatres, so drama on a modest scale was at least possible. It is quite probable, given its terminal placing in *Poems 1909–1935*, that Eliot intended *Burnt Norton* to be his final significant poem – and interestingly, he had at one stage considered ending it with the words 'Light / Gone'.[13] He may well have planned to devote himself to the theatre thereafter: *The Family Reunion* contains several echoes of his poetry, noticed by contemporary reviewers – almost as if he were consciously realigning the direction of his *oeuvre*. If so, the play's reception must have shaken his nerve, and given him cause to doubt that the drama really was the medium best suited to what he had to say and the way in which he was disposed to say it.

The 1930s had been a decade of both change and continuity in Eliot's career, from which he emerged as a (somewhat premature) elder statesman of English letters. Although this may have been his ambition, the means by which it had been fulfilled were sometimes unforeseen. In 1920, writing in her journal early on in her acquaintance with the young poet, Virginia Woolf perceptively applied to him the phrase 'dominant & subversive'[14]: it seems to have been the case that, if Eliot felt the need to dominate, this was accompanied by an equally strong urge to doubt the order that such dominance established. This can be seen in his relation to the Modernist movement: if his early energies were spent in attacking the literary standards prevalent in England around 1914, later on his rôle was, in part, to subvert the very subversives he had appeared to represent, by a provocative self-identification with the forces of orthodoxy. Yet these same forces, in their turn, were not safe from his subversion.

In certain respects his was a balancing act, a search for the middle way which, in religion, was represented for him by the Church of England. His increasing commitment to the Anglo-Catholic wing of that institution set him against the currents of the time, and estranged him philosophically from old associates such as Pound and Wyndham Lewis, as well as from the rising generation of poets whose most substantial and enduring figure was W.H. Auden; whose poetry, with its suggestions of secular apocalypse and its apparent summons to decisive action, defined and caught the mood of young intellectuals, even as they overlooked its more riddling obliquities. The Spanish Civil War, which broke out at the end of 1936, provoked *crises de conscience* amongst this predominantly left-wing group; many writers declared their support for the Republican (anti-Franco) cause, and some went so far as to enlist in its army. When, in 1937, Eliot was approached for his opinion on events in Spain, in a questionnaire circulated amongst contemporary writers, he replied – no doubt aware what the preponderant response would be – that he felt that at least a few men of letters should remain silent. Perhaps he intended a reproach of those who enhanced their reputations by speaking fearlessly about situations where the actual risks and misery were incurred by other people. When to his surprise his answer was published along with all the others, his failure to side with the Republicans was taken by some to be an expression of tacit support for Franco. Yet a principled middle ground, on which one could justifiably abstain from action, might well have been expected as the preferred position of the author of *Burnt Norton*.

What seemed like evasiveness might be more truly seen as a fundamental distrust of the political structures within which answers to such questions were being sought. During the course of the decade, Eliot grew less concerned with purely political debate, just as he grew less interested in pure literary criticism. His sense of the importance of economics, evidenced in some of his *Criterion* commentaries and in his interest in theories of Social Credit, diminished; and it is significant that he could not complete his projected political cycle, the 'Coriolan' poems. Although it is clear that his move away from the meditative inwardness of the *Ash-Wednesday* sequence to his work on *The Rock* signalled a desire to engage directly with social issues, these were perceived within a programme whose goal was religious, and whose concern was increasingly with the idea of a Christian society. This emphasis gave a curious slant to some of Eliot's pronouncements, as when, addressing the Harvard Classical Club in 1933, he expressed his hope for 'the revival and expansion of monastic teaching orders' ('Modern Education and the Classics', SE 515); the function of such orders would be to resist 'barbarism', but in the same year that saw the election of Hitler to the Chancellorship there was evidence of a barbarism that would need more strenuous opposition.

In the 'Last Words' of his final editorial in the *Criterion* in January 1939, Eliot, reviewing its development, explained how for him 'a right political philosophy came more and more to imply a right theology – and right economics to depend upon right ethics' (his detractors might remark that 'right' for Eliot also implied 'right-wing'). If he ventured onto political ground, it was as a Christian moralist rather than as a poet. He also made clear in these comments how profound was his 'depression of spirits' faced by the 'present state of public affairs'; which had led to his decision to close the *Criterion*. This in itself represented a change of direction, or an exhaustion of one: he could no longer wholly believe in a cultural community to which such a publication could address itself; and indeed it may fairly be said that, in failing to establish such a sense amongst a general readership, the venture had fallen short. In this editorial farewell Eliot reaffirmed his faith in 'literature', but envisaged this as likely to be written by authors who were prepared to forego immediate popularity. He was finishing *The Family Reunion* at this time, and since he had gone into the theatre in search of a wider audience his comments did not perhaps reflect his own intentions – although ironically, that play's unpopularity made him the undesigning practiser of what he had preached.

Some of his friends had sensed a mellowing in Eliot during the later 1930s, a relaxation after the turmoils of his marriage and separation. Outwardly, his life was that of a literary notable, with a busy calendar of lectures and committees; he also found time to approve merit in younger authors, writing in praise of Djuna Barnes, for example, whose experimental novel *Nightwood* was published by Faber in 1937. As well as this, he involved himself in work relating to Christian and charitable interests. He seems to have had a genial persona to put forth – displayed publicly in the avuncular personage of 'Old Possum' with his doggerels about cats (October 1939); yet co-existing with all this was his darker side, pessimistic about the future of civilisation and gloomy about his personal prospects in this world or the next. Political events of the closing years of the decade brought him close to despair; and, privately, it was during these years (he was later to explain to his confidante Mary Trevelyan) that his involvement with Emily Hale showed him he was no longer capable of love.

This point would be made in 1949 by a critic of his play *The Cocktail Party*, when he suggested that Eliot seemed 'incapable of love: of warmth towards the particular, as opposed to a diffused benevolence'.[15] Such a diagnosis was particularly relevant to the dramas, where Eliot's inability to interest himself sufficiently in his *dramatis personae* as characters made it difficult to stimulate an audience's interest. Who really cares what happens to Harry? Eliot's shortcoming as playwright is that he was too concerned with the emblematic or moral quantity of his plot to endow its agents with 'felt life'. That phrase is Henry James's; and whatever the similarities between the two transplanted American writers, Eliot's temperamental inability to carry out James's advice to 'dramatise, dramatise!' constitutes their most significant difference. Most unlike James, Eliot had an ascetic and even potentially monastic temperament, whose natural movement was withdrawal rather than engagement. His tendency toward a lofty disdain for what he dismissed in *Burnt Norton* as 'this twittering world' contrasts sharply with James's omnivorous fascination; and the 'social message' of both *Murder in the Cathedral* and *The Family Reunion* could be construed as being that it is better to disengage from a world which does not provide an adequate arena for spiritual exertion. Indeed, the technical problems with the presentation of the Eumenides, about which Eliot was to write amusingly years later (OPP 84), go right to the heart of the matter: the difficulty lay in manifesting them plausibly, in making them seem 'real'; yet for Eliot, the Eumenides were the truest level of reality in the play.

At the end of the 1930s, with the closure of his literary review and the poor reception of his play a little later, Eliot's career terminated one of its phases and experienced failure in another. Two areas of influence were in abeyance. There yet remained his function as an exponent of 'right theology', and he was still involved with the promulgation of a 'Christian society' (since 1620, we might note in passing, a quintessentially American project), but the very events by which the world was imminently to be convulsed must have cast doubt on how responsive the mind of Europe was likely to be to such thinking. There is, then, something of an irony in the fact that the war, which directly or indirectly interfered with his endeavours in these areas, was to furnish him with the circumstances in which the writing of a poetry of Christian affirmation would reach a very wide audience and prove to be socially useful; in which being a poet was a politically significant deed.

Lecturing at Corpus Christi, Cambridge in March 1939 (the three lectures were published that October as *The Idea of a Christian Society*), Eliot had made plain his dismay at the moral and political climate implied by Chamberlain's policy of appeasement toward Hitler. The abandonment of that policy, with Britain's declaration of war on Germany on 3 September 1939, did not immediately usher in a mood of national renewal, however, so much as produce a numbing dread of what was to come. Certain that gas-attacks would be a feature of this war as of the last (only this time directed against the civilian population), the authorities issued gas-masks to all and sundry; city children were evacuated to the country, in anticipation of a devastating aerial bombardment, which the popular imagination had been contemplating from the mid-thirties onward. But neither of these measures was necessary or effective, for remarkably little happened during the first months of the conflict. This period, lasting until the spring of 1940, would be referred to as the 'Phoney War'; and it was against this background of uncertainty, in which fatuous optimism about a speedy resolution mingled with vastly imprecise fears about the future, that Eliot embarked on the next phase of his career.

He was not unaffected by the mood of irreality or by fears of being bombed: this, after all, was his second experience of London at war. Letters of the period to Virginia Woolf show him confessing to his own listlessness in the dark time; on 12 October he was speculating half-humorously on the probable terminal dwindling of his reputation; and in a letter dated 'Holy Innocents' Day' (28 December) 1939, he wrote that the general 'restlessness' prevented mental activity. He told her that, offered a good spot on radio to air his views, he had turned it down because he didn't have anything to say. He was trying – on the whole unsuccessfully – to stimulate himself by reading the plays of Ibsen; he had derived no pleasure from the appearance of Cyril Connolly's new literary magazine, *Horizon*. Wartime was different from peacetime, but lives had not yet suffered the profound disruption that was to come. For Eliot, one personal consequence was that Emily Hale, whom he was accustomed to see at least once a year, had returned to the USA after an extended visit, and there was no way of knowing when, if ever, they would meet again. But at this stage he still lived at Emperor's Gate, and still kept an office routine at Faber's (added to which were his two nights' duty as fire-watcher and air-raid warden).

He also seems still to have had yearnings for the theatre. In 1958 Eliot said that his first reaction to the flop of *The Family Reunion* had been the wish to write a better play; Stephen Spender in his Journal recorded a lunchtime conversation in late September 1939, in which Eliot argued that the poetic drama might attain a lucidity not so easily achievable by the introspective monologue of a poem.[16] We have already seen that at the very end of the year he was reading Ibsen – perhaps in search of dramaturgical inspiration. There is no indication in that December letter to Virginia Woolf that Eliot had any literary project in hand (although he had in his remarks to Spender stressed the importance of keeping writing, no matter what); but within six weeks or so John Hayward would inform Frank Morley in New York that Eliot was working on 'a new poem in succession to "Burnt Norton" – the second of three quatuors – provisionally entitled "East Coker"' (C4Q 16).

From Hayward's paraphrase of Eliot's remarks (C4Q 16–17), it sounded as if the poem was progressing slowly, with only two of the five sections drafted; Eliot was worried about it seeming 'like an imitation of myself', but had at least expunged the line 'The Archer's Bow and Taurus' ire' (in January 1940 Eliot told Virginia Woolf he had been reading a book on astrology in manuscript, which doubtless left its deposit in such images). Later the same month (February 1940), however, Hayward reported that he now had a complete draft of the poem, which he pronounced 'prodigiously fine'; his comments on the draft, and the sequence of Eliot's own alterations, are set out in Helen Gardner's book. The poem was first published as a supplement to the *New English Weekly* on 21 March 1940; this rapidly sold out, necessitating reprints of the Supplement in May and June; the poem was then published as a shilling pamphlet by Faber's that September. The poem was certainly prodigiously successful, producing both self-doubt and self-assurance in the author; having in October 1939 expressed his doubts to Virginia Woolf about how his reputation would hold up, by May 1940 she was complaining in her Journal about Eliot's 'writer's egotism', evidenced in his phrase 'Coleridge and I'. By 10 March the following year, however, reflecting on the success of *East Coker*, he wrote that he found it 'hard to believe that a poem of mine which sells nearly 12,000 copies can be really good' (C4Q 109).

Helen Gardner comments on the enormous impact it had, by virtue of appearing 'at the dreariest moment of the war' (C4Q 17). Doubtless its apparent evocation of a timeless English village provided an ikon for what many, in the Second as the First World War, were prepared to fight for – irrespective of whether or not they lived in such a place themselves. It is worth bearing in mind, however, that when the poem was written and first published very little fighting had actually been done: in March 1940 Chamberlain was still Prime Minister, and France was still a sovereign power, whose own army was reinforced by a substantial British force on French soil. However eloquently *East Coker* would speak to the nation with its back to the wall – as was shortly to be the case – the poem was a product of the Phoney War (as is perhaps most clearly seen in its treatment of the wasted time of *'l'entre deux guerres'*).

Eliot had evidently found something to say since he turned down the offer of a radio broadcast. But even if this poem was a response to his desire to find a role for himself in the atmosphere of helplessness and futility, it was perhaps not quite what many of its contemporary readers supposed it to be. *East Coker* is concerned with originations: named after the Somerset village from which Eliot's seventeenth-century forebear, Andrew Eliot, set out for a new life in the New World. Eliot had inherited his mother's interest in the family's roots, and early in 1939 had spent time researching the Eliot line in the British Museum. He had visited the village once only, in August 1937, when staying in the neighbouring village of West Coker with Sir Matthew Nathan; he had taken some photographs – and that was all; he would not return during his lifetime. For if the poem is concerned with origins, and with the past, it is also concerned with the need to leave the past behind and head toward the new life, as Andrew Eliot had done.

Although it is probable that the poem's apparent association of English rural life with spiritual verities formed part of its immediate popular appeal (this, after all, had been the burden of some of Eliot's *Criterion* editorials), the case is more complex. It is clear to anyone who knows East Coker that the village is not represented with fidelity; indeed, the somewhat Audenesque landscape of factories and bypasses could be – and was meant to be – anywhere, then and in England. With Helen Gardner's publication of the drafts and relevant material, it is also clear how much of Eliot's American past was implicated: although the mouse behind the wainscot comes initially from Tennyson (a passage from 'Mariana' which Eliot quoted in his essay on the poet, with the spelling 'wainscoat' as originally proposed for *East Coker*), the fact that it is a *field*-mouse he justified to Hayward's query by saying that fieldmice were found in the Eliot summer house at Gloucester, Massachusetts. He went on to explain to Hayward that this house in the poem was deserted – just as the Eliot family no longer possessed their seaside retreat – and it is difficult not to suppose that the 'silent motto' referred to was the Eliot family motto, *tace et fac*. Eliot's memory of that house on the Atlantic goes some way toward explaining the appearance of the wrinkling sea (another Tennysonian echo), at the end of the first section: for East Coker is twenty miles or so inland, and in the village one has no sense whatsoever of the distant ocean.

Just as Andrew Eliot left East Coker behind him in 1669, to cross the Atlantic and join a society which represented itself as truly following God's word, so the poem withdraws from its cloddishly dancing rustics, in pursuit of the unchanging principle within changing appearances; and the village is seen no more. Moving from place to placelessness, *East Coker* returns to roots in order to enforce the necessity of deracination; it does not matter where you start from, it implies, so long as you are prepared to make a start, and it enjoins on its reader the duty of exploration: the setting forth, the act of 'beginning', becomes its own 'end', or purpose. There are some consistent Eliotian themes audible within the poem: the need to establish continuity with the past, but also to break from it; the ungenial dismissal of the things of this world, whether represented by 'the coupling of man and woman' or the priorities of merchant bankers; and the anticipation of purgatorial suffering.

As can be seen from his comments to Hayward, Eliot was at first concerned that in *East Coker* he might appear to be imitating himself. Not since his series of quatrain poems had the poetic form preceded the poetic impulse, and his instinct had consistently been to avoid repetition.[17] *East Coker* not only inherits the shape of *Burnt Norton*, it deliberately establishes correspondences – the 'deep lane' into the village echoes the 'passage' leading to the rose-garden in the earlier poem, for example. The later poem directly confronts the issue of repetition, of course ('You say I am repeating / Something I have said before. I shall say it again.'); and it does so because it is in many ways a retort to its predecessor, rejecting the 'intense moment / Isolated' evoked in *Burnt Norton* (and suggestive of Eliot's own lyric impulses), in favour of a less exalted world of continuity and consequence. What might have been the Garden of Eden, glimpsed amongst the roses, has become the Garden of Gethsemane in *East Coker*; and the later poem is concerned, not with unique experience, but with cycles of recurrence in the life of a community. This partly explains why, of all the Quartets, *East Coker* is the most allusive to other literature; for it is very much a rumination by Eliot on the role his individual talent can find for itself in the 'community' of tradition: whether that community is conceived as England, as English Literature, or as the Church of England.

The poem's immediate success illustrated an extraordinary con-fluence – such as Eliot had sought and failed to achieve through drama – between his private preoccupations and the public world; it even had a certain predictive quality. Doubtless, a good many of its 12 000 readers took *East Coker* as a high-brow version of the war-time favourite 'There'll always be an England'; but even the poem's ascetic urging to self-sacrificing confrontation with the unknown was a topical message, having its similarity to Winston Churchill's promise to the embattled nation of 'blood, toil, tears, and sweat' (May 1940). How easily its 'quiet-voiced elders' with their deceitful serenity could be associated with the discredited appeasers in the British government; how easy, also, to believe that Eliot's 'undisciplined squads of emotion' with their 'shabby equipment always deteriorating' were based upon the Home Guard – which did not, however, come into existence until mid-May 1940. In fact, events which took place between the poem's first appearance on 21 March and its publication by Faber in September 1940 endowed it with startling relevance: the government of Chamberlain fell after the failure of the Franco–British attempt to invade Norway, and Churchill became Prime Minister on 10 May; then came the German invasion of France, quickly followed by the evacuation of the British Army (minus equipment) from Dunkirk. France had capitulated by the end of June, and the Battle of Britain, in which the Luftwaffe tried and failed to destroy British air resistance in preparation for a German invasion, ensued in July and August. By the time *East Coker* appeared from Faber on 12 September, the intensive night-time bombing of London had begun.

In that context, Eliot's production of a long poem with an identifiably English setting could hardly fail to seem affirmative; the more so, as its publication made most visible his own decision to remain in England. For even had he not written anything, merely by staying in the country during wartime he performed an act of encouragement. More than one of the younger generation of writers who had come into fashion and prominence during the 1930s (and whose poetry had so fearlessly evoked a necessary apocalypse) had taken immediate care to place themselves well out of harm's way. Eliot had the offer of a bolt-hole at an American university, but declined it; and there is reason to suppose he disapproved of British citizens who sought that kind of safety: a letter to Mary Hutchinson of July 1940 suggests he had commented adversely on the exodus to America by those who could (typically, the monied classes).

He did not remain because he was not frightened of the bombing, however, and with the Blitz on London he felt obliged to alter his routine. In October 1940 he removed to Shamley Green, near Guildford, to stay with the writer Hope Mirrlees and her mother and aunt, commuting to London for one and then two nights each week, which he passed with Geoffrey Faber and his family at Hampstead. This was to be the pattern of life which he would follow for the rest of the war: trying to do his job and any public duties during his days in the city, and reserving his time in Surrey for composition (he was not, however, always able to keep to these demarcations). Looking back on this period, Eliot commented on how the later Quartets lent themselves to the conditions of their production, because he 'could write them in sections' and 'didn't have to have quite the same continuity'; 'it didn't matter,' as he put it, 'if a day or two elapsed when I did not write, as they frequently did, while I did war jobs'.[18] That such circumstances were conducive to this kind of poetry is evident in the speed with which Eliot went on to write the next poem in the sequence: in January 1941 Hayward reported to Morley that on New Year's Day he had received 'the typescript of the first draft of the third poem of Tom's trilogy' (C4Q 19). *The Dry Salvages* had been composed during the last three months of 1940.

It is unclear why Hayward should refer at this stage to a 'trilogy' of poems. Although in February 1940 he had been anticipating a sequence of 'three quatuors', by April that year he had told Morley that Eliot envisaged a series of four. It seems more than a slip of the pen, however, since in his further comments on the new poem's title Hayward complained of its failure 'to complete the pattern' begun by its two predecessors. Whether this is evidence of any uncertainty on Eliot's part we do not know; he was later to assert that the conception of the *Quartets* as a set of four came to him during the writing of *East Coker*; and the use of the four seasons and the four elements as patterning devices seems to corroborate this.

We can certainly see how *The Dry Salvages* follows on from the previous poem, suggesting the element of water where that had suggested earth; in addition, the ending of *East Coker* prefigured a sea-voyage, which leads into its successor but was also appropriate, of course, as the consequence of Andrew Eliot's decision to leave the village. The poem does not open with a 'sea picture', as Eliot had at first intended, but with an evocation of a strong brown river, obviously the Mississippi; and it may be that he chose this beginning more clearly to signal the American location to an English audience. The title of the poem, he explained to Hayward's objection, did denote a place name, and therefore did not break the pattern of previous titles; but commenting on that Hayward rather shrewdly discriminated a 'place-name' (such as 'East

Coker') from 'the name of a place', which this was. In fact, as a location the Dry Salvages differs from all the others in the sequence, in that it does not denote a human settlement; moreover, it is possible that Eliot never actually set foot on these rocks 'off the N.E. coast of Cape Ann', for although they are a seamark useful to navigate by, they are also a hazard to steer clear of.

In 1964 Eliot mistakenly believed his ancestor Andrew to have been involved in a famous ship-wreck near the spot (C4Q 53); if he also thought that in 1940, it would have been an additional continuity. Be that as it may, in evoking the Dry Salvages and the Mississippi Eliot was returning in imagination to what he more than once defined as the two poles of his American experience, at New England and St Louis. Hayward at once recognised that nostalgia for the sea, deriving from Eliot's boyhood and youth sailing off the coast of Cape Ann, which forms an emotional substratum in much of the poetry; nevertheless, this is not a poem of homecoming, but of nature seen as chaos: a 'backward look' toward 'the primitive terror'. There is an ambivalence, then, in the homage *The Dry Salvages* pays his native land, which Eliot divests of civilised amenities, and restores to something of that savagery by which his seventeenth-century forebear must have been confronted. For Andrew, America was a place in which to work out his salvation; but for Thomas it had been a place to get away from: in the final section he depicts a milieu reminiscent of the London of Madame Sosostris, and closes envisaging a distinctively English interment. This poem of water ends with an evocation of the life of 'significant soil'.

The Dry Salvages was first published in the *New English Weekly* at the end of February 1941; a week earlier, Faber had issued *Burnt Norton* by itself in a format similar to that of *East Coker*, thereby retrospectively incorporating the poem of 1935 into the growing sequence of what were now 'quartets'. In July Faber published an introductory selection of Eliot's prose, edited by John Hayward, and in September issued *The Dry Salvages* in a print-run of over 11 000. The *TLS* greeted the poem, like *East Coker*, with some misgivings, but on the appearance of this third quartet other reviewers took the opportunity to consider all three poems in the light of Eliot's development. Young scholars like Muriel Bradbrook and Helen Gardner, each of whom would later write book-length studies of the poet, inaugurated their critical interest with appreciative responses to his latest work, laying particular emphasis on the religious aspects of the Quartets. In the same year that their pieces were published (1942), George Orwell offered a less scholarly response, asserting that he found the Quartets unmemorable and devoid of enthusiasm; writing in the new magazine *Poetry London*, he contrasted their 'melancholy faith' with the 'glowing despair' of the earlier poetry.

This division of opinion between scholarly reverence, and scepticism on the part of a practising writer, foreshadows later discussions of the *Quartets* (although writers have also praised the poems, and academics have also deplored them). At the time of publication opinion was more for than against, and the high expectations indicated by the initial print-run for *The Dry Salvages* were not disappointed. The poem's prayer of intercession for endangered mariners was highly relevant to the beleaguered Atlantic convoys running the gauntlet of Hitler's U-boats; and whatever the privately personal impulse behind Eliot's imagination of his boyhood's scenery, he was hardly alone in fixing his mind upon America at this dark period of the war, when Britain desperately needed allies. The increasingly overt Christian references within the poem were unlikely to have upset the poem's readers, many of whom would gladly have accepted God's help, if offered; and its closing affirmation that we 'are only undefeated / Because we have gone on trying' struck a truly topical note.

Reporting on Eliot in July 1942, Hayward wrote to Morley that the three quartets had 'more than rehabilitated his current poetic reputation which was in some danger of becoming temporarily dimmed by the vapourings of the young' (C4Q 24). The context of his remark, however, was a letter in which he bemoaned the slow progress Eliot had been making with the final poem of his sequence, *Little Gidding*. He had started on this quite soon after the publication of its predecessor, and had produced a first draft for Hayward to inspect by 7 July 1941. The two men exchanged letters, with Eliot replying to Hayward's first comments in early August, at which stage he anticipated leaving the poem aside 'for a week or two longer'; but to Hayward's frustration this delay extended itself over months, and it was not until late July 1942 that Eliot again set to work on it. There were then interchanges of letters, revised sections, and a second complete draft on 2 September; minor details were still being changed at the proof stage. The poem was finally published in the *New English Weekly* on 15 October 1942, and subsequently was issued as a pamphlet on 1 December.

Little Gidding takes for its title the name of the hamlet where a small Anglican community was founded by Nicholas Ferrar (a friend of the poet George Herbert); this lasted for some twenty years, until its destruction in 1646 as a result of the English Civil War. What has survived is the unremarkable little chapel in which they worshipped, its red-brick subsequently dignified with stone facings to the west wall, justly described in the poem as a 'dull façade'. To this secluded spot of Huntingdonshire Eliot had come on a beautiful late-May day in 1936, roughly two years after his visit to Burnt Norton, and a year or so before his visit to East Coker; and it appears that, like those places, he came only once. But unlike Burnt Norton and the emotions released there by his visit with Emily Hale, and East Coker with its genealogical interest for the Eliot family (and unlike the Dry Salvages with their associations from his boyhood), Little Gidding had no particularly personal resonance for him; it seems to have embodied, rather, an approved type of Anglican devotion, a small-scale embodiment of a Church of England humbly outlasting reverses of fortune. We may well understand how a symbol for the survival of English spirit through adversities of history might suggest itself to a poet writing in England in 1941 (especially if he was not born an Englishman); but the association was willed rather than immediate.

This may have contributed to his obvious difficulties in composing this last quartet, as Eliot himself acknowledged when he wrote to Hayward in August 1941 that he felt it damagingly lacking in 'some acute personal reminiscence' that might animate its imaginative texture. There were other possible reasons for the delay: early in 1940 Hayward had expressed some impatience (to Morley) with Eliot's over-conscientious involvement in time-consuming committee-work and 'vestry intrigues'; this had not decreased: in April 1942 he paid a five-week visit to neutral Sweden accompanied by Bishop Bell, lecturing for the British Council; later he delivered lectures in Glasgow, Bristol and London (it should be remembered that Eliot was a nervous traveller, and that journies in war-time were seldom convenient). He wrote an introduction for his selection of Kipling's verse, which further bemused Hayward. All this was visibly fatiguing – Hayward described him in June 1941 as looking 'washed-out and dispirited' – added to which were Eliot's susceptibility to bronchial complaints and the extraction of all his teeth. That his poor health and congested diary retarded composition was likely, however, to have been symptom rather than cause of the poem's delay; for Eliot was finding the writing of *Little Gidding* a most challenging assignment, from whose 'solitary toil' (he told Martin Browne soon after it was published) he had been willingly diverted to 'external or public activity'.

Eliot was invariably diffident about work in progress, but in July 1941 his expressed reservations about the first draft were quite strong: he was sure it was not as good as the others; for him the question was, whether it was even good enough to keep company with them. Part of his difficulty lay in the need to be adequate to contemporary events; as he later explained in his letter to Browne (20 October 1942), 'in the midst of what is going on now it is hard, when you sit down at a desk, to feel confident that morning after morning spent fiddling with words and rhythms is a justified activity' (C4Q 21). But the greater difficulty lay in being adequate to the earlier quartets. For the third time, Eliot was breaking with what had once been his practice, by reverting to the form of a previous poem; and much more than the others, *Little Gidding* was a conscious recapitulation. As he explained to Hayward (14 July 1941), his doubts about it were 'partly due to the fact that as it is written to complete a series, and not solely for itself, it may be too much from the head' (C4Q 22). The prestige already acquired by its forerunners may also have been daunting; as we have seen, Hayward judged them to have restored Eliot's reputation to its height. Those who doubted were rebuked: George Orwell's comments were vigorously rebutted by Kathleen Raine, for example; and when *East Coker* received an obliquely sneering review in the *TLS*, F.R. Leavis immediately wrote to berate the paper for its condescension toward 'the greatest living English poet'. Leavis amplified his accolade when he came to review *The Dry Salvages* in the summer of 1942, concluding that 'it should by now be impossible to doubt that he is among the greatest poets of the English language'.[19]

Such laurels might well weigh heavily, on the brows of a writer who was attempting to match these earlier achievements; the more so given his sense, expressed in a letter to Mary Hutchinson of 25 October 1941, that 'in these times' it was necessary, as never before, that his work be good. In *Little Gidding* Eliot consciously set out, not only to complete the pattern of four, but in doing so to evoke the wholeness of his own *oeuvre*: in addition to the unifying echoes of the earlier Quartets there are, as his letters to Hayward made clear, allusions to his plays and to earlier poems such as 'New Hampshire' and even 'La Figlia Che Piange'. The word 'eviscerate', for example, chosen in his revision of section II, occurs in the 1918 'Ode', where it is also used, unusually, as an adjective rather than a verb; this poem was only published once, in *Ara Vos Prec*, whose title (when translated) is unobtrusively alluded to in the first three words of 'I pray you to forgive / Both bad and good'.

Little Gidding may have been intended to set a crown upon his lifetime's effort, thereby confirming the literary pre-eminence he had established; but there is within the poem an essential counter-current to such grand designings – 'the purpose is beyond the end you figured' – and which leads toward a meditation less on the greatness than on the pointlessness of such achievement. In July 1935, writing in the *Criterion*, Eliot had himself referred to Yeats as 'the greatest poet of his time'; and he had given the first Annual Yeats Lecture in Dublin in 1940 (the year after his death), in which he had deepened his appreciation of Yeats's greatness, and also of his rage. One of the most significant improvements made between the first and final drafts of *Little Gidding* lay in Eliot's altering the message delivered by the 'familiar compound ghost', from flat exhortation to a more resonant evocation of the vanity of human wishes; and although based on Dante's discovery of his old teacher Brunetto Latini in hell (*Inferno*, Canto XV), the major figure behind this ghost was Yeats (another component was Swift).

This was not because Eliot thought of Yeats as one of the damned, but because he respected him as a poet whose final achievement lay in making great poetry out of disappointment and remorse; and it was all the more appropriate that one whom he had himself described as pre-eminent in his time should remind Eliot – as inheritor of those laurels – of the emptiness of ambition. If the example of Yeats was before him as he composed *Little Gidding* (and it is interesting to note that in it he partly adopted Yeats's practice of writing initial drafts in prose), there were other writers he might well have thought of: in January 1941 James Joyce had died suddenly, and in March the same year Virginia Woolf committed suicide. Neither was a deep personal loss for Eliot, but here were two careers to ponder; and it may be that his reminiscences of Woolf (*Horizon*, May 1941), which seemed to some cold and neglectful of her literary achievement, reflected a sense of the insignificance of literature (she had killed herself within days of receiving the NEW printing of *The Dry Salvages* from Eliot). In addition to any possible professional gloom, there is also some evidence of personal gloom in a letter to Mary Hutchinson written on his birthday (26 September 1941), in which he comments on his limited social life, and asserts his doubt that anyone could value his friendship.

Assuredly, the international situation fed Eliot's depression; the war in Europe (and there was by this stage also war in Asia) threatened so much in which he had believed: how vulnerable the 'ideal order' formed by monuments of the past must have appeared. The circumstances of the war impinge most obviously on *Little Gidding*, whose imagery summons up the experiences of the air-raids on London; and it needs to be remembered that, when this last Quartet was being written, British defeat still seemed distinctly possible (it was not until November 1942 that Churchill hailed the Battle of Egypt as signalling 'the end of the beginning'). So although his declaration 'History is now and England' might itself seem to enact a quasi-Churchillian bravado, its mood is more muted, and is not unmindful of the possibilities of failure: the community at Little Gidding had, after all, been destroyed; and to subsume one's individual fate within the national destiny was no escape-route. The poem tries to learn how to care and not to care about personal and national survival – 'survival' being different from salvation.

In 1953, preparing his address 'The Three Voices of Poetry', Eliot wrote and then struck out a declaration that the last three Quartets had been 'primarily patriotic poems'.[20] Quite a few contemporary readers probably took them in this spirit; but *Little Gidding*, as the culmination of the sequence, is no exercise in poetic triumphalism, whatever its address to 'England'. As a series, the *Quartets* move away from the solitary and ambiguous exaltation of *Burnt Norton* toward the sense, in the last, of a life made meaningful by its wider relations. The first note Eliot wrote, as he started *Little Gidding*, stressed the redemption of individuals within a larger pattern, 'having their meaning together not apart' (C4Q 157); (if Eliot wished us to think of his collected poems in this light, his self-quotation becomes thematically relevant, rather than ostentatious). The situation of a nation at war, in which individuals are conscripted and even sacrificed for the common good, is a political instance of this fundamentally religious idea; and it may be that Eliot thought better of his definition 'primarily patriotic', not because he wanted to obscure that element in the poems, but because it is less true than to say that the last three Quartets are primarily religious poems.

The critical response to *Little Gidding* was overwhelmingly favourable; the *TLS* reviewer expressed some impatience with Eliot's relapse into accustomed patterns, and John Shand in *Nineteenth Century* (September 1944) implied that Eliot was too erudite for his own good; but these voices stand out from the chorus of approval. A reader who dared to dispute D.W. Harding's semi-ecstatic review in *Scrutiny* found himself imperiously rebuked by F.R. Leavis. The poem was particularly well-received, of course, by those to whom its Christian message was most congenial, and Eliot himself observed that the best notices were in the *Tablet* and the *Catholic Herald*; but it is unlikely that all its enthusiasts were Christians. In February 1943 Eliot told Montgomery Belgion that the poem had sold about 12 000 copies; the print-run for the Faber pamphlet was 16 775; each print-run had grown larger, just as each successive Quartet grew longer. These pamphlets had not been published in the USA, so the first collected edition of *Four Quartets* (Eliot having been dissuaded from his original wish to call them 'Kensington Quartets') was published in New York (May 1943), to be followed by a UK edition from Faber in October 1944. Although as usual the American print-run was smaller (3500 against 6000), the reaction of American critics was not markedly less favourable; even the doubters, such as the young poet Delmore Schwartz (who had dubbed the second 'East Coca-Cola') writing in *Nation*, were respectful, and the enthusiasts were generous: Horace Gregory described them in the *New York Times Book Review* (16 May 1943) as 'the best poetry of their kind since Wordsworth wrote "The Prelude"'.

It is notable that *Four Quartets* received intelligent and sympathetic treatment more or less immediately, on both sides of the Atlantic. The themes of intersection of time by eternity, the relevance of the epigraphs from Heraclitus, the musical analogy suggested by 'quartet', the inter-relations of the poems, the purpose of the allusions to other writers and the echoing of his own work, and the place of the sequence within the corpus of Eliot's writing – all these issues were addressed by early reviewers, some of whom showed an extensive familiarity with all his poetry and much of his prose. This was in part a consequence of the fact that Eliot was not exactly a voluminous writer (to borrow the phrase he applied to Ronald Bottrall), at least in terms of poetry; but beyond this it indicated how far his *oeuvre* had been assimilated by his readership, and how far he had trained them to read it: they carried his phrases and images in their heads, and used his own critical formulae to illuminate his poems.

Unlike *Burnt Norton*, the three later Quartets were composed with an audience in mind. This was doubtless a result of Eliot's intervening experience as a playwright, but was probably also due to the different circumstances of their production: he wanted to be useful in wartime. Moreover, he wrote with an increasing eye to posterity: John Hayward, the friend with whom principally he discussed the early drafts, was self-appointed keeper of the 'Eliot Archive'; Eliot had given him the printer's copy of *Burnt Norton* before the war, and subsequently gave him manuscripts and documents for the other Quartets, which the bibliophilic Hayward lovingly preserved. At one point in the correspondence with Hayward, Eliot humorously imagines 'some American freshwater college sleuth' of the future misinterpreting a remark in his letter (C4Q 173). Hayward's interventions during composition were rather those of a pedantic editor, than an inspired interpreter such as Pound had been for *The Waste Land*, and the nature of Hayward's concern with Eliot's career was also different from what Pound's had been.

It is appropriate that there should be so marked a contrast between the fugitive presences of *Burnt Norton* and the declamatory ghost of *Little Gidding*, because the last Quartet comes closest of all Eliot's poetry to making a public statement. His ever more conscious patterning doubtless encouraged the kind of exegetical appreciation the sequence received when seen as a whole. It can be read as a kind of spiritual journey, moving from a glimpsed Eden (*Burnt Norton*), through the fallen world (*East Coker*), across the river of death (*The Dry Salvages*), to arrive at the community of the transfigured faithful 'not in time's covenant' (*Little Gidding*). But if the sequence encourages such (reductive) pattern-making, it also subverts it; the distinction of *Little Gidding* is to oppose the teleological momentum of the earlier poems, by insisting that our beginnings truly never know our ends, and by abandoning the quest for spiritual distinction, substituting a more modest participation in communal purpose (costing not less than everything); which leads to no triumphant transcendence, but to an acceptance of 'place' and 'time' as preconditions of eternity.

'*Finis coronat opus*' had been Hayward's comment to Morley, having seen the first draft of *Little Gidding*; and it seems highly probable that Eliot knew that this would be his last poem of any significance. When John Lehmann asked him for a new poem for an anthology, Eliot replied, in August 1944, that he had written nothing since *Little Gidding*, and could not think it likely he would ever again write anything worth printing. He had, meanwhile, turned toward his social criticism, publishing what would, in revised form, be issued as his *Notes towards the Definition of Culture* (1948), in four successive issues of the *New English Weekly* at the beginning of 1943. He gave himself up to Church concerns, and was in unabating demand as a lecturer and cultural ambassador: Wyndham Lewis, replying in April 1944 to a letter in which Eliot had described his war-time routine, observed that his life seemed to be 'packed with official duties'. Although he continued to be a sympathetic and painstaking publisher, and always ready to offer practical assistance to aspiring writers; and although he continued to be a loyal friend, from the outset doing what he could to mitigate the desperate predicament in which Pound had placed himself, Eliot became more and more assimilated to the role of a public figure, combining the functions of lay preacher and literary elder statesman. With the coming of peace he would take up his interest in the theatre again, and achieve substantial success at the box-office; but he would do nothing to disprove his premonition that with the fourth Quartet he had come to an end of his poetry.

NOTES

1. The letter to More (who was a theologian at Princeton) was written on 2 June 1930 and is quoted by Margolis pp. 143, 144. For Eliot's comment on Kipling see *Criterion*, XV, 60, (1936), 462.
2. See Pound's Canto XXIX; the speaker of the line 'I am afraid of the life after death' is identified as Eliot in Carroll F. Terrell's *Companion to the Cantos of Ezra Pound* (Berkeley, 1980), vol. I, p. 117; the setting is the Dordogne, where Pound and Eliot had holidayed in 1919.
3. See Tate, p. 81. Spender's comment on Eliot comes from this volume.
4. First published in the *Little Review* IV (May, September 1917), 'Eeldrop and Appleplex' is one of the pieces collected in *The Little Review Anthology*, ed. Anderson (New York, 1953), pp. 102–9.
5. The reasons for this, and for Eliot's destruction of his letters from her (presumably equal in number), are set forth in Lyndall Gordon's *Eliot's New Life* (Oxford, 1988), and in Valerie Eliot's introduction to *Letters*, vol. I. Gordon's study offers the most detailed discussion so far of the relationship with Emily Hale. I have followed Gordon's date for the resumption of correspondence between Eliot and Emily Hale; Valerie

Eliot gives the date as 1932 (L xvi), but Gordon states that they met in 1930 (p. 159).

6. See Helen Gardner, *The Composition of Four Quartets* (London, 1978), p. 67. Hereafter cited in the text thus: (C4Q 67).
7. Quoted in R. Kojecky, *T.S. Eliot's Social Criticism* (London, 1971), p. 78.
8. According to T.S. Matthews, in *Great Tom: Notes toward the Definition of T.S. Eliot* (London, 1974), Father Cheetham was 'seriously addicted' to dress-making (p. 117).
9. VWL VI, p. 198. Conrad Aiken, *Ushant: An Essay* (New York, 1971), p. 168.
10. Gordon (see n. 5 above), pp. 80, 300.
11. See Martin Browne, *The Making of T.S. Eliot's Plays* (London, 1969), p. 107.
12. Gordon, pp. 227–8.
13. See Gordon, p. 102n. Dr Gordon kindly confirmed this variant of the ending of *Burnt Norton* in a letter to me (20 Jan 1989); her interpretation, given in her book, emphasises the evocation of 'Light'; I am struck more by 'Gone'.
14. VWD II, p. 67.
15. Desmond Shawe-Taylor, writing in the *New Statesman*; in Grant, vol. II.
16. See Bush, p. 273, n. 40; and Stephen Spender, *Journals 1939–1983* (London, 1985), p. 45. Hereafter cited as Spender.
17. Some time in the later 1930s Eliot told Bonamy Dobree that he had stopped writing poetry in order not to repeat himself (Tate, p. 83).
18. *Paris Review*, p. 87.
19. *TLS*, 21 September 1940; and *Scrutiny*, XI, 1 (1942), p. 71.
20. See A.D. Moody, *Thomas Stearns Eliot: Poet* (Cambridge, 1979), p. 203.

7

After the End

It may seem perverse to finish a survey of Eliot's career at 1945: for during the final twenty years of his life he was recognised as probably the most eminent living man of letters in the Western world, with a genuinely international reputation (which in the USSR, he gleefully reported in 1951, was that of 'a reactionary, anti-Semitic, pornographic hyena').[1] At the beginning of 1948 his prestige was acknowledged in the conferral of the Order of Merit by King George VI, and at the end of the same year it was augmented by the award of the Nobel Prize for Literature (in the first honour he equalled the achievement of his predecessor in expatriation Henry James, and in the second he matched W.B. Yeats). The following year his new play *The Cocktail Party* was well received at the Edinburgh Festival, and subsequently went on to do good business both on Broadway and in the West End; with it, Eliot achieved his long-nurtured aim of making a success in the commercial theatre. His poetry and criticism became ever more immovably embedded in the curricula of universities and then of schools; his influence in the world of modern letters was such that Delmore Schwartz described it, in an article of that title in *Partisan Review* (February 1949), as 'the literary dictatorship of T.S. Eliot'. There can hardly have been one who was so acknowledged a legislator in English letters in his own lifetime, since Dr Johnson. It was not surprising that Wyndham Lewis, contributing in 1948 to a symposium for the poet's sixtieth birthday, found himself reflecting on the very different fates suffered by his two early literary collaborators, Pound and Eliot: the first was in an asylum for the criminally insane, while the second dwelt, as Lewis put it, 'in the bland atmosphere of general approbation'.[2]

Neither Pound's nadir nor Eliot's zenith would be permanent. In any case, the bland atmosphere of fame and acceptance was not entirely congenial to Eliot, who near the end of his life told Groucho Marx that he had no wish to be 'required reading' in schools; in 1950, according to one memoirist, he complained that 'no one thinks of me as a poet any more, but as a celebrity'.[3] It was certainly a blandness of approbation which respectfully received the two plays Eliot went on to write, *The Confidential Clerk* (1953) and *The Elder Statesman* (1958); neither repeated the success of *The Cocktail Party*. In his pronouncements upon matters cultural and literary during this period, it was hardly surprising if Eliot's prose displayed more magisterial affectation than incisive judgement and analytical rigour; for his authority was practically unassailable. Stephen Spender, in his *Journals*, records a meeting with the New York publishers of Eliot's work, in 1953; Spender was proposing a book to them which amounted, he confessed, to an attack on Eliot's critical theories:

> 'Oh that's OK with us,' they said, producing the *Collected T. S. Eliot* they've just done – which is the size of a small suitcase – 'Every time anyone attacks Eliot we just sell another thousand copies of this.'[4]

In his role as a celebrity, Eliot received honours, gave lectures and wrote articles, and sat on committees. In his role as publisher (where he was 'always a part-time director'), he set about making the Faber poetry list the strongest representation of contemporary poets. He did what he could to alleviate the circumstances of older writers he admired, such as Lewis. His role as a poet was restricted to the production of occasional verse, and to poetry readings. These he disliked, complaining to Mary Trevelyan as she drove him to one that it felt too much like undressing in public (she reassured him that he didn't take much off). In her own case, particularly, Eliot remained obstinately dressed: some of his energies at this period went into fending off the proposals of marriage which she made to him.[5]

In the decade following the end of the war there continued to be something of a gap between Eliot's public profile and his private invisibility. He had accepted John Hayward's suggestion that the two of them set up home together (made, so Hayward explained, 'to get him away from all those parsons'); and visitors noted the contrast between Hayward's comfortable quarters in Carlyle Mansions and the quasi-monastic austerity of Eliot's rooms. Hayward suffered from a progressive disability, and his celebrated friend was regularly to be seen pushing his wheelchair. In January 1947 Eliot received the news of Vivien's unexpected death in her nursing-home; but this did not, as Emily Hale had supposed it would, make him feel able at last to marry her. It seems that, instead, he anticipated ending his days in a religious establishment somewhere (he had been accustomed since the 1930s to spend periods in retreat). Necessarily the relationship with Emily Hale modified and diminished, and that with Mary Trevelyan – whom, along with Hayward, Eliot called one of his 'guardians' – remained within prescribed limits.

In the context of all this, it was with enormous surprise that Eliot's friends learned that on 10 January 1957 he had married Valerie Fletcher in a secret early-morning ceremony at St Barnabas's Church, Kensington (where, he discovered to his amazement, Jules Laforgue had also been married). His new wife, much younger than Eliot, had been his secretary at Faber's since August 1949. The apparent suddenness and the secrecy (itself characteristic of most of the major decisions of his life) were upsetting to some of those who had considered themselves close to him; neither his friendship with Hayward nor with Mary Trevelyan survived this second marriage. In spite of some who disapproved, and in spite of his deteriorating health, it was clear to most that this late marriage was a source of enormous happiness to him, releasing a capacity for affirmation in one who had before been notable for his ascetic gloom. At the close of his life Eliot experienced the human love of which he had been sceptical for so long.

He died on 4 January 1965. There followed a memorial service at Westminster Abbey, to which the Queen, the British Prime Minister, and the President of the United States sent representatives. In mid-April Eliot's ashes were taken to St Michael's Church at East Coker, and placed near the interior north-west corner. This interment at East Coker struck Conrad Aiken, for example, as a rather stagey and inappropriate gesture on Eliot's part, given the tenuousness of his actual connection with the village. It should probably be seen as Eliot's final affirmation of his Englishness, as a result of which St Michael's has become a place of pilgrimage for the poet's devotees; and although we see no 'glittering jewelled shrine' such as the Fourth Tempter offered Becket, there is an oval plaque soliciting prayers for the repose of Eliot's soul. It is clear from the church visitors' book that many if not most come there because of the association with Eliot: its spaces for their 'comments' frequently contain snatches from the poetry, of variable accuracy and appositeness – and in some cases wilfully recondite.

On a recent inspection of the book, near the time of the poet's centenary, I rather warmed to the visitor who declared with gentle sarcasm, 'unfortunately I do not know any quotations from T.S. Eliot'. I'd like to believe that Eliot himself would have appreciated that.

His words echo, thus, in our minds, but there were some things he said that we might have challenged (to adapt lines from *Burnt Norton* and 'Mr Apollinax'). In the twenty-five years since his death Eliot's reputation has inevitably declined somewhat from its high-water mark. If to some degree his eminence both sponsored and benefited from the accruing prestige of English as a university discipline, so the subsequent uncertainties and debates within the subject have affected his standing. As perhaps the most influential spokesman for 'Modernism', Eliot has partaken of some of the retrospective scepticism visited upon that movement; as a writer who asserted the importance of discriminating the good from the bad in literature, his own work has necessarily been subject to revisionary estimates, on the parts of those who are deeply distrustful of the privileging of 'literature' over other discourses, or those who dispute the hierarchical perspective of a canon of great works and the means by which such a canon is established and maintained. Even F.R. Leavis – so absolutely wedded to ideas of a 'great tradition', so assertive of Eliot's central importance, and so deeply in Eliot's intellectual debt – came to review his earlier estimate, particularly of the achievement of the *Quartets*. The growth of 'American Studies' and, later, of 'Women's Studies' in universities has had an adverse effect on Eliot's status, since he estranged himself from the first by expatriation, and from the second by an apparently suspect attitude toward female sexuality in his writing.

Eliot's intolerance and that of his critics is most in evidence over the question of his alleged anti-Semitism. This was raised during Eliot's lifetime – and not only in the Soviet press – but has more recently been the subject of debate, coinciding with the centenary celebrations in 1988. Eliot's own response to such inferences was touchy, pointing out that anti-Semitism was unChristian (and that therefore by implication he could not be suspected of it; an equal and opposite reaction was that, because Eliot was anti-Semitic, his Christianity must be suspect). Such accusations were the more damaging, precisely because of the moral authority with which

Eliot had been endowed. It is beyond dispute that there are some extremely unlovely passages to do with Jews and Jewishness in Eliot's writing; the worst of these are the unpublished 'Dirge', rejected from *The Waste Land* (Ts 121), and the comments on the undesirableness of 'large numbers of free-thinking Jews' to a homogeneous society, made in *After Strange Gods* (a volume which Eliot did not allow to be reprinted). Also cited are 'Burbank With a Baedeker: Bleistein With a Cigar', and 'Gerontion', for its reflections on the unwholesomeness of the landlord. In addition, there is in the *Criterion* (XV, 1936, pp. 759–60) an intemperate dismissal of a book detailing Nazi persecutions of German Jews, in a brief unsigned review which as editor Eliot must have sanctioned, if he did not actually write it himself (unsigned reviews were usually his own).[6]

Eliot's letters show some of the characteristics; writing to Pound on 31 October 1917, he refers to 'a Jew merchant, named Lawson, (sc. Levi-sohn?)' (L 206); in the naming of men as of cats, Eliot was a man who noticed such things: a letter to Richard Aldington of 12 February 1926 mentions in passing a rumour that someone called 'Stallybrass' had changed his name from 'Sonnenschein'. This tells us something about the general atmosphere; in the case of the earlier letter, Eliot's style clearly echoes Pound's in its vulgarity and its vituperation. There is also a letter to John Quinn of 12 March 1923, in which Eliot wishes he had a 'Christian publisher' in the US, rather than the 'Jew publisher' whom he was finding difficult; here again, he seems at least in part to have been playing to his audience. This does not, of course, explain away such comments; but their significance as indicators of what Eliot actually thought should probably not be exaggerated. It is clear that he was aware of Jewishness as a ground for differentiation; but such discrimination was not necessarily pejorative: for examples, to his mother on 9 August 1920 he mentions his friends the Schiffs, 'very nice Jews' (L 400); and in a letter to Pound of 9 December 1929, he describes the poetry of Louis Zukofsky as 'highly intelligent and honourably Jewish'.[7]

It is also clear, however, that to Eliot's mind there were ways of being dishonourably Jewish, and it is these that are apparent in 'Burbank' and 'Gerontion'. The latter is the more alarming instance, in that unlike the quatrain poem, which seems rather a sterile performance, few would deny that 'Gerontion' is amongst his strongest; the presence within it of so potentially disfiguring an element as anti-Semitism needs explaining. In his recent book *T.S. Eliot and Prejudice* (1988), Christopher Ricks has argued that many of Eliot's effects come from the calculating operation of prejudice, most audible in the use of suggestively pejorative names: responding in imagination to these incitements, the reader discovers his own helpless collaboration with the dark power of prejudicial labelling. In the case of such a poem as 'Gerontion' (by contrast with 'Burbank' or, even more so, the unpublished 'Dirge'), a mind in control of prejudice – Eliot's – evokes a mind in the grip of it – Gerontion's. In his criticism, as well, we can see that Eliot's acts of nomination, the labels he affixes, can be weightily significant. They can also be part of an un-innocent adversarial strategy, originating in animosity rather than exactness, whose purpose is rather to justify disapproval than to establish an objective evaluation by the common pursuit of true judgement. Yet this tough unreasonableness is part of the combative energy that animates, more than it vitiates, his best critical writing.

Like all of us, Eliot could lack charity contemplating his neighbour, and could find reasons to hold him in contempt. Perhaps – again like most people – this impulse had its origin in insecurity. For the Jew, as an unfixed cosmopolitan (evidently the chief source of offence), might uncomfortably evoke his own deracination and displacement: the sense of which propelled Eliot toward elaborate rituals of association with his adopted country.[8] 'You were silly like us,' declared Auden of Yeats, in his elegy for the Irish poet. To suggest in Eliot's defence that his objectionable remarks on Jews reflected an attitude widespread in Europe before Hitler is not, however, sufficient; nor is the thought that his lack of charity or clarity on the issue makes him 'like us': a *semblable* for his *hyprocrites lecteurs*. Eliot sought for himself the position of arbiter in matters of culture and, to a degree, of morals; therefore his own credentials justifiably come under scrutiny, and shortcomings are more serious than they would be in those who don't aspire to establish standards. He found himself challenged by a correspondent over his notorious pronouncement in *After Strange Gods*, and Ricks rightly feels that his answer to the charge was less than satisfactory; but he also clearly feels that a difference in kind and culpability exists between Eliot and Pound over the issue of anti-Semitism. Pound's version was more virulent, more aggressively proclaimed, more lastingly nurtured, and so malignantly obtuse that he found himself backing the dictators in the Second

World War. This does not, of course, make Eliot's any better; but it provides a necessary perspective, and reminds us that to have published some ungenerous reflections on Jewishness in the 1920s and 1930s, albeit reprehensible, is not to have entered into complicity with the Nazi atrocities.

The case of Pound helps us to see that something else often underlies discussions of anti-Semitism in Eliot: for there are those who seem far more willing to forgive Pound his gross infringements than Eliot his early indiscretions. Given the magnitude of the difference between the two offences, this seems attributable to a straightforward dislike of the man Eliot was and the beliefs he held, which finds expression in the wish to devalue his writing. A tone which runs through much of the adverse commentary on Eliot, both during his lifetime and subsequently, is that however accomplished he was, the philosophy of life implicit in his writing is impoverished and flawed, and his achievement finally suspect. This is where the contrast with Pound is instructive: some critics clearly find the rampant Pound more admirable than the celibate Eliot, feeling that even the greatness of his errors shows a generous if wrong-headed response to life, giving us in Pound a man wartily himself, unlike the guarded Eliot's impeccability. Something of this is seen, for example, in a letter Richard Aldington wrote in 1930, admitting Eliot's 'genius as a poet' and his 'extreme skill as a critic', but at the same time asserting that his 'attitude to life' needed to be attacked, along with the 'over-intellectual' poetry he had created 'as a refuge from life'.[9]

More than one writer has regretted Eliot's influence on the poetry of his own and succeeding generations in terms similar to these. The burden of complaint is generally that the conscious difficulty and recondite allusiveness which were his trademarks seemed to turn the reading of poetry into an activity so specialised that only a very few could attempt it. William Carlos Williams has recorded his belief that *The Waste Land* marked a 'catastrophe' for the kind of poetry he himself had been struggling toward, and institutionalised a retrogression toward the academy. In England, later, Philip Larkin stated his opposition to the Modernist assumption that poetry needed to be difficult. It's possible that Eliot himself revised his requirement of difficulty: for as we have seen his move to the theatre, and the language of the later Quartets, both represented his attempt to reach a wider audience. In the eyes of other commentators, however, this very move toward intelligibility was made at the cost of a relaxation of the tautness of his language.

Looking back, Eliot adjudged the Quartets to represent the summit of his achievement; he expected to 'stand or fall' by them. Notwithstanding his uncertainties during composition, he also felt that each Quartet was better than its predecessors. This view reflected – and doubtless influenced – the critical consensus that prevailed for a time after his death, by which, satisfyingly, his best poetry was his last-written, and *Little Gidding* was seen as the triumphant culmination of his art – as indeed had been his intention. Later, however, doubts were increasingly expressed about the gratifying myth of this perfectly-ripening career. As early as 1956, Donald Davie had shaken some of the pillars of the temple by suggesting that the Quartets were not of equal merit, and that *The Dry Salvages* was actually 'rather a bad poem'[10]; but even Davie could not bring himself to believe the badness was unintentional, and suggested that the whole poem was a kind of parody. His suggestion did not take root, and Helen Gardner dismisses it as 'extraordinary' in her 1978 study of their composition, where the triumphalist view prevails (C4Q 4n). Other voices were scolding these poems, however, and the basis for complaint was precisely that they *were* over-intended performances; as C.H. Sisson put it:

> It would have been harder, perhaps, for Eliot to have written what he had to say in prose, but he should have done, for he already knew what he meant, as far as he was going to know.[11]

Since 1965 much more information about Eliot's private life has been assembled and disseminated, culminating in the (unauthorised) biography by Peter Ackroyd, the studies of Lyndall Gordon, and the ongoing publication of his letters, under the editorship of his widow, Valerie (of which at time of writing the first volume has appeared). Those who had supposed that Eliot's aversion to biography was the reaction of a man with guilty secrets to conceal, have not had their suspicions borne out by anything that has yet appeared. But in some ways Eliot's instinct toward separating the writer's life from judgements of his art was sound, for his own reputation has suffered from a confusion of the two. It is quite clear that many readers found (and find) the Christian emphases of *Four Quartets* congenial and reassuring, in spite of the fact that it is a somewhat obdurate version of the faith. But the merits of the writing were too closely identified with the supposed personal merits of the man, allotting him a role of secular sanctity difficult to justify and easy to subvert. A kind of mutual authentication between life and poetry was set up, whereby any failure of charity on the part of the man was taken to vitiate the work, and any lapses in the work were taken as signs of evil in the poet. Eliot's Christianity is not, perhaps, so very much more pronounced an element in his work than is, say, Evelyn Waugh's in his; but for some there seems more difficulty in reconciling themselves to Eliot's human shortcomings.

The gradual revelation of Eliot's private life as something less than an ideal order has been paralleled with regard to his poetry; and just as his idea that there is a relatively fixed literary canon is currently out of fashion, so the canonicity of his own writing has been increasingly subverted. Significant in this process was the rediscovery and publication of the original manuscripts relating to *The Waste Land*, which showed the turbulent and obscure genesis of what had been institutionalised as a Great Modernist Text, whose difficulties had been satisfyingly probed and mythically recuperated by many an erudite exegete; and furthermore, these drafts seemed to show the crucial importance of Pound's excisions. Eliot had not sought to hide the poem's chaotic origination, nor Pound's contribution to its final shape; but *The Waste Land* would never again look quite the same: its ideal order had been infringed upon by our knowledge of these excluded elements. On the other hand, this kind of textual destabilisation of a Major Work (as in the current controversy over *Ulysses*) can serve to reinvigorate interest in it. The revelations about the Quartets, in Helen Gardner's study, were less startling; and this is due not only to the different circumstances of production and the different collaborators, but most of all to the difference in kind between those poems and *The Waste Land*. In both cases, however, what might be termed the iconic self-containment of the familiar texts had been breached.

Readers now found themselves in a position to choose between the authorised version of rejected variants; and similarly, some critics felt inclined to dispute Eliot's reading of his own career. The major question is whether the *Four Quartets* really is his crowning achievement, or whether *The Waste Land* actually represents his best poetry. The argument runs close to the terms quoted by Eliot in his lecture on Matthew Arnold, by which Arnold sought to differentiate between the verse of Dryden and Pope, whose poetry 'is conceived and composed in their wits', and what he defines as 'genuine poetry', which is 'conceived and composed in the soul' (UPUC 117). Eliot did not sympathise with this distinction, but it is parallel to what emerges in some of the criticism which compares *Four Quartets* disadvantageously with *The Waste Land*: that the premeditated pattern-making of the later poems enforces a dully intellectual coherence, at the expense of the kind of spontaneous energy so evident in the earlier work, whose coherence could safely be left to a third party. Something had happened to the mind of Eliot between *The Waste Land* and the Quartets, which represented a diminution of poetic sensibility.

That is a way of putting it; not very satisfactory, because it obscures the truth that we are not obliged to make an absolute choice between the two, any more than we have to choose Eliot or Pound. It is probably the case that the prestige of *Four Quartets* has fallen, and that of the earlier work has risen – so that even a critic like Ronald Bush has serious reservations about the Quartets. But it is clear that, in writing them, Eliot was attempting a very different kind of poem from *The Waste Land*: a poetry which was less continuously intense and more discursive; indeed, a poetry whose very mode was to probe the relation between intensity and discursiveness. In his earlier criticism Eliot had wanted to convince himself that the excellence of a poet like Donne lay in his undissociated sensibility. He wished to reject the view that our intellectual part can only offer a kind of commentary after the event: the 'meaning' derived from the 'experience'. In his criticism he was a passionate advocate of 'intelligence', which for him constituted – in *The Sacred Wood* – the true method of Aristotle. This exemplified the 'scientific mind', by which we see 'intelligence itself swiftly operating the analysis of sensation to the point of principle and definition' (SW 11); for if to Donne a thought was an experience, to Aristotle an experience was a thought.

In an early *Egoist* article Eliot had declared, 'we must insist on the importance of intelligent criticism' (May 1918), and he never under-rated the importance of intelligent poetry. But whereas at one stage he might have been inclined to equate 'intelligent' with 'difficult', later on the equation might have been more with 'intelligible'. By the time of the Quartets he could not be content with a poetry of the unreflective instant, a distraction fit generated entirely in impenetrable 'depths of feeling'; he could not accept a poetry of soul without imposing on it a poetics of wit. It may be that the kind of ratiocinative control exercised in the Quartets is finally inimical to Eliot's truest creativity, which originated – as he himself knew – in the surprising and the inexplicable (the 'three white leopards' which he refused to explain survive because they are not simply allegorical). One of Wallace Stevens's aphorisms was that 'poetry must resist the intelligence almost successfully'[12]; and it can be argued that in Eliot's last poems that resistance has failed, because of too much responsibility toward 'meaning' and too little toward poetic 'experience', in a poetry whose beginnings know too much about their ends. One of the features of Eliot's verse is a certain linguistic irresponsibility, audible in much of the earlier verse (in such a poem as 'Gerontion' we can see this bordering on an irresponsibility of attitude), and occasionally in the later ('Sempiternal though sodden toward sundown' comes to mind). When the complete consort dances together the motions can be eccentric, because poetry presents a language freed from its purely denotative role, and celebrating to that degree a disengaged, aesthetic impulsion. As *The Waste Land* acknowledges, there is a splendour that is inexplicable.

If *Four Quartets* has lost the unquestioned, rather formidable, pre-eminence it once enjoyed, this may in the long term be for the best; the poems can now be discovered by readers unconstrained by a compulsion to venerate. What the sequence did establish was that there was a large audience for serious poetry; and it would be foolish to assume that the Quartets have entered a permanent eclipse. More successfully than *The Waste Land*, perhaps, they accomplish one of the primary tasks of literature, which is to give experience form; some of the phrases from *Four Quartets* have entered the collective unconscious of literary quotations. Their unevenness as poems cannot sensibly be denied; but I suspect that they will continue to find readers to respond to them; partly because in them Eliot speaks rather more as a man involved in living, by contrast to the Tiresian omniscience of *The Waste Land*. He predicted that his survival would be linked to the Quartets; but whilst it is probably true that his reputation has diminished somewhat, other factors than the prestige of *Four Quartets* come into play. In Britain, the Modernist appropriation of centrality in the canon of English Literature has been disputed, with the consequent assertion of a more important native strain running through Hardy (whom Eliot considered 'minor'). In America, William Carlos Williams has had a more apparent influence on the writing of subsequent poets, through his stress on the American speech rhythms. In both cases this may be evidence of a provincialism of taste against which the internationalist Eliot would have argued.

It is perhaps surprising that his own poetry has survived the sustained aversion therapy of being a set text, over and over again, in examinations in English. Yet even if readers' appetite for Eliot were to decline further, it is unlikely that the future will adjudge him to have been a figure inflated beyond his true importance. His influence, exerted both as poet and as critic, was decisive, in ways not necessarily dependent on his 'originality': he was responsible, for example, for putting the phrase 'objective correlative' into wide circulation, even if he had not invented the concept. His advocacy of Anglo-Catholicism or the ideal England was much less influential, and presents us, in Eliot, with the curious picture of an unavoidably central figure, many of whose beliefs were literally eccentric. Even though his career was importantly connected with the existence of a professional – one might say professorial – readership, he will survive, I imagine, because of his capacity to reach the unprofessional reader who does not, fortunately, know any quotations from T.S. Eliot. This differentiates him from Pound, whose *Cantos* are essentially sustained by specialist explication.

To talk of a decline in Eliot's standing may be to do no more than register the inevitable revaluation that follows great achievement. It is still difficult to conceive of a map of twentieth-century English literature on which he does not figure largely; yet it may also be the case that his will turn out to have been the last major literary career of its type, because the conditions in which it was possible may not recur. The ideological presumptions underlying Eliot's writing, about the nature and value of culture, religion and literature, with his emphasis on homogeneity and stratification, now meet with much less widespread assent; and this is in part due to different perceptions, stressing diversity and pluralism. In both his poetry and criticism Eliot was aiming for 'an easy commerce of the old and the new', but the nature and possibility of such transactions are viewed in some quarters with increasing scepticism. It would not have surprised him that his hierarchical construction of reality should be challenged by cultural relativism (of which he was not ignorant), nor that the notion of a literary canon, or of 'literature' itself, should be under attack in university departments of English (about which he entertained his own scepticisms).

More significant than the whirligig of academic fashion, however, may be the prevalent conditions of contemporary life, in which the book seems destined to increasing cultural subordination to the television, or film. It is unlikely that an influence such as Eliot's could in these days be wielded through the medium of the written word, rather than through other cultural channels. Again, Eliot had his own sense of cultural apocalypse, and would not have been surprised, nor perhaps distressed, by the diminishing place for poetry in people's lives. I suppose he would be content at the last, if this meant that his poetry was read less by people who were required to and more by people who wanted to. It is curious how little even the period details in the earlier verse, such as the 'lonely cab-horse' or the 'magic lantern' or Prufrock's Edwardian neck-tie, interfere with our sense that these are contemporary utterances. Eliot is likely to continue to reach the general reader – if not the 'illiterate' whom he once proposed as his ideal – and this accessibility will not be the consequence of an ideological content requiring philosophical belief, but of the poetic assent conjured by his mastery of words and the persuasiveness of his cadences: his 'conscious art' in 'the inexplicable mystery of sound'.[13]

NOTES

1. Spender, p. 107.
2. March, p. 24. Pound had broadcast anti-American sentiments on Italian radio, when Italy was an ally of Nazi Germany. At the close of the war he was arrested and returned to the USA for trial on a charge of treason. He was judged unfit to plead (had he been tried, the death sentence would have been possible), and was consigned to custody in a mental institution, from which he was released in 1958, with the charges dropped.
3. In *Affectionately, T.S. Eliot* by William Levy and Victor Scherle (London, 1968), p. 19.
4. Spender, pp. 112–13.
5. The comment on Eliot as 'part-time director' at Faber's is made by Peter du Sautoy (see n. 7, ch. 3). Eliot's relations with Mary Trevelyan are fully detailed in Gordon; see also Humphrey Carpenter, 'Poor Tom: Mary Trevelyan's View of T.S. Eliot', *English* XXXVIII, 160 (Spring, 1989).
6. This *Criterion* review (of *The Yellow Spot*) is reprinted and discussed in Bush, pp. 226, 274, and Stead, pp. 206–7. It is also given in Ricks's *T.S. Eliot and Prejudice* (p. 51).

7. This letter to Pound is in the Humanities Research Centre of the University of Texas at Austin; it is a transcription apparently made by Zukofsky himself, who presumably did not find the reference to his Jewishness offensive.
8. Eliot's awareness of his 'outsidership' is glimpsed in his use of the pseudonym 'Metoikos' ('resident alien'), for his last commentary in the *Christian News Letter* (21 March 1945). In a letter to Mary Hutchinson of 1919, Eliot reminds her of his status as 'a *metic* – a foreigner' (L 318).
9. See *Richard Aldington: a Biography* (London, 1989), by Charles Doyle (p. 141).
10. Davie's essay is reprinted in *T.S. Eliot, Four Quartets. A casebook*, ed. Bergonzi (London, 1969).
11. C.H. Sisson, *English Poetry 1900–1950* (London, 1971), p. 153.
12. This is one of Stevens's 'Adagia', in *Opus Posthumous* (London, 1959), p. 171.
13. From Eliot's poem 'To Walter de la Mare'.

Further Reading

It would be very easy to compile an immensely long list; but I take it that the purpose of this section is not to convince the reader how much I have read. I also suspect that lengthy bibliographies can have a discouraging effect. What follows, therefore, is an extremely selective and highly personal choice of books which I hope the reader may find useful and interesting; it should certainly not be taken to imply either that books not listed are worthless, or that I have not benefited from them. My aim is to present the reader with a manageable selection, and I intend no offence to omitted authors.

Primary Material
In addition to CPP, Valerie Eliot's edition of *The Waste Land: a facsimile and transcript* (London, 1971), and Helen Gardner's *The Composition of Four Quartets* (London, 1978) are essential.

With regard to criticism, Frank Kermode's *Selected Prose of T.S. Eliot* (London, 1975) contains a useful range of material, together with a lucid introduction.

Biographical
Valerie Eliot's edition of the *Letters of T.S. Eliot* (London, 1988 onward) will be an essential source.

There are several biographical studies, but the most exhaustive so far has been Peter Ackroyd's *T.S. Eliot: A Life* (London and New York, 1984). Lyndall Gordon's *Eliot's New Life* (Oxford, 1988) contains interesting new information about Eliot's relations with Emily Hale, as well as with Mary Trevelyan.

Critical
Ronald Bush, *T.S. Eliot: A Study in Character and Style* (Oxford, 1984)
Hugh Kenner, *The Invisible Poet: T.S. Eliot* (London, 1959)
A.D. Moody, *Thomas Stearns Eliot: Poet* (Cambridge, 1979)
C.K. Stead, *Pound, Yeats, Eliot, and the Modernist Movement* (London, 1986)
Frank Kermode's *An Appetite for Poetry: Essays in Literary Intepretation* (London, 1989) contains a new appreciation of Eliot.

There are innumerable essays about Eliot in literary periodicals; one that I found interesting is Barbara Everett's 'Eliot In and Out of the *The Waste Land'*, *Critical Quarterly*, 17, i (1975), pp. 7–30.

Index

Ackroyd, Peter, 6, 7, 8, 24, 29, 174
Aiken, Conrad, 6, 20, 23, 28, 29,
    33, 35, 36, 43, 44, 45, 47, 48,
    50, 59, 65, 66, 67, 69, 96, 102,
    106, 129, 144, 169
Alain-Fournier, Henri, 24
Aldington, Richard, 4, 39, 40, 41,
    44, 46, 55, 56, 58, 62, 69, 97,
    98, 101, 128, 129, 171, 173
    Stepping Heavenward, 128, 129
Alice in Wonderland, 138
Andrewes, Lancelot, 100, 110–11,
    113, 117
Anglo-Catholicism, 113, 115–16,
    178
Aristotle, 79, 176
Arnold, Matthew, 175
Athenaeum, 42, 55, 56, 65, 111, 116
Auden, W.H., 81, 103, 120, 125,
    126, 128, 147, 172

Babbitt, Irving, 23–4, 26, 51
Barker, George, 132
Barnes, Djuna,
    Nightwood, 149
Bateson, F.W., 80
Baudelaire, Charles, 20, 21–2, 59
BBC, the, 112, 136
Becket, Thomas à, 111, 135
Belgion, Montgomery, 163
Bell, Clive, 54, 58, 96
Bell, George (Bishop of
    Chichester), 131, 135, 159
Benda, Julien, 46, 98
Bennett, Arnold, 55, 101
Bergson, Henri, 25–6, 27, 28, 39,
    41, 44, 52
Betjeman, John, 51
Blake, William, 112
Blanshard, Brand, 46, 47
Blast, 15, 35, 42, 43, 44, 53, 55
Bloomsbury, 54, 55, 69
Blue Review, 55

Boni and Liveright, 95
Bottrall, Ronald, 163
Bradley, F.H., 1, 30–1, 35, 46
Bradbrook, Muriel, 157
British Museum, 47, 153
Brooks, Cleanth, 113
Browning, Robert, 62
    'Childe Roland to the Dark
        Tower Came', 92
Browne, E. Martin, 131, 135, 136,
    160
Bubu de Montparnasse, 24
Burnt Norton, 137, 138, 140, 159
Bush, Ronald, 111, 176

Cambridge (University), 49, 57,
    80, 90, 105, 111, 113, 128, 150
Calendar of Modern Letters, 109
Canterbury, 135, 136
    Catholic Anthology, 58, 64
Catholic Herald, 163
Chamberlain, Neville, 146, 150,
    152, 155
Chandos Group, 142–3
Chapbook, 43
Cheetham, Fr Eric, 144
Christian News Letter, 143
Churchill, Winston, 155, 162
Cobden-Sanderson, Richard, 100
Coghill, Neville, 81
Commerce, 117, 126
Colefax, Lady Sybil, 54
Coleridge, Samuel Taylor, 130, 152
    Rime of the Ancient Mariner, 92
Connolly, Cyril, 151
Conrad, Joseph, 89, 92
    Heart of Darkness, 89
Coterie, 61
Cowley, Malcolm, 142
Criterion, 43, 48, 69, 76, 81, 84, 87,
    88, 95, 96, 97–100, 101, 103,
    104, 105, 107, 114–15, 116,
    125, 127, 128, 133, 135, 142,

143, 148, 153, 161, 171
Cummings, E.E., 66

Dante, 20–1, 22, 23, 27, 46, 76, 78,
    92, 112, 115, 118, 120, 134,
    161
Davie, Donald, 174
Day Lewis, Cecil, 126
Dial, 65, 81, 82, 83, 88, 95, 101,
    116
    'London Letter', 82
Dickens, Charles,
    Our Mutual Friend, 92
Dobrée, Bonamy, 132, 134
Donne, John, 78, 101, 110, 111
    112, 176
Doone, Rupert, 105, 136
    'The Group Theatre', 105
Douglas, C.H., 143
Dryden, John, 79, 86, 112, 175
'Dry Salvages, The', 157, 159
Dukes, Ashley, 136
Dunne, Annie, 12

East Coker, 153, 159, 169
Edinburgh Festival, 167
Egoist, 43, 55, 56, 58, 64, 176
Eliot, Andrew, 13, 153, 156, 157
Eliot, Charlotte Champe (mother),
    1, 2, 12, 13, 15–16, 19, 26, 50,
    57, 58, 59, 66–7, 82, 84, 126,
    153, 171
Eliot, Henry Ware (father), 12, 13,
    15, 24, 50
Eliot, Henry Ware Jr (brother), 12,
    34, 48, 50, 82, 87, 105
Eliot, Marian (sister), 82
Eliot, Thomas Stearns,
    LIFE AND CAREER:
    Americanness of, 12–18, 44, 46,
        47, 67, 89, 122, 140, 153,
        157
    appetite for squalor, 17, 19–20,
        21–2
    attitude toward Jews, 130, 170–3
    British citizenship, 3, 103, 115
    Christianity, 2, 8, 9, 27, 33, 49,
        94, 103, 112–13, 115, 118,
        123–4, 133–4, 142–3, 148,
        150, 158, 163, 169, 174–5

Church of England, 27, 100,
    103, 110–11, 115, 124, 131,
    147, 159, 165
    baptism and confirmation, 115
'Classicism', 'Romanticism', 3,
    74, 76, 77
composition of poems, 28–9,
    31–6, 57
contrasting aspects of, 8–9, 11,
    17–18, 53, 54, 56, 59, 64, 70,
    89, 96, 104, 109–11, 118–19,
    122–3, 140, 144, 147, 149,
    176, 178, 179
decision-making, 3, 141, 169
distrust of public world, 7, 32–3,
    126, 135, 145, 148, 149
as dramatist, 101, 104–5, 125,
    130, 131–2, 135–7, 144–6,
    149–50, 151, 167–8
and Eastern religion and
    philosophy, 23, 29, 94
education, 18–20, 23–4, 29–30
Englishness of, 4, 48, 54, 115,
    125–6, 127, 153, 154, 155,
    159, 162, 169, 172
as extension lecturer, 51–3
and his family, 1–2, 12–18, 24,
    28, 47, 49–50, 82, 126, 145
fear of exhaustion as poet, 4,
    48, 58–9, 109, 116, 126, 130,
    132
formality of, 54, 106
and France, 3, 24–8
and French, 57, 58–9, 60
and hell, 124, 133–4
hidden force of, 106, 144, 172
ideal of Europe, 46, 78, 112,
    114, 120, 150, 162
ill health, 16, 84, 94, 97, 130,
    159
'impersonality' of writer, 7,
    74–5, 89, 115
'Krutsch, Gus', 82
literary allusions in his poetry,
    70–2, 89, 154, 173
    allusions to own work, 146,
    160–1, 162
literary ambition, 5, 55, 67
literary background to early

Eliot, Thomas Stearns – *continued*
London years, 37–45
literary periodicals, 42–3
literary influence of, 61, 66–7,
100, 113–14, 168
literary influences on, 20–3, 61,
138–9
Lloyds Bank, 57, 81, 83, 97, 98,
99, 100
and London churches, 28, 82,
111, 131
marriage, first, 2, 5, 6, 46,
47–50, 69, 82, 87, 97, 103,
107, 121, 129
second, 2, 5, 10, 169
in Munich, 28
nature of poetic creation, 74–5,
88–9, 177
Nobel Prize, 167
Order of Merit, 167
philosophy, studies in, 1, 3, 28,
29–30, 35, 46, 50, 53
poetry and criticism (apparent
contrast), 3, 4, 77–8, 89
reception of his work, 64–6,
95–6, 109–10, 119, 120,
141–2, 157–8, 160, 163, 174,
175–6
differing popularity in UK and
USA, 136
respectability and remoteness,
128–9, 131, 142, 144, 167
scholarliness of, 56, 71, 80
as schoolteacher, 51, 57
secretiveness of, 5, 6, 69–70,
116, 169, 174
as social/political commentator,
9, 125–6, 143, 147–8, 172
and the specialist reader, 70–1,
80–1, 113–14, 170, 173, 178
squeamishness of, 108, 145
'the void', his sense of, 33–4,
109, 133
WORKS:
After Strange Gods, 5, 119–20,
124, 128, 130, 136, 171, 172
'Andrew Marvell', 73, 82
'Animula', 16–17, 109, 117–18,
140

Ara Vos Prec, 5, 31, 37, 61, 65,
67, 72, 80, 161
'Ariel' poems, 117–18, 122, 126
Ash-Wednesday, 9, 89, 117, 120,
121–3, 124, 125, 126, 139,
148
'Aunt Helen', 47
'Baudelaire', 108, 134
'Ben Johnson', 53, 66, 74
'The Boston Evening
Transcript', 65
'Burbank . . .', 60, 62, 171, 172
Burnt Norton, 4, 135, 137–41,
144, 145, 146, 148, 149, 151,
154, 157, 162, 164, 170
Clark Lectures (Cambridge), 81,
111–12
'Catholicism and International
Order', 142
The Cocktail Party, 34, 149, 167,
168
Collected Poems 1909–1935, 139,
141, 142, 146
*Complete Poems and Plays of T.S.
Eliot*, 31
The Confidential Clerk, 168
'Conversation Galante', 31, 32
'A Cooking Egg', 42, 61
'Coriolan', 126–7, 148
'Cousin Nancy', 47
'The Cultivation of Christmas
Trees', 117
'Dans le Restaurant', 60, 87
'Dante' (1929), 120, 122
'Descent from the Cross', 35–6
'Difficulties of a Statesman',
126, 127
'Dirge', 171, 172
The Dry Salvages, 156–8, 160,
161, 164, 174
East Coker, 4, 13, 151, 152–5,
156, 157, 160, 164
'Eeldrop and Appleplex', 58, 134
The Elder Statesman, 168
Essays Ancient and Modern, 142
'Experience and the Objects of
Knowledge in the
Philosophy of F.H.
Bradley', 30

Ezra Pound: His Metric and Poetry, 60

The Family Reunion, 134, 135, 137, 139, 141, 144–7, 149, 150, 151

'La Figlia Che Piange', 22, 35, 160

'Five-Finger Exercises', 127

For Lancelot Andrewes, 118–19, 142

Four Quartets, 4, 10, 94, 127, 143, 146, 156, 162, 163, 164, 170, 173, 174, 175, 176, 177

'Fragment of an Agon', 104

'Fragment of a Prologue', 104

'The Function of Criticism', 76, 77

'Gerontion', 9, 37, 61–4, 65, 70, 88, 108, 117, 123, 127, 171, 172, 177

'Hidden under the heron's wing', 35

'The Hippopotamus', 60

'The Hollow Men', 9, 82, 89, 101, 102, 108–9, 116, 121, 123, 139

Homage to John Dryden, 70, 100

Idea of a Christian Society, 143, 150

'In Memoriam', 144

'Inventions of the March Hare', 32

'John Dryden', 82, 86

'John Marston', 140

'Journey of the Magi', 116, 117

'King Bolo and His Big Black Kween', 35

'Landscapes', 127

Little Gidding, 74, 139, 158–62, 164, 165, 174

'The Love Song of J. Alfred Prufrock', 3, 22, 28, 29, 31, 32–4, 43, 45, 48, 57, 58, 62, 64, 70, 90, 106, 108, 123, 179

'A Lyric', 16, 31

'Marina', 117, 118, 127

'Mélange Adultère de Tout', 18

'The Metaphysical Poets', 75, 78, 82

'Mr Apollinax', 47, 170

'Modern Education and the Classics', 142, 148

Murder in the Cathedral, 4, 134, 135–7, 139, 141, 145, 146, 150, 169

'New Hampshire', 160

'Nocturne', 32, 59

'A Note on the Verse of John Milton', 144

Notes Toward the Definition of Culture, 143, 165

'Ode' 31

'Ode' (*Ara Vos Prec*), 5, 31, 161

Old Possum's Book of Practical Cats, 131, 149

On Poetry and Poets, 75, 150

'Perch'io non spero', 117

'Philip Massinger', 71

Poems (1919), 61, 65

Poems 1909–1925, 69, 81, 102, 105, 106, 108, 109

Poems by T.S. Eliot, 61

'Poems Written in Early Youth', 31

'Portrait of a Lady', 4, 22, 29, 31, 32–4, 50, 58, 62

'The Preacher as Artist', 111

'Preludes', 29, 32, 35, 53

Prufrock and Other Observations, 37, 58, 64

quatrain poems, 58, 59, 60–1, 62, 63, 65, 154

'Reflections on Vers Libre', 60

'The Relativity of Moral Judgment', 49

'Religion and Literature', 134, 142

'Rhapsody on a Windy Night', 25, 29, 32, 33, 34, 53

The Rock, 4, 104–5, 131, 132, 135, 136, 146, 148

The Sacred Wood, 15, 37, 53, 55, 56, 64, 66, 67, 70, 73, 74, 76, 77, 80, 81, 83, 101, 112, 118, 119, 176

'Salutation', 117, 122

'Second Caprice in North Cambridge', 19

Eliot, Thomas Stearns – *continued*
  Selected Essays, 128
  'Shakespeare and the Stoicism
    of Seneca', 75, 112, 115
  'Som de l'Escalina', 117
  'A Song for Simeon', 117
  'Song to the Opherian', 82
  'Spleen', 32
  Sweeney Agonistes, 90, 101, 104,
    105, 126, 134, 144
  'Sweeney Among the
    Nightingales', 60, 61
  'Thoughts After Lambeth', 124
  'The Three Voices of Poetry',
    75, 162
  'To Walter de la Mare', 179
  'Tradition and the Individual
    Talent', 56, 66, 73–5, 76
  'Tradition and the Practice of
    Poetry', 11
  'Triumphal March', 117, 126,
    127
  '"Ulysses," Order, and Myth',
    77
  *The Use of Poetry and the Use of
    Criticism*, 28, 75, 128, 130,
    136, 176
  The Waste Land, 7, 10, 31, 34, 46,
    53, 57, 59, 60, 61, 64, 69,
    80, 81, 82, 83, 89–95, 96, 98,
    99, 100, 101, 103, 104, 108,
    109, 111, 115, 116, 118, 119,
    121, 123, 127, 164, 171, 173,
    175, 176, 177
    composition of, 83–8
    publication of, 95
  'Whispers of Immortality', 60
  'William Blake', 76, 112
Eliot, Valerie (second wife, *see also*
    Fletcher), 18, 174
Eliot, Vivien (first wife), 5, 46, 47,
    48, 49, 50, 57, 64, 81, 82, 84,
    85, 87, 97, 99, 107, 116, 121,
    126, 129, 130, 131, 144, 145,
    168
  as 'Fanny Marlow', 107
Eliot, W.G. (grandfather), 12–14,
    17
Elyot, Sir Thomas, 13

Emerson, R.W., 13, 47
Empson, William, 113
  Seven Types of Ambiguity, 113
Enemy, 113
English Review, 42
Eumenides (Aeschylus), 145

Faber and Faber, 100, 104, 117,
    126, 129, 131, 136, 143–4, 149,
    151, 152, 155, 157, 163, 168,
    169
Faber and Gwyer, 69, 100, 102,
    103, 105, 118, 125
Faber, Geoffrey, 100, 156
  Mrs Geoffrey Faber, 129
Ferrar, Nicholas, 159
Fitzgerald, Edward,
  Rubáiyát of Omar Khayyám, 20
Fletcher, Valerie, 169
Flint, F.S., 39, 40, 41, 69, 97
Ford, Ford Madox, 42
Forster, E.M., 98, 105, 123
  Aspects of the Novel, 105
Freeman, 65
Frost, Robert, 39
Fry, Roger, 54, 98, 131
Fussell, Paul,
  *The Great War and Modern
    Memory*, 78

Gallup, Donald, 36, 136
Gardner, Helen, 152, 153, 157,
    174, 175
Gautier, Théophile, 60
'Georgian' poetry, 38, 43
Gloucester (Mass.), 17, 153
Golden Legend, 111
Gordon, Lyndall, 137, 138, 140–1,
    145, 146, 174
Gourmont, Remy de, 46, 59, 76–7
Gregory, Horace, 163

H.D. (Hilda Doolittle), 39, 40, 41,
    44, 46, 58
Hale, Emily, 29, 46, 129, 137–8,
    140–1, 145, 149, 151, 159, 169
Harcourt, Brace, 136
Harding, D.W., 142, 163
Hardy, Thomas, 177
Harvard University, 1, 16, 20, 47,

48, 66, 128, 129, 148
TSE undergraduate studies at,
    18–20
TSE M.A. studies at, 23–4
TSE doctoral studies at, 28–31
Harvard Advocate, 31, 32
Hawthorne, Nathaniel, 50, 109
Hayward, John, 139, 141, 151,
    152, 153, 154, 156, 157, 158,
    159, 164, 168, 169
Heraclitus, 30, 140, 163
Herbert, George, 159
Hesse, Hermann, 98
Hinkley, Eleanor, 29
Hitler, Adolf, 148, 150, 158, 172
Hogarth Press, 54, 61, 95, 96, 100
Horizon, 151, 161
Hulme, T.E., 39, 41–2, 44, 51
Hutchinson, Mary, 155, 160, 161
Huxley, Aldous, 50, 54

Ibsen, Henrik, 151
Imagism, 38–41, 44, 54, 58, 59–60,
    88
  Des Imagistes, 40, 58
  Some Imagist Poets, 41
International Journal of Ethics, 56

James, Henry, 29, 50, 67, 109,
    149–50, 167
  'The Jolly Corner', 138–9
Joachim, Harold, 46
Johnson, Samuel, 133, 167
Joyce, James, 3, 43, 57, 77, 79, 83,
    103, 110, 111, 129, 161
  Ulysses, 83, 92, 110, 127, 175
  Nora Joyce, 129

Kenner, Hugh, 32
Keynes, J.M., 99
Kipling, Rudyard, 133, 159
  'They', 138
Kreymborg, Alfred, 58

Laforgue, Jules, 20, 22, 23, 27, 55,
    59, 61, 112, 169
Larkin, Philip, 173
Lawrence, D.H., 38, 103, 125, 130
Leavis, F.R., 101, 113, 128, 142,
    160, 163, 170

New Bearings in English Poetry,
    128
Lehmann, John, 164
Lewis, P. Wyndham, 6, 7, 35, 42,
    45, 46, 47, 53, 55, 56, 62, 64,
    67, 69, 79, 82, 85, 98, 113,
    114, 129, 147, 165, 167, 168
  Apes of God, 69
  Literary World, 64–5
Little Gidding, 159, 162
Little Review, 55, 58, 61, 65, 66
Liverpool Daily Post, 97
London Mercury, 38, 66, 109
Lowell, Amy, 40–1, 43, 59–60, 114

MacCarthy, Desmond, 65, 72
MacDonald, Ramsay, 127
MacNeice, Louis, 126
Mairet, Philippe, 143
Manchester Guardian, 96
Mansfield, Katherine, 54, 55
Marburg, University of, 1, 36
Marsden, Dora, 43
Marsh, Edward, 38
Marvell, Andrew, 79, 101
Marx, Groucho, 10, 167
Masefield, John,
  The Coming of Christ, 135
Mathews, Elkin, 58
Maurras, Charles, 25, 26–7, 28, 52,
    59, 118, 120, 125
  Action Française, 26, 27
Methuen, 64, 119
Midwives Gazette, 106
Milton Academy, 18
Milton, John, 78, 144
Mirrlees, Hope, 155
Mond, Sir Alfred, 42
Monro, Harold, 43, 45
  Selected Poems (TSE's foreword
    to), 128
Monroe, Harriet, 39, 43, 45, 57
Moore, George, 95
Moore, Marianne, 61, 65, 66
Moore, Sturge, 98
Moot, The, 143
More, Paul Elmer, 133, 142, 144
Morley, Frank, 131, 141, 151, 156,
    158, 159, 164

Morley, Frank – *continued*
Morrell, Lady Ottoline, 6, 49, 50,
    53–4, 59, 84, 129, 137
  and 'Eliot Fellowship', 97
Muir, Edwin, 141
Munich Pact, 146
Murry, John Middleton, 42, 54,
    55, 56, 65, 76, 109, 110, 114,
    115, 116, 133

Nathan, Sir Matthew, 153
Nation, 99, 109, 116, 163
New Age, 43, 88
Newbolt, Sir Henry, 38, 42
New English Weekly, 143, 152, 157,
    158, 161, 165
New Freewoman, 43
New Republic, 109
New Signatures, 128
New Statesman, 53, 56, 60, 65, 109
New Voices, 128
New York Times, 109
  NYT Book Review, 163
Nichols, Robert, 61
Nineteenth Century, 163
Nouvelle Revue Française, 24, 26,
    116
Noyes, Alfred, 38, 42

Oedipus the King (Sophocles), 73
Oldham, J.H., 143
Orage, A.R., 43, 143
Orwell, George, 125, 158, 160
Others, 58
Ouspensky, P.D., 83
Oxford (University), 1, 46, 47, 48,
    80, 81, 122
Oxford Book of English Prose, 110

Partisan Review, 167
Perse, St John,
  Anabase, 116
Petronius,
  Satyricon, 92
Pirandello, Luigi, 98
Poe, Edgar Allen, 20
Poetry, 39, 40, 43, 45, 55, 65
Poetry and Drama, 43
Poetry London, 158

Poetry Review, 43
Pope, Alexander, 86, 93, 175
Pound, Ezra, 5, 26, 37, 38, 39–46,
    47, 49, 50, 53, 55, 56, 57, 58,
    59, 60, 61, 64, 65, 66, 67, 69,
    81, 82, 83, 84, 85, 92, 95, 96,
    98, 102, 114, 115, 116, 118,
    128, 137, 142, 143, 147, 164,
    165, 167, 171, 172–3, 175, 176
  TSE's collaboration with, 60–1,
    85, 86–91, 93–4
  schemes to help TSE, 81, 97
  Cantos, 115, 124, 178
  Hugh Selwyn Mauberley, 60
  Selected Poems (TSE's
    introduction to), 61, 72, 75
Powell, Anthony, 55
Princeton University, 138
Prothero, G.W., 42

Quarterly Review, 42, 58, 64
Quennell, Peter, 141
Quiller Couch, Sir Arthur, 110
Quinn, John, 31, 45, 50, 56, 58,
    61, 64, 81, 83, 84, 85, 90, 95,
    99, 171

Raine, Kathleen, 160
Ransom, John Crowe, 96
Read, Herbert, 5, 62, 69, 77, 98,
    106, 120
'Rebel Art Centre', 42, 44
Reeves, James, 80, 81
Richards, I.A., 6, 57, 80, 81, 109,
    113
  Principles of Literary Criticism, 81
  Science and Poetry, 113
Richmond, Bruce, 55, 100
Rickword, Edgell, 96, 109
Ricks, Christopher,
  T.S. Eliot and Prejudice, 172
Rivière, Jacques, 24
Roberts, Michael, 128
Robinson, E.A., 45
Rothermere, Lady, 43, 83, 97, 100,
    125
Rousseau, Jean-Jacques, 23, 51
Royce, Josiah,
  The Problem of Christianity, 29

Russell, Bertrand, 6, 13, 14, 16, 19, 26, 30, 47, 48–51, 53–4, 55
St Louis (Mo.), 12, 13, 17, 157
Saintsbury, George, 98
St Stephen's, Gloucester Road, 132, 144
Sandburg, Carl, 114
Santayana, George, 26
Saturday Review of Literature, 117
Schiff, Sidney, 86, 171
Schwartz, Delmore, 163, 167
Scrutiny, 128, 142, 163
Shakespeare, William, 20, 78, 92
  Antony and Cleopatra, 62
  Coriolanus, 126
  Hamlet, 80, 90
  Measure for Measure, 62
Shand, John, 163
Sisson, C.H., 174
Sitwell, Edith, 54, 55, 69, 129
Sitwell, Osbert, 54, 55, 61, 69, 129
Sitwell, Sacheverell, 54, 55, 69
Soviet Union, 126, 167, 170
Spanish Civil War, 147
Speaight, Robert, 136
Spender, Stephen, 77, 94, 126, 128, 134, 151, 168
Squire, J.C., 38, 53, 96, 109
Stead, C.K., 38, 85
Stead, William Force, 100
Stevens, Wallace, 89, 177
Strachey, Lytton, 54, 55, 57, 110, 111
Stravinsky, Igor,
  Rite of Spring, 82
Sunday Times, 141, 145
Swift, Jonathan, 161
Symons, Arthur,
  The Symbolist Movement in Literature, 20, 22

Tablet, 163
Tate, Allen, 96, 109, 123
Tennyson, Alfred, Lord Tennyson, 144, 153

'Mariana', 153
Thayer, Scofield, 81, 83, 95
Times (London), 136
  TLS, 42, 53, 55, 56, 64, 65, 66, 71, 81, 82, 96, 98, 101, 110, 111, 116, 119, 135, 140, 157, 160, 163
Trevelyan, Mary, 149, 168, 169
Tyro, 82

Unitarianism, 14, 115
Untermeyer, Louis, 65, 96

Valéry, Paul, 98
Verdenal, Jean, 24
Virginia, University of, 128, 129, 130
Vorticism, 41–2

Waugh, Arthur, 58, 64
Waugh, Evelyn, 175
Weaver, Harriet Shaw, 43, 56
Webb-Odell, Revd, 131
Weston, Jessie,
  From Ritual to Romance, 90
Whibley, Charles, 100, 110
Williams, William Carlos, 40, 65–6, 96, 173, 177
Wilson, Edmund, 95, 109
Woods, Professor J.H., 66
Woolf, Leonard, 54, 99, 100, 108, 109, 120, 131
Woolf, Virginia, 6, 29, 54, 69, 95, 98, 100, 106, 108, 116, 119, 120, 129, 131, 133, 137, 142, 144, 146, 147, 151, 152, 161
  and the 'Eliot Fellowship', 97
Wordsworth, William, 163
Worringer, Wilhelm, 41
Wren, Sir Christopher, 111

Yeats, W.B., 46, 58, 98, 115, 161, 172

Zukofsky, Louis, 171